A PLUME BOOK

GOING SOMEWHERE

BRIAN BENSON grew up in the Northwoods of Wisconsin. He now lives in Portland, Oregon, where he teaches writing at the Attic Institute. This is his first book.

GOING
SOMEWHERE

A Bicycle Journey Across America

BRIAN BENSON

P A PLUME BOOK

PLUME
Published by the Penguin Group
Penguin Group (USA) LLC
375 Hudson Street
New York, New York 10014

USA | Canada | UK | Ireland | Australia
New Zealand | India | South Africa | China
penguin.com
A Penguin Random House Company

First published by Plume, a member of Penguin Group (USA) LLC, 2014

P REGISTERED TRADEMARK—MARCA REGISTRADA

LIBRARY OF CONGRESS CATALOGING-IN-PUBLICATION DATA
Benson, Brian, 1982–
Going somewhere : a bicycle journey across America / Brian Benson.
   pages cm
ISBN 978-0-14-218064-8 (paperback)
1. Benson, Brian, 1982—Travel—United States.   2. Bicycle touring—United States.   3. Cycling—Psychological aspects.   4. Man-woman relationships—Psychological aspects.   5. Cyclists—United States—Biography.   I. Title.
GV1045.B38   2014
796.6'40973—dc23   2013045251

Printed in the United States of America
10 9 8 7 6 5 4 3 2 1

Set in Sabon
Designed by Eve L. Kirch

For my family

To be interested in the changing seasons is a happier state of mind than to be hopelessly in love with spring.

—George Santayana

PART I

A BRIDGE
TO WHO KNOWS?

CHAPTER 1

Here or There or There or Here

I pressed my cheek to the clouded glass, took a deep pull of diesel and wood smoke and rain-kissed leaves and sweat-soaked cotton, and watched as *ayudantes* swarmed the pavement, hoarsely exhorting ancient women in Technicolor *traje* and cow-eyed backpackers in full-zip rain pants to go here or there or there or here. "¡A Guate a Guaaaate! ¡A Sololá! ¡A Xela a Xela, a Huehue!" My heart was pounding. My skin tingling. Because, here or there or there or here. Because maybe I was on the wrong bus. Because Cuatro Caminos looked a lot like Los Encuentros looked a lot like every other traffic-jammed junction town I'd seen from a sticky vinyl seat on *El Madre de Dios* or *El Don Diego* or the dozen other buses that had carried me from destination to destination, from this dusty market to that Mayan pyramid, from that must-see waterfall to this realization: I had mistaken distraction for destination. I *had* no destination.

Beside me, Dave choked on a snore. I turned to see his head

listing toward port, his drooping lower lip on the verge of spilling saliva onto a faded brown T-shirt. Somehow, amid all this, he was sleeping.

El Madre coughed a Rorschach of smoke, shuddered to life, and lurched forward. Again we were moving, and again that goddamn song was looping through my head: *The wheels on the bus go round and round, round and round, round and round. The wheels . . .*

I knocked my forehead against the window, hard enough to wake Dave. He blinked his eyes open and rolled his head from shoulder to shoulder.

"Almost there, Barney?" he asked, yawning.

I'd met Dave two years earlier, back in Madison. He'd instantly forgotten my name and the second time we saw each other had called me Barney Bosworth. I'd been Barney ever since.

I nodded. "I think it's like fifteen more miles to Xela."

"So three hours, then."

"Right."

He pulled a ratty paperback from his bag and opened to the bookmark. I slumped down, jack-knifed my legs against the seat in front of me, and stared out at the roadside market, at the mangy dogs and roasted corn and stacked tortillas and seven-cent avocados and people, so many people, headed here or there or there or here or . . . Honestly, I could no longer tell the difference.

Just a year earlier, I'd graduated from UW–Madison with a fill-in-the-blank lib-arts double major, a glut of idealist energy, and the deeply felt conviction that I was meant to be a union organizer, or a high school history teacher, or a writer, or the second coming of Che Guevara, or, ideally, all of the above at once. But I'd missed the app deadline for Union Summer, and getting a teaching certificate seemed like a lot of work, and I hadn't ever written anything more than term papers and student-rag op-eds, and so, having just watched *The Motorcycle Diaries* for the third time, I decided what I really needed was that whole "if you want to change the world, let the world change you" thing. I thus used my degree to land a job waiting tables at a suburban Chinese restaurant, spent a year shoe-boxing tip money and highlighting Lonely Planet pages with Dave, and soon enough we were buying plane tickets, packing bags, and setting off on an epic, yearlong journey from northern Mexico to southern Argentina to Real Life.

I slid deeper into my seat, my knees now above my head. Already, just four weeks in, I was ready to admit it: I *hated* backpacking. I hated the waterfalls and the ancient ruins and the repetitive conversations with wayward Scandinavians, and most of all I hated how, in the space between these supposed highlights, I always felt so lonely, so indecisive, so guilty. I had a college diploma and no debt and a supposed commitment to Fighting for Social Justice, but somehow I'd ended up here, folded into a bus seat, being not just a pampered tourist but an *unhappy* pampered tourist.

I couldn't keep this up. I needed to stop somewhere, do something. I needed some sense that by going somewhere I was going somewhere.

I reached into my bag, pulled out the guidebook, and flipped to the pages I'd read a dozen times over the past few days— pages focused on the Guatemalan city of Quetzaltenango, also known as Xela. It was supposedly a beautiful spot, frequented but not defined by foreigners, full of Spanish schools and seemingly righteous nonprofits. Also, it was like fifteen miles away. Xela was the closest emergency exit, and I was about to kick the crash bar.

I turned to Dave. He was still holding his book, but his eyes were shut, his mouth an oval.

"Dave," I said.

He opened his eyes. "Barney."

"We need to talk."

Two days later, I was at Xela's bus terminal, waving good-bye to Dave and my delusions.

Those first few weeks in Xela, I was desperate for a sense of be-longing. I needed to meet real people, not just the ghost people who moved in and out of hotels and hostels, and so I enrolled in Spanish classes and joined a gym and helped pour the foundation for an elementary school and chatted up strangers in coffee shops and city parks, and soon enough I found a room in a house with a Guatemalan, two fellow gringos, and an Irish guy named Carl. The night I moved in, Carl invited me to catch a jazz band—a woman from his Spanish school was the vocalist.

The band was already playing as we walked up to El Royal Paris, a warmly lit fishbowl on a second-floor balcony. From the stairs, I could hear a lazy walking bass line, a keyboard tinkling over guitar triads, and horns murmuring in harmony. We approached the door, and through floor-to-ceiling glass walls I saw that the band appeared to be a mix of Guatemalans and gringos, all men.

Carl shrugged. "Maybe she's sick, eh?"

He grabbed a table, and I headed to the bar for bottles of Moza, the least offensive of Guatemalan beers. As I set the bottles on the table, I noticed a woman stepping through the door and slipping a phone into her purse. She was unfairly, disorient-ingly attractive: silver-blue eyes against olive skin, watercolor collarbones over a silky subcollarbone swell, and a downright mythical strawberry blonde mane. Now she was shimmying past four-tops and awkward couples, sliding onto a stool by the gui-tarist. She noticed Carl and waved, and he waved back. I half-raised my own hand, then dropped it, unsure of the etiquette for greeting a beautiful woman who doesn't know you exist.

Over his shoulder, Carl said, "That's Rachel."

"Cool," I heard myself say.

I watched Rachel lean toward the keyboardist, a scruffy gringo in a baggy button-down. They exchanged whispers, and she tossed her head back in laughter, then theatrically pulled the mic to her lips. The band stayed silent as she sang the first few bars of "In My Solitude." All around, conversations stopped. Heads turned. I felt my jaw dropping, my eyes deadening, but I could not control myself, could not do anything but absorb. That someone so young could sing like this, with such smoke and power and clarity, seemed impossible.

Minutes, hours, millennia passed. Glaciers advanced and retreated. And suddenly the band was starting an instrumental, and Rachel was walking over to say hi to Carl, and I was panicking, because I hadn't prepared for this, hadn't considered that I might need to *speak* to her, and so I just did the midwestern thing and defaulted to effusive praise.

"You've got a really amazing voice," I said.

"Thanks." Rachel pulled up a chair, sat down, and produced a pack of American Spirits. "Really, I owe it all to these. Do you mind?"

I did not mind. She could do whatever she wanted, so long as she stayed at this table.

As Rachel exhaled cones of smoke and surveyed the room, I tried to make conversation, but her friends kept interrupting, stopping by to plant kisses on her cheek and ask about evening plans. So I just sat back and listened as she talked about an upcoming nonprofit fundraiser–cum–dance party and some guy named Paco and how tired she was of organizing *despedidas* for every freaking student who'd spent five days studying Spanish at her school, and, well, at some point I lost track of what she was saying and just listened to how she was saying it. That *voice*. So sexy and strong, so utterly entrancing, even offstage, even when she was just talking about . . . Actually, she now appeared to be talking about stomach parasites.

Whatever. She plainly had a life here, a community, and her rootedness and confidence added to her beauty. Or rather, they complicated it. After a few minutes, I wasn't sure if I wanted her or wanted to be her.

Now the band—apparently called Soltura, which roughly translates to "flowiness"—took a set break, and Rachel introduced me to Andrew, the guitarist, and his brother Galen, the scruffy keyboardist. I peppered them with questions about the whens and hows and whys of their lives in Xela, and as I listened to their responses, my gut twisted and clenched. They were speaking a language of shared experience, a language of belonging. I wanted to learn it.

The next weekend Andrew invited me to sit in at a show. I knew next to nothing about jazz but I'd played guitar for years, and so I kept up, even shone from time to time, on twelve-bar blues and A-minor bossa novas. As for all the other standards, with their dizzying modulations and impossible melodies, I just held on to whatever I could grasp and focused on not falling off.

As the weeks passed, I sat in for more shows, every one a roller-coaster ride, terrifying and exhilarating. Most afternoons, I'd lock myself in my room for a DIY crash course in music theory. I practiced scales and voicing, obsessed over these "Rhythm for Dummies" worksheets I'd gotten from Andrew, and soon, rather than watching her from the crowd, I was tucking arpeggios under Rachel's melodies and eliciting the occasional smile or compliment.

One night we all headed from a gig to El Duende, a reggaeton-all-day-every-day bar that was hosting a fundraiser for the shelter where Rachel volunteered. We ordered Cuba Libres and pulled stools around a table. That night's show had been particularly good, and I was swimming in booze and endorphins, was witty and sharp and asking all the right questions, and soon it was just Rachel and me, leaning close and straining our voices over the music. We were laughing and buying more Cuba Libres and grasping arms while asking, "Could you repeat that?" And then she was asking if I'd like to walk her home, and I was saying yes, yes, I would.

As we wound through cobblestone streets, I was sure this was the moment I had been waiting for. We would have earth-shattering, teeth-shaking, uninhibited-but-of-course-respectful sex, and then do it again, and then fall in love and never grow old but stay young together, making beautiful music and saying beautiful things and being beautiful forever. But when we got to her place, Galen was there—supposedly displaced by houseguests, definitely ruining my life. He followed us into Rachel's room, grabbed a guitar, and started playing Silvio Rodríguez covers. An hour later he finally headed to the couch. By this point I'd lost my buzz, my momentum, my moment. Rachel and I kissed for a few minutes, but we were both exhausted. She told me she couldn't keep her eyes open, but that I should stay, and so I tucked up beside her, not removing my jeans or my button-down shirt. I didn't want to be presumptuous.

The next day Rachel told me she thought we should keep things platonic. I thought keeping things platonic was a terrible idea. But I nodded as if I had been thinking the same thing.

Andrew soon left Guatemala, opening up a spot in Soltura and a room in Galen's house. I took both and began pouring all my energy into the band. I spent my days studying and practicing and talking about how much more I'd need to study and practice if I was ever going to keep up with my bandmates. Galen joked that if he were to make a talking doll in my image, its catchphrase would be, "I suck! I suck!"

My newfound status as sucky guitarist meant Rachel and I were together pretty much daily. I felt increasingly comfortable around her, and the less I acted like a tittering, wide-eyed fan, the more she seemed to enjoy my company. It turned out we had a lot in common, from our lefty politics to our crazy Jewish aunts to our mutual tendency to go a bit too far with vulgar humor. We got into long conversations that ranged from bell hooks to Boyz II Men, and stuck our tongues out at Galen every time he forced us to play "My Way," and one night, at a postshow dinner, when I blurted to the band that I'd sell my best friend's firstborn to see Beck in concert, Rachel not only laughed but responded with something frankly unpublishable.

Soon enough, I again found myself sitting around with her and Galen until well after midnight. Again Galen bid us adieu, but this time Rachel and I stayed on the couch, listening to music, playing nostalgic favorites, and sharing for what or whom that nostalgia was reserved. Eventually a silence fell between us. Rachel stood and started for her room. Over her shoulder, she said, "You can come with."

We took our time that night, preserved some boundaries, all of which evaporated within days. But in the weeks that followed, we remained cautious. We decided not to tell Galen or anyone else in Soltura, didn't even talk about it to each other. This thing was new and fragile, and I was afraid if I looked too long it might explode. At any rate, I knew it would be over soon, as we both had commitments that would call us back to the States, she to Oregon and I to Wisconsin.

So we just enjoyed the moments we had. I loved how she would look at me during a set, tilting her head and smiling. I was by no means the first or last guy to admire Rachel from afar, so sitting up there with her—*with* her—felt like the sweetest secret in the world. And I looked forward all week to Sunday afternoons, when we would finish our last gig, walk back to her house, climb into bed, and spend the rest of the day intertwined, drifting in and out of sleep.

During the week, it was harder to find these quiet moments. Whereas I had little going on outside Soltura, Rachel's days were ridiculous. Between her Spanish classes, her *despedida* planning, research for her thesis on machismo, volunteer work at a domestic-violence shelter, and her quasi-religious yoga regimen, she barely managed to make our gigs, let alone the biweekly practice sessions. But she made time for me. Soon we were seeing each other every day. And as my departure date crept closer, I began to question where I was going, why I was going there, and whether the answer to both questions might be Rachel.

The trip was her idea, really. On an August afternoon, a few weeks before I was to leave Guatemala, we were walking back toward San Pedro, having just spent a few hours at an ugly but secluded beach on the shore of Lake Atitlán—*el lago*. An immense crater formed by an ancient volcano and filled with sapphire blue water, this was our go-to vacation spot when we needed a break from the tough life of getting paid to play music in a foreign country.

The path back to town was bumpy and overgrown, and I was out front as always. Whenever I'd walk behind Rachel, I'd fall prey to my long legs and unbridled extroversion and ride her heels, so she always insisted I lead. We'd been walking in silence, enjoying the sun and the lake view, when Rachel spoke.

"Es matamoscas."

She barely got the words out before bursting into a laughing fit.

I flipped her off. *Matamoscas*. The night before, we had been making gnocchi in our hotel. We were cooking with a cheap pan, and the onions were starting to scald, so I scrambled around, found what looked like a spatula, and poked at the veggies. A few seconds later, the hotel's housekeeper walked into the kitchen, gasped, and said, "Es matamoscas."

I hadn't heard the word before, but it sounded familiar, because, yes, I knew *mosca*, and it meant . . . Fuck. I was cooking with a flyswatter.

"Hey, it looked like a spatula," I muttered.

Rachel, who could accelerate from zero to gasping and teary-eyed in a matter of seconds, paused in the path and started laughing so hard that she was barely producing sound. I turned to find her doubled over, heaving, tears coating her cheeks. I had been mortified about the flyswatter, but I no longer felt embarrassed. Just happy. Happy that I was here with Rachel, this woman who was so full of life, so dynamic, and so completely with me, even if I had stirred dead flies into our marinara sauce.

After a solid minute of laughing, nearly composing herself, then losing her shit all over again, Rachel caught her breath. I kissed her, and when I pulled back, I had the overwhelming urge to tell her I loved her. But I wasn't sure those were the right words or, for that matter, what they even meant. What I did know was that I was leaving town in two weeks, and two weeks didn't feel like enough. Not at all.

My mind drifted to a conversation we'd had earlier that day about backpacking and its pitfalls. Rachel had mentioned that while she couldn't see herself traveling that way ever again, she had for years dreamed of biking across the States. When I asked why, she shrugged and said, "I don't know. It just kind of sounds fun." I waited for one, two, five seconds, and then she added, in concise, bullet-pointed afterthoughts, that she (a) biked everywhere in Portland but had never ridden farther than forty miles, (b) hadn't really seen the Midwest or the Plains, and (c) figured that riding the Rockies would give her "really tight buns."

I got the impression she'd produced those bullets on the spot. And I knew she'd now repeat them verbatim. This was how Rachel made decisions. Clearly. Finally.

I turned and started down the path, and Rachel fell in behind me. After trying to come up with a clever segue, and failing, I looked over my shoulder, and not breaking stride, said, "So, this bike trip. Is it really something you're thinking about?"

"Yeah, I guess." She wiped the final tears from her eyes. "I'll finish school next May, and I was hoping to maybe go then."

"Sounds amazing. I've been thinking about taking that kind of trip forever." Depending on one's conception of space and time, this was true. I had indeed been thinking about it incessantly since Rachel first mentioned it, twenty-five minutes earlier.

"What if we did it together?" I asked, still walking.

"Well, it *would* be nice to have someone carry my gear. And, yeah, of course I'd love to ride with you."

For the rest of the walk and the bus ride back to Xela, and during my final weeks in town, we batted the idea around. We figured we'd start in my rural Wisconsin hometown and head to—or at least toward—Portland, Oregon, where Rachel had grown up. We weren't sure which states we'd ride through or when we'd leave or what gear we'd need. The details could be worked out later. The important thing was to have an idea, a commitment, and *this* was it.

Time came, we said good-bye. As I sat on my Wisconsin-bound flight, I was already missing her but thrilled I had something to hold on to. I would follow Rachel into this bike trip, and she would pull me westward, over lakes and plains and mountains, over a twenty-five-hundred-mile bridge, toward something new, something shared. And when we reached the horizon, breathless and ecstatic, we would have solved its mysteries and begun searching for new ones, on new horizons.

CHAPTER 2

The Water Beyond

As usual, the intersection of East Buckatabon and West Buckatabon was sprinkled with loose sand and gravel, and, as usual, I was coming in way too fast—because how could you *not* bomb that corkscrew downhill?—so I veered into the opposing lane and slalomed through a gap in the debris, dropped a hand from the bars, and pointed tireward in hopes that Rachel would follow my lead. And, what with all the slaloming and stones and signals, I didn't even notice the bald eagle until it was right there, maybe thirty feet overhead, its shadow slicing across the pavement like a giant black boomerang.

I coasted to a stop on the shoulder. Rachel parked beside me, and together we watched the bird soar south over the marsh, its snow-white tail feathers popping out against the latticed evergreen and sun-silvered water.

"I still can't believe you grew up here," Rachel said.

I shrugged. "Believe it, lady."

She pulled a water bottle from the silver cage on her down tube and, her eyes still on the eagle, took a long pull. She swallowed and asked, "Do we really need to leave?"

"Nope," I said. "We can totally move in with my parents. It'll be romantic."

"Deal." She smiled and nodded eastward. "Let's go tell them."

She pushed off and, after a few unsuccessful clacks of metal on metal, snapped her cleated shoe into its pedal and started spinning. I slid onto my saddle and followed behind.

We had been in northern Wisconsin for nearly a month, staying with my folks, playing some gigs—on the patio of a local country store, at the wedding of family friends—and, of late, trying out all the gear we'd acquired during a bewildering three-day shopping spree in Madison. We now owned panniers and racks, headlights and headlamps, Lycra shorts and moisture-wicking shirts. Also bikes. Matching bikes.

We'd had them for weeks, but even now, as I watched Rachel power hers up a steep, pine-shaded slope, I had to shake my head. Hers was a silver and black 52 cm, mine a brown and gold 58 cm, but in all other ways they were identical. Both had "Fuji Touring" emblazoned in a sloping font on the top and down tubes. Both had wide bars with a second set of brake levers near the stem, so we could change hand position as we rode. Both had black seats, black bar tape, black spokes and rims, black tires, and black racks that held our black-and-gray panniers. And both had small square stickers down by the gears, stickers that screamed in big black capital letters that the bikes had indeed been purchased from the same shop.

We hadn't planned it this way. Hadn't planned it, period. No, we'd just shown up in Madison with a monster shopping list and a fantastically unrealistic timeline and pretty much zero idea what we were doing, and we'd quickly discovered that Madisonian shops had a limited selection of the affordable, steel-frame bikes that, according to our sources (my daddy and Rachel's Internet), were the only option for long tours. It turned out Fuji's touring bike was the only "only option" in Madison, and so after visiting every shop in the city, after manically scouring Craigslist posts and estate sales, we'd sucked it up and bought the same bike.

Brown and silver. His and hers.

By now Rachel was well ahead of me, nearly at the top of the hill. I downshifted and gripped the bars tight and drove the pedals, and the Fuji rocketed forward. I gripped tighter, pushed harder, and the bike responded so instantly and enthusiastically that I had the urge to dismount, carry it into the woods, and cuddle it for a little while.

Until a week ago, I'd only ever owned a one-speed blue Huffy and, come puberty, a Trek that I'd theretofore believed to be the best bike in the universe. But now I'd found the Fuji. After test-riding it for like six minutes, I'd come to the conclusion that the Fuji and Huffy were both bikes in the way a greyhound and papillon were both dogs. Even with twenty pounds of cargo—we'd half-packed our panniers for this, our first loaded training ride—it felt impossibly fast and light and powerful. This was a bike that could take me anywhere.

I rode up beside Rachel and said, "I'm surprised how easy this is. I mean, the bags are kind of heavy, but my legs feel good. Like they're inflated or something."

Rachel nodded, kept riding.

"How about you?" I asked.

"My legs are tired."

"Oh. Well, yeah, mine are kind of tired too. But in a good way. It feels good, right?"

"Yes, Brian. I'm tired in a good way." She flashed a toothy smile of questionable sincerity, then said, "Honestly, this does feel a little hard, but I like it. I'm going to be so buff and hot by the time we get to Portland."

I was about to tell her she was already pretty buff and hot, but I got tripped up on that last word: Portland. "Well," I said. "I'm glad you've made that decision for us."

She smiled, brought her eyes to mine. "Excuse me. By the time we get to the end—wherever in this big, bright world that may be. Is that better?"

"Yes," I said. "Much better."

This was by now a familiar exchange. Rachel obviously saw us ending up in Portland. I did not. I didn't know where I wanted us to end up, but I was pretty sure it wasn't Portland.

It wasn't that I disliked the city. Quite the contrary. Months earlier, at about the halfway point between my departure from Xela and our rendezvous in Wisconsin, I'd taken the train out to visit Rachel and had fallen in love with her city, with its cozy neighborhoods and laid-back feel, its cool color palette and damp, mossy intimacy. But Rachel *owned* the place. She had all kinds of odd jobs and volunteer gigs, and tons of friends, and this immutable morning routine of sipping coffee and eating granola and listening to OPB and chiming in with her own opinions. She had a hundred favorite cafés and parks and bars, and knew multiple equally awesome bike routes to all of them, and understood which stop signs to blow and which to respect, and was always wearing this one outfit, a form-fitting black jacket over faded gray corduroys, that made her look put together and sexy even while riding through pissing rain. As she led me through her Portland life, a life that seemed to reflect exactly who she was and wanted to be, I felt swoony and off-balance and aroused and terrified.

I knew she'd spent years building that life.

I wasn't sure I'd fit into it.

I didn't want to find out.

What I wanted was to find a new place, a place unlike Xela or Portland, a place where she'd be as wide-eyed and clueless as I was. And at the moment, I was enjoying having her here in Wisconsin. In *my* place.

From behind, I heard the growl of an engine. I stood on the cranks and pedaled hard, pulled past Rachel, and waved on the boat-towing truck that had crept up behind us. It rumbled past, the passenger power-waving through an open window. I coasted, waiting for Rachel to pull beside me, and as she did I caught a glimpse of the little lake glimmering through the pine.

A couple of years earlier, after graduating from school but before leaving on my ill-fated backpacking trip, I'd spent the autumn up here, staining cabins and coaching soccer while living with my folks in their beautiful lakeside home. Halfway through my stay, they'd left town on a trip, and I found myself alone, in the woods, for three weeks. I'd never spent much time on my own and feared I might be lonely, bored, sad. But I loved it: loved the quiet, the lack of dizzying choice, the unusual joy I felt whenever I walked deep into the woods to read a book on a bed of pine duff, or whenever I dove into still black water under a star-studded sky, or whenever I did something—anything— just because I wanted to, even (especially) if nobody else knew I was doing it. It always felt like I was telling myself a secret.

The little pine-rimmed lake was my favorite secret of all. Most nights, just as dusk was settling in I'd grab a beer, step into the canoe, and paddle across the lake my parents lived on, up to the northwestern corner, where a finger of water disappeared into marshland. I'd move slow and quiet, my paddle barely breaking the surface as I slipped past lily pads and high grass, bullfrogs and blue herons, painted turtles on downed trees and, on lucky nights, a beaver with a mouthful of branches. Soon enough, the creek would open into a tiny, placid lake whose name I never learned, and I would lay the paddle across my lap and open the beer and sip it as I floated. A few houses dotted the south shore, but no one ever seemed to be home. It was just me out there, alone and unseen, and upon recognizing this, I'd swell up with the unusual joy, just about the sweetest feeling I'd ever felt. But by the third week of feeling that feeling, I found myself wanting someone else there with me: someone who would know better than to speak, someone who would sit with me and sip beer and listen for loons and know when and how to smile in such a way that I understood they understood what neither of us could ever say.

I turned from the lake and looked at Rachel. Her eyes were on the trees, maybe on the water beyond. And I'm pretty sure she was smiling.

We leaned our bikes against the house, then unracked the panniers and carried them into the garage. On the opposite wall, between the cross-country skis and bags of birdseed, was our gear. It was a knee-high pile, about four feet wide, a mess of bags and poles and bright fabric. Somehow we were going to carry it all, for thousands of miles, on two bicycles.

I wasn't sure how we'd ended up with all this crap. I mean, of course I remembered those days in Madison, rushing around, hemorrhaging money. But the gear still felt separate from, even at odds with, the *idea* of the bike trip. Since the day we'd dreamed it up, I'd envisioned an exodus from the trappings of society, an iconoclastic, anticonsumerist journey into the unknown. And yet here were the Camelbaks and Clif Bars, the shiny new helmets and factory-fresh panniers.

For the millionth time, I asked myself if we really needed any of this—if we needed anything more than a bike and a bag. That, after all, was what Galen had.

Galen—the guy who had moved to Guatemala at sixteen and started a jazz band; the guy who had dreamed up an epic concert that featured music from across the Americas and packed an eight-hundred-seat theater; the guy who could play piano like nobody I'd ever heard and make these fantastically weird balloon animals and speak flawless Spanish, on the phone, with octogenarian Cubans; the guy who, on better days, I looked to for inspiration and, on other days, I wanted to bury in a deep, deep hole—was, as it turned out, about to embark on his own cross-country bike trip. From Boston to Who Knows? Maybe even the same Who Knows? as Rachel and me.

A few days earlier, I'd called him and we'd talked routes and gear. Apparently he had bought a hammock, rather than a tent, so he could sleep wherever he found two trees or an abandoned barn. He'd made himself a stove, from two beer cans and a penny, that ran on HEET, the stuff I'd once used to prevent gas-line freeze during Wisconsin winters. He'd found a sweet steel-framed eighties road bike and was bringing little more than shirt and shoes and shorts and jacket, and was now on the hunt for his final bit of gear, a duffel bag—not a trailer or set of panniers but a fucking *duffel bag*—in which he would carry his meager supplies.

By the time I'd hung up the phone, I'd convinced myself that we were doing it all wrong. But when I mentioned my doubts to Rachel, and told her about Galen's super-spartan setup, she'd said, "A hammock? That sounds awful. And I'd much rather haul some weight than wake up every morning and put on the same sweaty socks and poopy shorts."

Now, as I stared down at our piled panniers, at the tent and rain fly, the cleated shoes and moisture-wicking socks, I told myself that Rachel was right, that these purchases were not exorbitant but practical, that Galen would end up regretting his thrift, that—

"Hey." Rachel was waving a hand in front of my face.

I blinked and turned toward her.

"Something interesting down there?" She smiled and set her panniers on the pile.

"No," I said. "I was just zoning out."

"You sound like your dad."

"You sound like my mom."

"Your mom sounds like your mom."

I nodded, vanquished, and followed Rachel from the garage into the kitchen, where we found my mom sounding very much like my mom, singing "Nappy Pooby Time" (a Barb Benson original) to our astronomically dumb golden retriever, who, gauging by the glassy eyes and open mouth and statuesque stillness, seemed convinced that "Nappy Pooby Time" was edible.

Now Mom turned to ask us how the ride went, and if the bags were too heavy, and if we'd maybe decided we were just going to stay in Wisconsin forever. Rachel told her we'd decided exactly that. Then she headed upstairs, to change into a bathing suit, and I moved to follow her. But Mom stopped me, her hand on my shoulder, her eyes on the Lump.

A couple of weeks earlier, a Ping-Pong-ball-size growth had appeared on the right side of my neck. It looked like an overly pronounced Adam's apple running away from home. Rock-hard and hot to the touch, the Lump had pulled my skin taut, reddening the flesh so my neck appeared to be permanently blushing. And throbbing. It hurt whenever I moved my head, which is to say, whenever I was awake and often when I was asleep. I had no idea why the Lump had appeared. Luckily, my crack team of nonexperts was more than happy to offer opinions. Everyone and their mother—mine especially—was convinced it was a harbinger of something terrible. Pneumonia. Cancer. An embryo sac full of flesh-eating aliens. At first I'd figured it was just a lymph node—I'd once had an equally gross inflammation in my armpit—but I eventually got paranoid enough to see a doctor. He'd looked it over for a minute, sat back on his stool, and told me that, yes, it's an inflamed lymph node and likely nothing to worry about, though it could be something worse, and that'll be two hundred dollars. I left with a new flavor of paranoia and a deepened hatred for our health care system.

Now Mom was touching the Lump. I recoiled, less in pain than embarrassment.

"Mom, I'm fine."

"Does it still hurt?" she asked.

"Mom, I'm *fine*."

"Do you want some ibuprofen?" My mom believed everything—headaches, fevers, racism—could be cured with ibuprofen.

"I'll be okay," I said. "It actually feels like it's a bit less swollen today."

This was a lie, but Mom seemed to buy it. She looked off at the steps leading to my room, then back at me. "I know this is going to be a great trip for you two," she said. "But I'm only half-kidding about wanting you to stay. We'll miss having Rachel here. And you too, I guess."

My folks hadn't met Rachel until I'd brought her to their doorstep, some three weeks before, but already they loved her and were stunned—as was I—by her utter comfort in Conover, this tiny Northwoods town where she knew no one and spent all her time with the family. I mean, I'd expected her to enjoy the Friday fish fries and Fourth of July fireworks, the afternoon swims and walks in the woods, whitetail deer and pileated woodpeckers, and she certainly had, but what she seemed to like most of all was just being at the house, reading books, hanging out on the dock with my family, and, of course, indulging in her immutable morning routine. Every day around eight, she'd pull on a hoodie and head downstairs, yawning and stretching and moaning "Coffee"—and looking, as Mom described it, like a baby bird waiting to be fed. Even if no one else was up, she'd eat and read and opine, just as she had in Portland.

For the past few weeks, I'd again been thinking what I'd thought the night we met: I not only wanted Rachel but wanted to *be* her. She was self-confident enough to lean into the unknown and self-aware enough to be herself wherever she landed. I wanted that: I wanted to keep moving. I wanted to figure out how to be myself anywhere. And I wanted to do it all with her.

Now Rachel came back to the kitchen, in swimsuit and towel, and I lifted swim trunks from the porch railing and followed her down to the lake. We stayed all afternoon, diving into the water and drying on the dock, diving and drying, again and again, Rachel shrieking when her toes got tangled in slimy stalks of invasive Eurasian milfoil, me yanking up handfuls and sticking them in her hair. Later, after helping with dinner, we returned to the dock, to play music and watch the sunset, then lingered as stars burned the blue-black sky. And as I lay beside Rachel, staring up at the night, my legs faintly aching from our afternoon ride, I thought not of Galen or gear, of Portland or Who Knows? but only of this quiet moment. I wondered how many such moments might await us out there. I was ready to find out.

PART II

THE WISCONSIN GLACIAL EPISODE

CHAPTER 3

Big Picture, Little Moment

We stood alone in my parents' driveway, I in a freshly laundered gray polyester T-shirt, Rachel in a sleeveless beige version of the same, both of us in crotch-hugging Lycra and baggy black shorts whose sole purpose was to hide said Lycra. Our heads were helmeted, our laces tied. Tires pumped, chains lubed, panniers packed and racked. It was a prime photo op—golden light peeking through pine needles, dappling bikes and bikers—but nobody was around to take the photo, and I hadn't figured out the timer on my clunky old digital, so I settled for an extended-arm head shot, the kind that fills the albums of many a mediocre photographer.

I pulled up the image and we huddled over the screen. Our huge helmets blotted out the bikes, but we were smiling, leaning into each other.

"Look, honey!" I said. "This was back before we hated each other."

Rachel nuzzled her helmet into my armpit. "You always know just what to say."

We had by this point heard every imaginable quip about how the bike trip would destroy us. We would break down after weeks of sore butts and scarce showers, brutal winds and grueling climbs. We'd explode under the pressure of having to agree on decision after decision. I'd want to go faster, and she slower, and sometimes one of us wouldn't want to go at all, and, well, what were we going to do about that? We'd shrugged this off, all of it. Wisconsin had been good to us, and we'd never been more confident about our ability to take this trip and move forward, together.

"This is pretty good, right?" Rachel said, still staring at the screen. "I'm sure your mom will appreciate that we took it. Speaking of, I'm surprised she hasn't called again."

I nodded, shaking off a mild guilt tremor. My folks were in Chicago, and I knew it was killing them to miss out on a dramatic send-off. But it felt right, leaving like this: alone and unseen.

"Do you have the map?" Rachel asked.

"Of course." I gave her an are-you-really-asking-me-that smile, but as soon as she looked away, I slid my fingers into the pannier pocket and dug for the folded sheets in question. She looked back from the lake just in time to catch my hand releasing the paper. Busted.

The map was actually nine separate maps photocopied from a gazetteer and taped at the seams. I'd sketched out our route with a yellow highlighter, and it stretched from edge to edge, bottom right to upper left. We'd had other options—an association called Adventure Cycling offers dozens of compact, waterproof, intricate route maps for cross-country bikers—but we'd agreed that buying those babies was out of the question. Our trip was about independence, about adventure, about us, and we didn't need to be coddled or constrained.

This super-map was just one of a hundred things in my four panniers. Port side, I'd packed my blue goose-down mummy bag and school-bus-yellow tent, a one-quart Ziploc full of tools (patch kit and tire levers, spoke wrench and chain breaker, adjustable wrench and multitool with screwdrivers and hex heads galore), and a smaller bag with my toothbrush and paste, my deodorant and peppermint Dr. Bronner's. The pannier on the starboard bow held two sporks, a spice kit, some hand-me-down tinware, and the penny-alcohol stove I'd built days earlier with a drill bit, needle-nose pliers, three tin cans, and a lot of long-distance tech support from Galen. My final bag teemed with clothes: extra shirt and shorts, wool hat and thermals, socks and boxers, flip-flops and rain poncho, some hideous but functional quick-dry pants, and a gray fleece with a dime-size hole in the breast, courtesy of a rogue campfire ember I hadn't noticed in time. Atop the rear rack, I'd bungeed on tent poles, a sleeping pad, and a pleather case that held my brand-new ukulele. And in the front panniers' zippered pockets, I'd packed the stuff I'd use most often: on the left, I had the super-map, a dog-eared copy of *The God of Small Things*, two rollerball pens, and a hardback journal with a blue and silver honeycomb cover; and on the right, my camera and sunscreen and Cub Scouts pocketknife, the latter a welcome-to-manhood reward I'd earned, at age nine, by selling the requisite load of corporate candy to my sweet, defenseless neighbors.

Rachel's bags brimmed with clothing and gear nearly identical to mine. The main pouches held shorts and shirts and socks and sandals, and in the zippered pockets were her journal and pens, postcards and stamps, Tom Robbins paperback and blocky flip phone. In exchange for my taking the tools and tent, she had packed the rain fly and all the food we'd carefully chosen: flour and baking soda and powdered milk for pancakes, a huge bag of homemade granola, some energy bars that Dad had pulled from his dresser drawer, and a dozen other things I can't remember now because we would discard them within days. One full pannier was reserved for her enormous, and enormously cheap, sleeping bag. Bulky and built for fifty-degree nights, it was the antithesis of "performance" gear. Its pannier bulged, tumorous.

As I looked down at said tumor, I instinctively raised my hand to the Lump. It was bigger and throbbier than ever, had gotten painful enough that I'd at last made the Mom-pleasing decision to start eating ibuprofen a couple of times a day. And though I'd never have admitted this to her, it was starting to worry me. I couldn't help but wonder if the Lump might indeed be a harbinger, not of any specific illness, but of my all-around unfitness for this trip. Maybe it was a sign that I should do it more like Galen, or shouldn't do it at all.

Or maybe it was just some inflamed tissue.

I shook away the thought and looked back to the bikes. Including the Lump, which was hard to isolate on a scale but probably weighed at least two ounces, we'd be hauling over forty pounds apiece, not including the Fujis, which weighed over twenty pounds themselves.

I raised my eyes to meet Rachel's. "I think we have everything, right?"

"Yeah, I think so." She stared down at her bike for a moment, then snapped her fingers and said, "Wait! Did you remember the bowling ball?"

"Yep." I pointed at one of the rear bags. "It's right under the shingles."

"Great. I'd have forgotten those." She looked down the driveway, turned back to me, and shrugged. "Well? Ready?"

I nodded. I didn't quite feel ready, didn't feel the moment was momentous enough. But we were as ready as we'd ever be. We'd made our plans, survived the anticipation, amassed the gear. Now there was nothing to do but pedal to the Pacific.

We rolled down the driveway, whooping at any forest creatures that may have been listening, and when the gravel met the asphalt, we turned west, coasting, laughing, and looking at each

other with twinkling eyes, as if one of us had just told the other
"I love you" for the first time. We were doing it. After months
and months of daydreams, we were riding, together, away from
here or there, toward somewhere west, and Rachel was all
gooey-eyed, and I was too, because this was a glorious beginning, the chickadees chirping, sun shining, overhead oak nudging paisley shadows across the—

I winced, grunted. We'd hit our first hill and it was steep and
my legs were pissed. I geared down and squeezed the bars and
strained to pull my bike and body and bags up the slope. This
was hard. I was now carrying twice as much as I had on any of
our training laps around the lake, and on those rides I'd known
where we were going and how long it would take to get there.
Now, as heavy as the weight was the knowledge that I'd be
bearing it for the foreseeable future. We crested the hill, and I
found myself too out of breath to cheer. Already, maybe a minute into the trip, I felt like we were just taking a bike ride.
Which, well, duh. But I really was surprised. I hadn't spent
much time considering the details, by which I mean anything
beyond the romantic idea of disappearing into the world with a
woman I loved, and so I'd figured we would just sort of float
over the American West, as if in hot-air balloons, incorporating
localized swatches of topography and culture into a big picture
that would always stay in sight.

I started up a second hill. My bike was not a hot-air balloon. It
was a tank. I'd always loved bikes because they were so sleek, so
fluid, so simple—because I could go from zero to twenty in seconds, bunny-hop onto curbs, shimmy through two-foot gaps in
fences, and tuck hard into turns, all atop two wheels and a few
steel tubes. But now I was riding a bike-tank, and there would be
no rapid acceleration, no hopping, no shimmying or tucking. Just
hauling freight.

I looked over my shoulder at Rachel, who was five feet

behind, her eyes on the pavement. She glanced up, puffed out her cheeks, and said, "Is it nap time yet?"

I turned back to the road, rose from my saddle, and pedaled hard. The Fuji began wobbling with every stroke, tilting right, then left, then right, then veering hard to port. I regained control and sat back in the saddle; bike-tanks, apparently, weren't meant to be ridden standing up.

Now the grade leveled off into a gentle, winding downhill, and I relaxed off the bars, leaned back in the saddle, and took a deep gulp of lake breeze. Twigs snapped as squirrels scurried through underbrush and a hint of spilled gas wafted over from the boat landing. Maybe, I thought, I couldn't see the big picture, but I owned the little moment.

I turned to Rachel, eager to share this revelation, but I couldn't figure out how to word it, and what ended up coming out was, "This is awesome."

Rachel nodded encouragingly, as if I were a child just learning to speak.

We followed West Buckatabon past the marsh where we'd seen the eagle, past the tidy little cabin with its towers of exquisitely stacked firewood. We'd ridden these miles many times, and I couldn't help but feel we were just taking a lap around the lake, headed not for the horizon but for the house, where we'd spend yet another afternoon sipping pints of Spotted Cow and playing Gillian Welch covers on the dock. But then Buckatabon dead-ended at County K, and rather than turning right, back toward home, we headed leftward, westward. Just like that, the big picture came back into focus. The potholed pavement had never looked so potholed, the roadside pine so lush. I'd traveled this road for years, but always as part of a loop, a predictable path where the beginning was the end. This was my first time seeing it for the last time.

"I've always loved these trees," I said, glancing at Rachel

and then shifting my gaze to the boughs above, hoping her eyes might follow. They did, and I rejoiced, because appreciating these sun-dappled trees—*these* sun-dappled trees—felt like a fleeting moment, and I was determined to engage with this moment, to have a dialogue or at least a monologue, to make it a Moment. If I had my way, the trip's every moment would be a Moment—ripe with meaning, worthy of at least a sidebar or infographic in my personal history book.

I looked back to the road, followed the pavement to the point where it disappeared into oak and pine. At last it was happening. We were out here, moving forward, focused on the few things that now mattered. Pine and pavement, moments and Moments.

The next dozen miles were hilly as hell, and since Rachel didn't quite share my affinity for charging up or bombing down, our average speed took a nasty hit, dropping down into the tweens, which, really, was for the better. Had I been alone, I might have succumbed to the speedometer and lowered my head and all but missed this quiet, lake-spattered, tree-lined stretch that had long been one of my favorites. But now, thanks to Rachel, my head was up, my breath slow, my mind full of County K memories: the lakeside birthday party for my one true middle school love, the countless bike rides to visit my only friend within a ten-mile radius, the nine hundred deer I barely missed hitting while speeding to soccer practice.

Fifteen miles in, we stopped for a swim at Lost Canoe Lake. As we sat on the sand, looking out over the water, Rachel said, "I'm really going to miss this place."

To which I nearly responded, "I love you too."

We headed back to the bikes, which we'd "parked" by dropping them on their sides, the overstuffed panniers acting like big cushions. Easy enough. Pulling out of the lot, though, was proving to be a more involved operation. First you had to pick the bike up, which was a lot like row-lifting a sixty-five-pound barbell. Then you needed to somehow swing a leg over the top tube without letting the overloaded front wheel pivot and squirrel away. And finally you had to push off and attempt to snap your cleated shoe into its pedal while sustaining enough forward momentum to keep your bike from falling over.

"This was a lot easier when I was leaning against the garage," Rachel said.

I agreed, though I refused to admit it.

We continued on, past pine groves and waveless lakes, and mile by mile the grade relaxed from hilly to bumpy to steamrolled. By the time we passed through the town of Boulder Junction, and on to an even quieter stretch of County K, the light was dusky. Birds stopped chirping. Evergreen blackened. The sky went windless and golden and nectar sweet. After a few miles, we turned onto a one-lane dirt road, and I looked at Rachel, and she at me, and a thousand words came to mind but none could compete with the backwoods silence. I drank it up. For so long, I had envisioned the two of us melting into the countryside. Now I could feel it happening. We were disappearing, tucked under a canopy of maple, massaging gravel on a winding road.

The road led to a cabin owned by Bob and Terry Simeone, longtime friends of my family. They'd offered to let us crash in their yard, and we'd accepted, figuring we may as well take advantage of cush campsites while we still had the chance. The plan had been to roll in quietly and set up our tent by the lake, taking pains not to disturb the family's peaceful evening, but as we turned in to the driveway, I heard laughter bouncing off the trees. We continued into a clearing, where we came upon a picture-perfect log cabin, a pine-laden bank backlit by sun-freckled water, and in front of all this, a crowd of bearded men, Bob among them, hoisting beers and tossing golf-ball nunchakus at PVC goalposts.

Bob dropped his chucks and gave us bear hugs and back-slaps, and Terry stepped off the porch smiling with such warmth that I couldn't help but feel I'd gotten an A+ on my big book report, and as the two of them wheeled our bikes away, Bob's brothers handed us beers and bright blue golf-chucks, which we tossed for one game, then two, then many more. Somewhere in there the night just kind of sped up, as nights do, away from sun-dappled trees and potholed pavement, toward comfort food and conversation, and soon it was pushing eleven, and I was half-drunk and bloated, my cheeks sore from laughter, my mind racing from cozy kitchen to county highway to moments whose meaning I was already questioning, doubting, forgetting. Just before midnight, Rachel and I tiptoed to the lake, set up the tent, and walked to the end of the dock. I closed my eyes and took a deep pull of Wisconsin summer and listened to the feral howl of a distant loon. And I remembered.

CHAPTER 4

Where Everything Happens

We were on the move at the crack of ten, riding quiet county roads through classic Wisconsin. The sun was low, the wind a whisper, water everywhere. Here were Big Lake and Clear Lake, Rest Lake and a dozen nameless ponds and puddles, all nestled in a carpet of coniferous bog. I was feeling proud of the landscape, as if I'd designed it myself, but also sad, because I was leaving it behind, and so when we came upon the little boat landing at North Bass Lake, and Rachel suggested we stop for some snacks, I said yes, because *snacks*, and also because I just wanted to sit and stare and soak this all up one last time.

We pulled into the lot and dropped the bikes in the gravel. Rachel dug up a tub of yogurt, and I grabbed some cookies, and we walked to the end of the small, sun-bleached dock. The lot behind us was empty of cars, the water untouched but for a bright orange canoe skirting reeds on the opposite shore. It was all ours.

I pulled off my shoes and socks, dipped my toes in the water, and looked at Rachel looking across the lake. I followed her gaze, hoped she was noticing the right things. How the canoe's Day-Glo orange played off cattail brown. The way the lily pads and reeds, the tamarack and pine, the maple and oak formed a spectral ring of green around the water, and how the wispy clouds sat so perfectly on its glassy surface. And maybe she did notice all that. Maybe that's exactly what she was thinking about as she sat there, in silence.

Just like that I wanted her. Yogurt-stained spoon in my hand, cookie crumbs on my lap.

I leaned in, brushed her hair back, and kissed her. And when she kissed back, it wasn't the being-a-good-sport kiss I'd been expecting. It was a yes-I-notice-the-Day-Glo-and-cattails-now-get-this-fucking-Lycra-off-me kind of kiss.

If you think putting on a condom can kill the moment, try helping your partner, who is straddling you, peel away a second skin of Lycra. I pulled off her hide-the-stupid-Lycra shorts with a snap of the wrist, but the Lycra . . . the *fucking* Lycra. Rachel hovered over me and buried her face in my neck while I fought the fabric. After a few seconds, she called it in favor of the fabric and rolled off. Lying on her back and squirming around, she managed to get the shorts past her knees, then pulled herself back on top. I wrapped an arm up the curve of her back, and with the other I braced my weight against the dock. My fingers slipped over a jagged ridge in the wood, and for an instant I found myself worrying about taking a splinter in the ass. Or worse.

Then Rachel pulled me inside, and I forgot about splinters, real or imagined. Her hands found the steel pipes supporting the dock, shaking it beneath us, and my hands clawed for her hair, her hips, anything I could hold on to. My vision tunneled, and I burrowed my face into her chest, and still the world followed, closing in on itself, on me. I felt the breeze curling up my neck, the sun hot on my cheek. Shimmering diamonds jumped from the lake and sunk into the soles of my feet. The blues and browns and greens bled into each other, into me, filling every capillary, filling me completely, and I held it all in, I held it, I—

Moans melted into gasps, then into laughter and some standard postcoital eloquence.

"Wow."

"Yeah."

Rachel pulled away and, after some rather deft cleanup work, settled onto her back and resumed battle with the Lycra. Just as the waistband made its satisfying snap against her hips, I heard a low rumble behind us. A beat-up Ford Ranger was pulling into the lot, kicking up dust and tugging an equally beat-up boat.

I put my hand on Rachel's knee, trying to look as wholesome as possible. Behind us, a door slammed shut, and I looked back to see two men popping the latch on their topper window and pulling out a pair of poles. The one nearer to us turned, peering out from under the brim of a camo trucker hat, and gave us a wave and a nod. I waved back, then returned my attention to the lake. The canoe had drifted from sight, but the cattails still traced the shoreline, and the clouds still hung in the sky and peered up from the waters below.

"Can you believe this?" I asked.

"Hmm?"

"We're out here," I said. "This is where everything happens from now on."

I let my eyes wander across the lake, over the evergreen, up to the open sky. Rachel smiled, then looked down and dragged her spoon around the container, finding the final pockets of yogurt. She cleaned the plastic deliberately, completely, just as if she were in the kitchen at my folks' house or on the couch in her old Portland apartment. As if this dock were home.

"Fuck. Me."

This was *not* happening.

"Is it a flat?" Rachel asked, pressing her elbows onto the bars and waddling toward me.

We'd ridden just fifteen miles from the lake, but gone was the pleasant bright of morning. Now it was sunny in the bad way. No breeze, no water. Just harsh light filtered through floating dust. And there was plenty of dust. Bob Simeone had said County Road FF would be winding, gentle, and tree lined, and that it was. But it was also being repaved and at the moment wasn't paved at all.

I dropped to a squat and rolled my bike fore and aft, keeping my eyes focused on the hub of my rear wheel. The hub's outer lips—I would soon learn that "flange" was the technical term—were both drilled with eighteen holes, each of which was meant to accept the nubbed head of a highly tensioned spoke. Thirty-six spokes in all, exerting equal force on the rim, sucking it in toward the hub. But one of these spokes had snapped, right where it emerged from the hub. The head spun freely in the flange, while the rest of the shaft dangled from the rim, amputated. One out of thirty-six, I thought, was small peas. My wheel disagreed. The injury to one spoke had distressed the whole system. I lifted the bike and spun the wheel, and the section of rim with the broken spoke swayed to the left, dragging on the brake pad with every revolution.

"No, it's not a flat," I said, looking up at Rachel. "I blew a spoke."

"Already?" she asked. "Wow."

"I know."

I looked back to the Fuji, shook my head, and said, "I thought we were friends."

Rachel stepped off her bike. "Well, at least we've got extra spokes, right?"

We did have extras, neatly attached to special notches that had been brazed onto each of our frames. And replacing spokes, in theory, had always seemed easy enough. Just pop off the tire, pull out the bad spoke, and slide in a new one. Bing, bang, boom. But my blown spoke was on the drive side of the rear wheel, the side facing the chain, and I could see I wouldn't be able to do anything until I removed the cassette: the cluster of gears that hugged the hub. I thought back to the weeks before Rachel and I left. We'd made a couple of trips to the nearby town of Minocqua, where we learned basic repairs and nifty roadside tricks from my dad's local mechanic, a kindhearted if laconic guy named Jeff. He had explained how to boot torn tires with dollar bills, had insisted on the importance of regularly oiling our chains and tightening every bolt on the bike. He had even mentioned a few things about replacing spokes. But I couldn't recall him saying anything about removing a cassette.

I squeezed my eyes shut and exhaled through my nose, the breath forceful enough to whip up dust from the earth between my knees. This was, in fact, happening. Thirty miles into our second day, I had already come across a problem I couldn't fix.

I spent a few minutes trying to use my pliers to loosen the nut holding the gear cluster on the axle, then tossed them in the dirt, feeling ridiculous. There was clearly a tool for this, and I didn't have it.

"Want one?" Rachel asked.

I looked up and saw her holding a couple of sandwiches. I had been looking forward to these sandwiches all day, had envisioned us eating them beside a placid lake while whitetail deer tiptoed through the forest and a lone bald eagle soared overhead. It was going to be beautiful.

"I guess so," I said, not making eye contact. I grabbed one of the sandwiches with my greasy, incompetent hands and began pawing at the plastic. Then I caught myself. It wasn't Rachel's fault we were stuck here, eating in the dirt. She was just trying to help.

"Thanks, Rach." I forced a smile. "This might take a little while."

"I'm sure it will be fine," she said. "Let me know if you need the phone or anything."

I joylessly inhaled the sandwich and considered my options. I knew there was a solution to this problem but also knew it was going to take a while and would probably entail hitching a ride. I didn't want to hitch a ride. I wanted to figure this out on my own. I stuffed the sandwich bag into a pannier and dug around for my tools. The spoke wrench, I decided, would at least buy me time. Using said tool, which looked like a cross-section from a tiny light bulb, I could loosen and tighten spokes until the wheel was somewhat true. Dad had given me pointers on this, and I felt confident I'd understood them. I would just straighten the wheel out, and then I'd ride to the next town, where I'd find someone who could help me remove the cassette.

As I worked, I stole glances at Rachel, who had propped herself against a stump and opened *Still Life With Woodpecker*. She looked content and had given no inclination that she was impatient. But I was. It was forty miles to the campsite we were shooting for, and now we were going to have to move fast, especially since we'd be stopping again in nearby Butternut to get everything really fixed. I worked anxiously, feverishly. Within ten minutes, I had the wheel back on the bike. I rode a couple of circles, twisting around and watching my wheel as I pedaled. It looked wobbly but good enough to get me to Butternut.

The construction only lasted a few miles, and the next stretch of road was beautiful. Here the pavement was perfectly flat, an arrow shot straight to the western horizon. The sun still shone above, its heat pulsing down and rebounding off the asphalt, but it was now joined by a light easterly. West-bearing winds, we'd heard, were a midwestern rarity. Something to be savored.

I considered this as I walked.

When Rachel and I had gotten back on the move, we'd almost immediately come upon a half-dozen guys working for the county. They told us the next two miles would be impassable on bikes, and one of them, seeing the defeated looks on our faces, offered to ferry us past the rough patch. In five minutes we were back on asphalt, on our way west. My bike felt weird, but I told myself it was in my head. I'd made a temporary fix, and soon we'd be in Butternut, and—

Ping!

The sound was muffled and benign, like an egg timer ringing under a throw pillow. I hadn't heard anything like it when the first spoke blew, but I just knew. Head hung, I hit the brakes. I started to say something to Rachel, but she must have heard it too and was already slowing to a stop. I didn't even need to get off the bike to see that a second spoke had snapped.

So now we were walking, straining to balance our bikes as we lugged them along. Walking a bike had always felt easy enough, like pulling a wheeled suitcase, but with loaded panniers, the experience was more akin to taking a rowdy Saint Bernard for a leashed walk. I had to use both hands to keep my bike from veering toward the ditch or the center stripe. My feet pointed due west but my upper body contorted in more of a northwesterly direction.

This was no way to cross the country.

"Not a bad place for it to happen," Rachel said. She was being a real champ. I forced a smile, and she pulled her hand from the stem and reached up to squeeze my arm. Her bike made a break for the ditch, and she caught it just as the front tire hit the shoulder. She walked in silence for a few moments, then said, "This isn't a huge deal, Brian. We'll figure it out."

I nodded, unconvinced. It *was* a huge deal. I had two blown spokes that I couldn't fix, we weren't eating our sandwiches by a lake, and on the second day of our trip we were going to have to get a ride. In a car.

We soon came upon a group of men framing up a shed just off the road. Their pickups were lined up on the shoulder, and the one nearest the site had its passenger door open, its radio blaring Heart's "Barracuda." I had worked on dozens of similar sites over the years, and the scene felt familiar. Too familiar. I found myself avoiding eye contact, staring at the stud walls as if inspecting them for shoddy craftsmanship. I was suddenly very aware of my bright blue, moisture-wicking shirt. My brand-new bike and brand-new gear. And my inability to operate my fancy equipment. In my teenage years, I'd sat on many a tailgate, sipping soda and wiping crumbs on Carhartts while watching a tourist ineptly try to back his brand-new boat, on its brand-new trailer, down a driveway. Now I was that tourist.

So it was Rachel who rolled her bike up to the music-playing truck, where one of the men was digging around in the passenger seat. He looked to be well into his sixties, tall but sagging, as were his pants, which were held up with suspenders. Rachel introduced herself and asked how far it was to Butternut. She was fearless, shameless, about asking strangers for help, asking for what she needed. It was one of the first things I'd noticed about her in Xela, one of the first things I'd fallen in love with. But now she was asking for what *I* needed.

"Butternut?" he asked. "What are you looking for in Butternut?"

"I blew a spoke," I cut in, grasping at a shred of dignity. "And I don't have the tool I need. Hoping I can find one there."

"In Butternut? Doubt it. Closest bike shop is up in Ashland." He cocked his head and looked up the road. "You know, I'm headed to Butternut in a couple of minutes. I'd be happy to take you to Park Falls. Just a bit further, and if you're lucky you might find someone there. Either way, there's a nice park you can camp in."

We thanked him, climbed into the bed of the pickup, and discussed our options. It was already midafternoon, and even if we were able to fix the wheel in Park Falls, it would probably take all day. This "nice park" sounded like a solid fallback. If we couldn't find help, Rachel could hang out there the next day while I hitched to Ashland, sixty miles north. I'd visit the bike shop, get the wheel sorted out, and hitch back. This plan made me want to puke. But it was a plan.

A few minutes later, we were again moving westward. Moving *fast*. I peered into the cab, convinced we were about to break the sound barrier, but the speedometer read fifty-two. Fifty-two miles an hour. Under the legal limit, but at this rate he'd still cover more ground in a couple of hours than we could in a full day on the bikes, even if said bikes were in working order. And at present there was no reason to believe they would be. We'd spend the next few months breaking things, hitching rides, and finding someone else to solve our problems.

My hand found its way to the Lump. It felt bigger than ever and lava hot. I was more sure than ever that something was in there, something more than blood cells and swollen tissue. I had no idea what it was, but it felt like an omen. I couldn't control my body or my bike, let alone the miles that lay before us.

I leaned against the wheel well and looked at Rachel. She had her arms spread across the bed's rusty sidewall, her eyes closed. Her hair danced in the breeze, trailing behind her like a meteor tail. I had to smile. As a kid, I had loved few things more than riding in the back of Dad's truck. Even when it was just parked in the driveway, I'd climb in and poke around the bed liner for treasures, watch Dad chop wood or just sit and daydream about going somewhere. We are going somewhere, I told myself. I closed my eyes and repeated the words. Once.

Twice. Five times. And then, for a few moments, I thought nothing. Just listened to the engine's muted drone and felt the wind tousle my hair.

A half hour later, our chauffeur dropped us off at Hines Park, a pretty little spot that hugged the river running through Park Falls. After offering a few suggestions for what to check out and refusing our offer to give him some gas money, he gave us a wave and drove back in the direction he'd come from. I got the feeling he hadn't really needed to go to Butternut, much less Park Falls, and was probably headed straight back to work.

I moped as we set up the tent. We'd ridden a mere thirty-four miles, hitched another nineteen, and now we were going to pay five bucks apiece to camp in a cushy park with picnic tables, bathrooms, and barbecue grills. I figured we'd occasionally pay for camping, but only when we craved luxury after some particularly hard riding. Only when we'd earned it.

"Ridiculous," I muttered, loud enough for Rachel to hear. I wanted to make sure she noted my turmoil. "On the second day. This is so goddamn frustrating."

"It's fine," she said. "We'll figure it out."

"Yeah, I know, but I just feel bad. I mean, it'd be different if it was just me." As I said this, I noted it was utter bullshit. Then continued. "But now you have to wait while I figure out why my bike hates me."

Rachel stood and wrapped her arms around my waist. "Brian," she said, hanging on the *i* in the way people often did when I was making them feel tender or exasperated, "I'm fine. I mean, I wish you didn't have to hitch to Ashland, but why worry? This is a beautiful park and we get to check out a new town."

I considered this. It *was* a pretty nice park, with bathrooms, picnic tables, and barbecue grills. And though I'd grown up close to Park Falls, had watched their basketball team destroy ours on a regular basis, I'd never seen the town.

"Want to take a walk?" she asked. "We can set this stuff up later."

We threw everything in the tent and locked our bikes to a pine. Just north of the park was a bridge spanning the river, and we crossed it, staring up at a wall of concrete. The entire eastern bank seemed to be property of Flambeau River Papers, whose logo was pasted onto an array of profoundly drab buildings, most prominent among them a windowless mill that looked not unlike a prison. We continued past the mill and into town, passing the standard beacons: grocery store, post office, seven bars. As we walked by an old theater, which, owing to a neon marquee that spelled out "Park," looked like the world's classiest parking garage, a man on a bike rode past, towing a yellow trailer containing one bag of groceries and one tiny child.

Rachel gave me a pat on the ass and mouthed, "Go."

I caught him at the intersection, where he'd dutifully stopped and looked both ways. Turned out he was a middle-school teacher and was headed for the library to return some books. We were going there too, I mentioned, but seeing him had made me wonder if there wasn't a bike shop in town. He sort of shrugged and nodded at the same time, and pointed to a corner store a couple of blocks up. It was more of a secondhand shop, he said, but the guy who owned it always had bikes for sale and probably knew how to fix them.

We walked to the store. Through the windows, I could see dusty chairs, stuffed animals, board games, and, yes, bikes. Some items sat on shelves, but most were piled on the floor, on each other. The place looked like it hadn't been open for some time. We were just about to turn for the library when we heard a boy's voice behind us.

"Can I help you?" The kid looked to be thirteen or fourteen, brown haired and scrawny. He was carrying some DVDs from the tiny rental spot across the street.

Nope, I thought. But it was sweet that he'd asked. I quickly explained our plight.

"That's my dad's store," he said.

"Really?" I was suddenly interested in this conversation. "Will he be open tomorrow?"

The kid sat with this for a second, then replied, "I can call him right now. He's at home." He pulled a phone from his pocket and dialed. There was something oddly severe about him. I didn't think he'd blinked since we started talking, and he definitely hadn't smiled. Now he spoke quickly, mentioning only that someone needed help. I wanted to snatch the device from his hands, or at least coach him on how to sell this situation, but in a few seconds he was folding the phone and putting it back in his pocket.

"He'll be here in a half hour."

Twenty minutes later, an old blue Chevy coughed to a stop in front of us. The driver's door swung open, creaking loudly, and out slid one booted foot, followed by another, followed by a man. A big man. When he pulled his frame from the cab, the entire truck relaxed off its shocks. The big man walked slowly around the front of the truck, his hand sliding across the hood. At six foot one, I'd always felt fairly tall, but this guy made me look like one of the toys inside his store. He had to be pushing seven feet and four hundred pounds.

"I understand you two are in a bit of a bind," he said, a smile spreading across his face. I don't know what I'd been expecting, but his voice was kind, as was his face, wrinkled in the right places. He put out his hand and I did the same, noting how delicate my fingers felt as they disappeared into his. I watched as he turned to Rachel, taking hold of her even tinier hand.

"I'm Jeff," he said, looking back and forth between us. "How can I be of service?"

I explained the problem. Better said, I tried to. My bike vocabulary was for shit. So Jeff just asked where the bike was, and before we knew it he was driving us back to Hines Park. On the way, we covered our essentials: coming from the Eagle River area, headed to Oregon; yes, we were dating; no, we'd never done anything like this; no, we didn't have a clue about how to fix our bikes. At the park I tossed my wheel and spare spokes into his truck, and by the time I hopped back in the cab Rachel had turned the questions on Jeff. He wasn't from Park Falls, but he'd been there for a decade or so and had opened his shop a few years back. Aside from running the store and doing some odd jobs, Jeff spent a lot of time working with the church.

"The church," he said, "gave me a second chance." I tried to figure out a vague question to get him to say more, but before I'd found the words, we pulled up to the store.

Jeff led us through the back entrance and went in search of his "truing stand." This was apparently a thing you used to straighten wheels, but I'd never heard of it. As he waded through a maze of boxes, toward what appeared to be an office, Rachel and I poked around the store. It was a disaster. The shelves teemed with old board games and ugly vases, and the floor was covered with more of the same, much of it sports related: a pyramid of tennis rackets, a dirty Playskool basketball hoop, half a dozen kids' bikes in various states of disrepair.

Jeff appeared from the office, walking as gingerly as was possible for a man of his size and hoisting up what I guessed was a truing stand. He stepped up to a long metal table, pushed aside a pile of papers, and set the stand down. "Let's have a look at that wheel, eh?"

Using another tool called a "chain whip," which despite its medieval-sounding name was little more than a length of chain bolted to a steel shaft, Jeff removed the cassette and set it aside. He pulled off the tire, popped out the broken spoke, and slid in a new one—bing, bang, boom—and sat the wheel in the stand. To my eyes, the stand had looked like some sort of giant staple remover, but now it made sense. Two steel columns rose perpendicular to a square platform, and they each accepted one side of the hub. Another shaft angled out from the base of the columns, sporting two opposing claws—"calipers," Jeff called them—that could be adjusted to trace the rim as the wheel spun. Wherever the rim surface scraped the caliper, Jeff explained, he'd make adjustments. I'd done the same thing using my brake pads, but this seemed way more precise.

Rachel stepped out back to make some calls, and I stayed inside, chatting with Jeff while he worked. Turned out he'd been an auto mechanic for years, and had always enjoyed working on bikes, though he hadn't been able to ride one since he was a kid. "They don't make bikes for my size," he said, chuckling. "I've broken quite a few and just don't try anymore. I can fix 'em, but I'll never ride 'em."

Ten minutes passed, then twenty more. He was having trouble with the wheel, and his good mood was souring. I appreciated the situation. It was one thing not to know how to fix something and quite another to fail in front of an audience. I busied myself as much as possible, checking on Rachel, scoping out his shop, trying to make conversation about the ramshackle inventory. "Yeah, I've got people coming by all the time to look at that stuff," he said, still squinting at the spokes. Based on the reply, I guessed he was close to having to shutter the store.

By now he was sweating and breathing hard. Truing wheels wasn't exactly a workout, but it was hot in his shop and the work was tedious, and I was starting to feel bad about taking up his night with said tedium, especially because I'd just real-ized I only had ten bucks in cash.

"Jeff, it's no problem if you can't fix it," I said, not fully meaning it. "I rode a few miles after blowing the first spoke and might have screwed something up. If I have to hitch to Ashland, it's my own fault."

He grunted but didn't look up. I took the hint and went out-side and found Rachel on the phone with her mom. I got her at-tention, waved my ten around, then pointed at her and raised my eyebrows. She frowned and held up one hand. Five dollars. So we had fifteen total. And my debit card was at the park. Shit. I headed inside and Jeff was on his feet, spinning the wheel. Sweat swam on his brow and through his hair. His baggy T-shirt now clung to his frame.

He turned at the sound of the door shutting, smiled weakly, and said, "It's ready to go."

"Really? Wow! Thank you, Jeff. I can't begin to tell you how much I appreciate this."

I started to explain our cash situation, but he walked back to the office, as if he hadn't heard. I figured he maybe just wanted to settle up at the park, so I circled the shop, shutting off lights, trying to appear helpful, and then followed him out the door. We all piled back into the truck, and I again thanked him for his help.

"No need to thank me. I've needed help and haven't always gotten it," he said. "I've done some bad things, but I've got a second chance to do some right." He shot us a sidelong glance, then started the engine. It seemed like he wanted to say more about this. So I fished for it.

"You don't seem like such a bad guy to me," I said.

"Well, you didn't know me when I was beating up cops. They chased me halfway around the state. Took four of 'em to wrestle me down, and two ended up in the hospital."

Rachel shifted beside me. Jeff had said this without remorse, almost boastfully, as if describing a football game where he'd scored a big touchdown. I pictured him beating up cops. Pictured him angry. The image was terrifying.

"That's behind me now," he said, as if reading our thoughts. "I've got a second chance and I'm taking it."

For the rest of the drive he talked jovially about his church, his relationship with God, his conviction that life was about helping others. To his credit, he didn't ask the questions I was expecting, didn't try to tie up the night with a "this is what Christians do—now, why don't you become one?" sermon. He just invited us to see where he'd come from and where he'd arrived. He didn't invite us to pay him, though. Didn't permit us, despite my blubbering protestations. "That's not what this is about," he said finally, and I understood I'd better leave it alone.

By the time he dropped us at our tent, night had fallen. Jeff had spent nearly three hours of a beautiful Monday night driving around and tinkering in his shop, all for two hapless strangers. We asked if we could get him breakfast in the morning, but he said he had work to do. And with that, he got back into his truck, accepted our final thank-yous, and drove out of the park, leaving Rachel and me to eat a string cheese and cookie dinner and gaze up at the stars and wonder what, exactly, we'd done to deserve all this.

CHAPTER 5

To Carry It with Me

I woke to the sound of a distant lawn mower. For a few minutes, I lay in my bag, drifting in and out of sleep, but the drone of the engine got louder and louder, until eventually, through the door of the tent fly, which Rachel or I must have left unzipped after the last of our overnight trips to our pine-tree bathroom, I saw a flannel-clad man ride by on a John Deere.

Hines Park was getting a haircut.

Rachel sat up and stretched. It had been a cool night, and she was covered head to toe in the blindingly white long underwear she'd picked up before we left. The first night she donned the outfit, we'd discovered it glowed in the dark, and now, even in the low light of morning, there was a powdery aura about her. With the form-fitting fabric, its snow-white radiant glow, and her long, flowing hair, she looked like some kind of winter-themed superheroine.

I stuck my head out of the tent. It was another gorgeous summer day, popcorn clouds on blue sky, and we were going to spend all of it riding toward a small town called Washburn, seventy miles to the north, on the shore of Lake Superior.

We dropped the tent, packed and racked the bags, and got dressed. Today I opted for the gray T-shirt, having decided I'd only wear that shiny, blue, I'm-a-stupid-rich-tourist shirt when I absolutely had to. Rachel had similarly buried her eyeball-burning pink tank top, opting instead for the beige number she'd worn on our first day out.

I was about to saddle up when Rachel asked, "Should we butter up today?"

"Yeah. I guess we should."

I dug into a pannier, found the tube of chamois butter. Squirted a dollop into my palm, shoved my hand down my shorts, and coated every inch of skin that might contact the saddle.

"Mmmm," Rachel purred, throwing her arms over my shoulders. "That . . . is so . . . *hot.*"

I yanked my hand up and wiped the final traces of lotion on her arm. She shrieked, then smeared the mess on my neck.

Chamois butter. The name sounded innocuous enough, like something you might spread on a baguette. It was not something you might spread on a baguette. It was crotch lubricant.

My dad had told me about chamois butter—a trademarked product, spelled (groan) Chamois Butt'r—years before, when I'd taken a long ride with him and some of his biking buddies. We were to ride a hundred miles that day, and though I'd never ridden half that far, I was nineteen, which meant I was all knowing and indestructible and didn't need to rub any stupid-old-man cream on my butt. By the end of the day, I felt like someone had attacked my perineum with a belt sander. I'd been a Chamois Butt'r true believer ever since, and had sold Rachel on the stuff.

Now she rubbed a palmful between her legs, scrunching up her nose in disgust. "I feel," she said, "like I just sat in a bucket of mayonnaise."

We were on the road by eight. Despite the previous day's short ride, my legs now felt weak. Not sore. Just heavy. Like they'd been injected with pudding. Thankfully, we had a light tailwind nudging us northward, and we rode the first seventeen miles, to Glidden, without a break.

Just south of town, I noticed a hand-carved "Black Bear Capital" sign atop a roadside berm, and then, a few hundred feet farther along, a gas station with "Bear Crossing" emblazoned across its canopy. We turned onto the main drag, and I looked left to find a white, two-story bungalow that housed a restaurant called the Bruin. On my right, in a squat brick building, sat the Glidden Black Bear Bakery. This place knew how to project an image.

Rachel and I bought some bear claws, and at the baker's urging, headed across the road to check out Mr. Bear, a town mascot of sorts. Back in the sixties, apparently, some hunters near Glidden had shot, killed, and stuffed the largest black bear ever seen, and he now lived next to the elementary school, in a little log cabin with floor-to-ceiling windows. A brushed steel sign said that Mr. Bear weighed 665 pounds, and that it had taken seven men to drag him from the woods. I believed it. He was immense, a mountain of fur and teeth and claws. As I looked him over, I thought about how it must have felt to install him here. To take the wild and rugged, place it behind lock and key. In his new digs, Mr. Bear was looking not rugged but regal. It appeared he had recently been groomed. His fur was luminous, his eyeballs polished, his nose gleaming.

I leaned my forehead on the glass, stared into those shiny, lifeless eyes. I got it, this scene—knew Mr. Bear was a symbol for the big bad world, his stuffed carcass a celebration of Glidden's residents and their mastery of their surroundings. And I knew that Mr. Bear was a gimmick. Glidden had gussied him up and adopted the whole black bear theme with the hope of attracting folks from the big city (i.e., anywhere with a highway off-ramp, an outlet mall, and/or a Fuddruckers), because that was where the tourists came from, and those tourists brought the tourist dollars that kept so many Wisconsin towns from shriveling up and dying.

Rachel and I had already encountered several such towns. There was Boulder Junction, musky capital of the world; Mercer, loon capital of the world; Park Falls, ruffed grouse capital of the world; Butternut, which isn't world capital of anything but does boast the "best-tasting water" in Wisconsin; and, of course, the town where I went to high school, Eagle River, also known as the snowmobile capital of (you guessed it) the world. Every one was holding up a billboard to tourists, inviting them to come catch the musky, drink the water, listen to the loons, get shitfaced and snowmobile from bar to bar, go ahead and shoot all the fucking grouse, but please, please, please just come and rent a cottage and buy a T-shirt and have a hamburger.

I pulled back from the glass, turned to look at the street. Empty. Something inside me flipped. I had loved growing up in a small town, but as soon as I graduated, and without a second thought, I'd left the area. I came back for countless visits, even returned for a few summers to work construction and play in the area lakes and bars with my friends. We visited, all of us, and then, like the tourists, we left. Not for a moment did we consider staying. This was the other half of the small town equation. Glidden and Conover wouldn't have had to work so hard to get tourists to come if they could only get their young to stay.

"Hey." Rachel's hand was on my shoulder. "You ready to ride?"

I snapped out of my daze and looked at her. Now she was

pulling on her helmet, squinting into the late-morning sun. In front of me, in this woman and these bikes and the bags that adorned them, was everything I was moving toward. And behind me, Mr. Bear.

"Yeah. Let's go."

We rode north through a sliver of the Chequamegon-Nicolet National Forest, a 1.5 million-acre, second-growth preserve planted after loggers failed to preserve the first growth. To either side, pine and maple and fir stretched and stopped as one, as if the entire forest had been trimmed with a giant lawn mower. On our super-map, the Chequamegon appeared as a chunky green polygon, and I'd been looking forward to riding through it, had expected the world to go all mossy and majestic. Life imitating cartography imitating life. But now that we were inside, I found it didn't really look or feel or smell different from the stretches we'd just ridden through. On the map those areas had simply been the white space between the towns and forests. But this stretch, this Forest, had the same mix of deciduous and evergreen, the same lava-hot pavement, the same scent, that oddly sweet blend of pine needles and animal droppings and decomposing leaves, and gasoline.

"CB!" Rachel yelled. She was behind me, but from the way she said it, I could tell she was smiling. "Wait, no, BFTB!"

I knew this meant something but couldn't recall what. The day before, we'd begun to develop a code language to communicate essentials out on the road, and I knew CB stood for "car back," TB for "truck back." But BFTB? I glanced at the rearview. In the glass I could see Rachel hunkered over the handlebars and, behind her, a wall of twisted metal. As an oddly localized gust rushed up my spine, I remembered.

A big fucking truck blew by, not three feet from my

shoulder. It was a double-trailer semi, loaded to the brim with thick slabs of hardwood, and as it passed I couldn't help but think of the opening scene from *Star Wars*. This semi was the Imperial Star Destroyer, appearing from the periphery and floating, slow and sinister, into full view. As it thundered past, I inhaled its sickly sweet diesel-pine perfume, felt its pulsing heat on my neck, struggled to keep my bike from getting sucked into the lane. In its wake the Destroyer left a yawning vacuum, and I careened toward it, pedaling furiously, riding the current, feeling for a brief, ecstatic moment like I might be capable of flight. And then, just like that, the wind was gone, and with it the semi, disappearing around a bend in the road ahead.

"Holy shit," I said. "That was incredible!"

Rachel appeared to have other thoughts on the matter, but before she had the chance to respond, my rear wheel cut in.

Ping!

Rachel heard it too. "Was that . . . ?" she asked.

I slid over to the shoulder, got off the bike, and discovered that, yes, it was *that*. Another broken fucking spoke.

This time it was on the nondrive side, meaning I could, in theory, fix it without removing the cassette. I did my best to ignore the rising anxiety and looked up at Rachel. "You might want to get comfortable," I said, straining to smile.

Her face betrayed a hint of impatience, or maybe doubt, but she shrugged and waddled toward the grass. "I'm going to make a couple of calls, 'kay?"

I nodded and set to undressing the bike. As I pulled the uke and sleeping pad from the rack, detached the panniers, and flipped the bike over, I thought about Jeff and how he had worked with the wheel. My mind started to travel to an awfully ungracious place, and I shooed away the thought. Jeff had done all he could to help, for free, and this wasn't his fault.

I followed the steps he had taken: removed the wheel, pried away the rim liner, and extracted the broken spoke. Once I got the replacement situated, I slid the wheel back into the dropouts, prayed a godless prayer, and, using the brake pads as a guide, set to straightening it. I remembered Jeff saying that if I made tiny adjustments on the spokes, using quarter turns, loosening and tightening, all would go well. And, miraculously, it did. After ten minutes, the wheel was clearing the pads. After twenty, it almost spun true. It appeared I had fixed something.

Soon enough I was back on the road, riding hard, Rachel hugging my back tire, the forest filling my vision, the wheel doing precisely what a wheel was supposed to do, and even though I couldn't quite pin who I was competing against, I knew I was totally winning.

My sense of triumph lasted about a half hour. As we rode north toward Ashland, I began to feel sluggish, and I kept hearing these disconcerting clicks and clacks from below, and so every five minutes I found myself pulling over, kneeling and searching for blown spokes. But I found no blown spokes, no flat tires, nothing worse than a stray pannier strap smacking against the tent poles. Eventually, begrudgingly, I accepted that this had nothing to do with the bike. I was just plain beat. My legs were saturated with lactic acid, my back and neck knifed by the slightest of movements. My temples were claustrophobic in my stupid fucking helmet, and I felt like a county road crew had spent all day jackhammering my crotch. I'd heard somewhere that male cyclists not seeking a DIY vasectomy should stand from the saddle every thirty minutes, for thirty seconds, and I was doing so, but still I was aching, and soon enough I was numb.

I asked Rachel if we could take a break. She said, "Oh my God, yes." As we dined on candy in the driveway of an abandoned lumber mill/steampunk playground, she complained of aching knees and pain in both wrists. I mumbled something about changing hand position, but she interrupted. She'd been doing that all day. I didn't know what else to tell her. This didn't seem like something that would fade over time. I imagined it would only get worse. But it was just beginning, and neither of us knew what to do about it, short of taking breaks before it got to be too much.

It was late afternoon by the time we rolled up to Ashland, a small college town on the Superior shore. Well before the water came into view, I felt its breath curling through city streets, up my arms, into my helmet. And that scent. So subtle and singular, the no-salt-please alternative to your standard ocean breeze. Superior, as ever, smelled just how it felt. Cold.

We pulled up to a shoreline park, and I called Donn and Ann Christensen, some friends of the Simeones who had invited us to camp on their lawn. Donn answered, his voice sweet and mellow, saying things like "welcome" and "take your time" and "spaghetti."

I liked him already.

It was eleven more miles to Washburn. Eleven *windy* miles. Though the lake was now out of sight, hidden behind a finger of forest, its icy breath wound around tree trunks, up over undergrowth, and into our faces. The wind was low, maybe ten miles an hour, but that was enough to make us fight for every foot, and by the halfway point I was tanking hard. Unreasonably hard, come to think of it. All day I'd blamed my aching muscles and raspy throat on the climbs and smoke-belching semis, but the present aches and rasps felt, well, different. I released the bars and raised my fingers to my neck. The Lump. It was throbbing, up to something.

Donn and Ann were the sort of well-muscled, ruddy-cheeked fiftysomethings who appeared casually, almost accidentally fit, and as I sat with them at a tastefully ginghamed picnic table, inhaling garden-fresh salad and homemade marinara with the desperate velocity of a six-year-old from a ten-child family, I learned—thanks to Rachel, who had the composure to speak, and breathe, between bites—that they both skied all winter, biked all summer, and had taken many tours of their own, including a four-thousand-mile journey that put ours to shame. They were bike-trip sages, and total sweethearts. By sunset, when Rachel and I retreated to the tent, I was full and content and barely thinking about the Lump.

The next morning, I woke feeling like I had swallowed sandpaper. Shit.

Rachel and I wandered into the house to find Donn, a doctor, getting ready to head to work. I raised my hand to my neck, where the Lump was doing its thing, being red and gross and painful. The night before, I had been relieved that he hadn't mentioned it, but now I asked if he might check it out.

Donn took the Lump between his fingers, pressed it like a button. "Looks like it's just a swollen lymph node," he said. "But, actually . . . Have you had mono?"

"Um, no," I said. Mono hadn't been on my radar since high school, when kids brought it up as an excuse to talk about kissing and, by extension, sex. "Do you think I have mono?"

"I really couldn't say. But swollen lymph nodes are a symptom." He must have noticed the color draining from my face, because he added, "Don't worry about it. If you're still feeling sick in a few days, you can always stop at a clinic."

Rachel and I decided to lay over in Washburn for the day, partly because of my maybe-mono and partly because, oddly enough, we already had errands to run. While we ran them, I pretty much without interruption thought about mono. I thought about it while riding to Ashland; while buying a nifty, portable cassette-removal tool for future spoke explosions; while helping Rachel pick a proper inflatable pad to replace her piece-of-shit, sleep-depriving foam mat; while getting groceries for the thank-you-for-hosting-us chili we were planning to whip up; while drinking coffee in a park and sitting on the Superior shore and riding back to Washburn.

We returned to the house by midafternoon, and I told Rachel I was going to take a nap, by which I meant I was going to lie in the tent and have a mild anxiety attack. I stretched out on my bag, felt my heart slamming against my sternum. If I had mono, I told myself, we'd have to head back to Conover for at least a couple of weeks, and by the time I was back on my feet it would be too late to ride all the way to the West Coast, and—

I cut myself off there. It was probably nothing more than a nasty head cold.

I ate a handful of ibuprofen and headed inside. Rachel was tucked up in a chair, paging through a *National Geographic*. We got started on the chili, combining our groceries with canned tomatoes from the pantry and fresh greens from the garden, and finished just before Donn and Ann got home. The chili was tasty, and it felt good to offer something to our hosts, even if it was simple, and even if we had created it mainly from things that already belonged to them. That night we had more great conversation, and Donn and Ann offered more advice about where to ride and who to stay with, but soon the drugs wore off and I got all hazy and shivery. I dried some dishes, then headed to the tent to be alone with the Lump and my thoughts.

Rachel grabbed a handful of blueberries from the bag in my lap and began popping them into her mouth, one by one, taunting a scraggly seagull that had camped out in front of us.

"These aren't for you, pal," she said.

The bird took a step toward the bench we were sitting on, his head bobbing sporadically, as if to some polyrhythmic beat only he could hear.

"Didn't we just talk about this?" Rachel frowned. "I feel like you're not listening to me."

I smiled and slid my hand onto her knee. Just after dawn, I had woken feeling even worse, so I'd swallowed more pills and done my best to ignore what my body was telling me. Sniffles or no sniffles, we'd needed to get moving. And now, sitting in the sun, awash in endorphins and caffeine, I was feeling good about being back on the road, and especially, here in Bayfield, the (wait for it) berry capital of Wisconsin. Rachel and I had made the obligatory stop at a u-pick patch, and we'd brought our spoils down to a bench in a little park overlooking the harbor.

"I'm pretty sure this is where we docked."

"Yeah?" Rachel asked, still staring down the seagull. "Whose boat was it?"

"Hmm. Honestly, I have no idea."

When I was a little kid, my family had taken a few sailing trips to the nearby Apostle Islands. I had only the vaguest memories of those trips: Dad calling me first mate as I weakly tugged on a line that may or may not have been attached to a sail; my sister, Leah, and I scrunching up in the triangular bed at the aft of the cabin; Leah barfing on Mom. I hadn't ever considered who the boat belonged to. It hadn't mattered to me then and, I decided, it still didn't.

"I can see why you talk about this lake so often," Rachel said, looking out at the water. "It does kind of feel like the ocean." She'd offered these words on a few occasions, and every time I took them as a personal compliment.

"Yeah," I replied. "And we get to follow the shore for another hundred miles."

We were headed for the town of Cornucopia, better known as Corny. Turned out Donn and Ann knew a young couple who lived up there, and that morning Donn had called to see if they'd put us up for a night. At first I had wanted to decline his offer. It was time, I thought, for Rachel and me to step out on our own. Then I reminded myself that I felt not like a conquering hero but like shit. I decided I could suffer a bit more generosity from perfect strangers.

West of Bayfield, the forest gave way to farmland, vast expanses speckled with solitary trees and five-foot rolls of hay. We stopped at a particularly picturesque spot and walked into the field and both emptied our bladders on hay bales. It occurred to me that this scene, minus the peeing, would be stunning in autumn, by far my favorite Northwoods season. The grass underfoot would be shorn to stubble; the trees a blur of crimson, orange, and yellow; the air crisp but for a hint of smoke from a nearby burn pile. Regret shot through me. All year I looked forward to autumn in Wisconsin, and even amid my recent travels, I'd managed to get back home and catch the colors. Now, for the first time, I'd miss them.

I turned to take in more scenery, and my gaze fell upon Rachel, who was on her way toward me, moving in a way I could only describe as frolicking. She was bounding through the field, weaving around hay bales, giggling wildly. In a few seconds, I was laughing with her. If there was any reason to leave the Wisconsin autumn behind, this was it.

We continued on, riding side by side, the road now nearly

empty of cars. The pavement began rolling with the surrounding farmland, and I tucked into a tear-jerking descent, fought up a leg-stabbing climb, then did it all over again as the highway wavered up and down and up, finally plunging back to lake level. At the base of the final hill, I saw a sign pointing to Meyers Beach. Blew right by it. But the words tore through my head, setting off sirens.

I squeezed the brakes, spun around, told Rachel I wanted to check out the beach. I didn't say why, and she didn't ask. She just rode beside me as I followed the impeccably smooth pavement into the lakeside parking lot. By the time I waddled up to the sign near the beach, I knew where I was. I was *here*. At the sea caves. And though I didn't need to read the sign—didn't want to—that's exactly what I did, aloud, to Rachel, who had been staring at me staring at the words.

Sea Cave Catastrophe: UW student perishes in Superior kayak accident

The sea caves are beautiful but can be dangerous. There are no landings and the cliffs cannot be climbed. When turbulent conditions capsized the kayak of a six-foot-three, 170-pound college athlete in the prime of life, he was not strong enough to survive being beaten against the cliffs by the waves.

I had gotten the call three summers earlier. The message, actually. I'd been hiking and camping in Yosemite National Park, at the tail end of a Wisconsin-to-California road trip with my friend Vijay. I'd had no cell reception in the woods. It was only as I was driving back to San Francisco with Vij that I felt the buzz in my pocket and pulled out the phone. Seven new voicemails. My gut flipped. It had only been two days since we were in the valley, where I'd had perfect reception and last checked my messages.

The first was from my mom, and for a moment, I thought she might have left all seven. She defined the term "helicopter mom," could work herself into a frenzy of worry over anything and nothing. Maybe she'd seen reports of nearby forest fires, or a yeti sighting, and had been calling incessantly to make sure neither had consumed me.

But the second message was from Josh. "Bri." His voice was shaky, oddly formal. "I need to talk to you. It's about Sam Larsen. Please call as soon as you're able."

I didn't need to listen to the rest of the messages. I knew. And looking back, I think it was the way Josh said his full name. Sam Larsen.

Josh and I both knew damn well that there was only one Sam. When we said Sam, we were talking cartoonishly big ears and the ever-present smile between them. Big, brown eyes, often brimming with tears from a spastic fit of laughter, a missed free throw in the final seconds of a conference game, a massive bong rip. We were talking about a lanky frame, all of it wrapped in sinewy muscle, that folded up awkwardly in busses and at desks but moved with astonishing, gazelle-like grace on the soccer field. A sensitive soul who, even as his friends goofed off in the basement, would spend hours in earnest conversation with my mom. A boy who actually enjoyed talking about his feelings, who made everyone feel he was their best friend.

Sam was the eldest of our group. Me, Beau, Joe, Joey, Josh, and Sammy: The guys with whom I'd spent every minute in high school. The group I loved fiercely. The group that popped into my head when I thought of home. Together, we had launched ourselves into lakes from docks and rafts and cliffs and airborne tubes; had made a sport of fishtailing pickups and hatchbacks on wintertime ice and summertime sand; had gotten our first citations for underage drinking and speeding and vandalism; had stayed up until dawn having achingly sincere conversations about the conversations we didn't know how to have with the girls we were sure we loved.

We were a family. And with family, you only used full names when you were preparing to dole out punishment.

I asked Vijay to pull over. There was a ditch just past the shoulder, and I slid down the slope, seeking some semblance of privacy. I dialed Josh, and there, amid the crushed beer cans and the empty bags of Doritos, the diesel fumes and the relentless whine of passing traffic, I heard Josh's voice, three thousand miles away, telling me that Sam Larsen had been at Lake Superior, that Sam Larsen had been kayaking around the Bayfield sea caves with Lenny, his dad, that the weather had turned ugly, that Sam Larsen had been knocked from his boat, that the six-foot waves had kept Sam Larsen from getting back in his boat, that Sam Larsen's lips had gone blue, that Lenny—"you know Lenny is such a strong swimmer"—had swum to shore for help because he had no other choice, that help had arrived in a helicopter, that Sam Larsen had lost consciousness by then, that Sam Larsen had been in the near-freezing water for far too long, and that the rescue team had done everything it could but could not bring Sam Larsen back. That Sam Larsen had passed away, an hour before I called.

I don't remember what I said to Josh, other than "I love you" and "I'll be home as soon as possible."

I sat there for some time, staring at the ratty grass between my feet. Eventually I got up and walked to the car, opened the door, slumped into the seat.

"You all right?"

I kept my eyes on the windshield. "Sammy was in an accident. He's dead."

Vij drew in a sharp breath and rocked his head back. "Jesus, Bri." He looked at me for what felt like an hour, then turned back to the road. "I can't believe Sam's fucking dead."

I cringed but couldn't fault him those words. I was thinking the same thing.

We'd just been talking about Sammy. An hour earlier, almost exactly.

Over the years, Sam and I had drifted. There had been an initial falling-out, over some trivial shit I barely remember, and then a longer, deeper divergence. We still exchanged e-mails, still saw each other a few times a year, but our friendship was in a holding pattern. Sam was a vivid presence in my past, and I imagined there would be a point where we'd reconnect and build an even stronger friendship, one in which we were mature enough to appreciate the ways we'd each grown and changed. But we weren't there yet. Given the distance between us—three hours, if you were pushing it, between Madison and Eau Claire, our respective college towns—we weren't able to be in the present with each other. We were stuck in the in-between.

I'd been feeling hopeful that Sam and I were on the verge of breaking out of this stasis. Just a few months earlier, I had visited him in Eau Claire, arriving late on a Friday and walking into an already packed party at his place. After giving me a big hug, wrapping his lanky frame around mine, he had grabbed me a beer and tossed his arm over my shoulder. "Bri," he'd said, grinning and raising his voice over the deafening hip-hop billowing up from the basement, "I'm so glad you're here." He paused, his foot-wide smile somehow stretching further, his watery brown eyes locked on mine. He had clearly been drinking for hours, but I knew those eyes, knew there was something else going on behind them. Still, I was unprepared for him to say, without warning or preamble, "All this shit from the past few years, it's so *stupid*, right?"

I coughed out a laugh. Before I could respond, a few of his soccer teammates walked up, and then he was off to play party host, I to abuse my liver with his friends. We didn't continue the conversation that night, or the next day. We didn't need to. It wasn't about a conversation. It was an opening. An invitation to take the yawning space between us and begin to fill it.

I had missed that opening. That invitation.

That point on the horizon, the place where we would use what we'd picked up to build something new, it had vanished. I was left with the in-between.

Rachel and I headed to the shore. I was hoping we'd have a view of the caves, or at least the bluffs above. I wanted this to hurt. But now, when I looked east, I saw only an evergreen tail disappearing into blue water.

I sat down beside Rachel, who'd gone quiet after reading the sign. We'd talked about Sam before, but only briefly. I never knew quite what to tell her, beyond the rote details, and so usually she did what she was doing now, which was grab my hand and massage it and ask if I was okay. I was, I told her. For three years running, whenever I thought of Sam I'd felt not sad but empty. Even in the week after his death, spent at a lakeside cottage in the company of my closest friends, I had been unable to cry. A few times I'd needed to leave, not because it was too hard, but because it didn't feel hard enough. And it wasn't a question of love. Of *course* I loved Sam. I'd just gotten used to a world where he lived only in the past and future. I still had the past. And I didn't know how to mourn our future. In many ways, I was still waiting for it.

Now I turned to Rachel and said, "This is my first time here."

She kept massaging.

"I'd been waiting. I wanted to . . ." I trailed off, stared at the water. "Honestly, I'm not sure what I was waiting for. I guess I figured if I chose the right time to come, I'd feel . . . I don't know. Something different. Something, period."

Rachel's eyes were on mine. For a moment it looked like *she* might cry.

"I'm sorry," she said, squeezing my hand. "I can't imagine what it must feel like."

I squeezed back and chose not to say what I was thinking, which was: me neither. Instead I stood, and smiled, and said, "I'm going to take a walk."

Rachel nodded and gave me a smile-frown. "Okay."

I headed east, toward the caves. I tried to make myself feel something. Anything. But I was empty. I knew only that I missed Sam, even as I couldn't fully feel his absence; that I missed Wisconsin, even as I stood on its soil; and that, in deciding to follow Rachel wherever she chose to take me, I'd for the first time in my life made plans to leave this place but none to return.

I looked over my shoulder. Rachel was now lying in the sand, the sun bright on her skin, revealing what was already a pretty impressive farmer's tan. I turned back and stepped toward the shallows. I let the frigid water lap my feet, looked out over the blue, and thought of how many times I'd found myself here, or beside a thousand other Wisconsin lakes. I thought about the Simeones and the Christensens, my folks and friends, the Gliddens and Bayfields, black bears and berries. About everyone and everything that made this place, for me, a place.

I wanted to carry it with me. Wanted to pack my past in my panniers, haul it to the horizon, use it to build something new with Rachel. But we hadn't yet arrived at the horizon. We didn't even know where, exactly, it was. We only knew we were on the verge of heading into unknown territory, into that place I'd learned to avoid. The in-between. There was nothing to do now but accept it, live in it. We'd picked a point in the distance and were moving toward it, mile by mile. And we needed to believe we couldn't lose what we were carrying along the way.

CHAPTER 6

To Leave a Mark

West of Meyers Beach, the highway climbed through farmland and fourth-growth oak, then dipped back toward Superior, and as the slope steepened, I dropped my head and drove the pedals, spinning faster and faster, until pedaling was of no use and I was just chin-kissing the bars, tucking elbows to hips, and plunging shoreward, lungs full of lake air, eyes on distant blue.

The grade leveled out, and I coasted into a shore-hugging gravel cul-de-sac. Rachel pulled up beside me, and together we backhanded tears from cheeks and gaped at the north end of the lot, where, just as Donn Christensen had promised, a farmers' market was in full swing. It all looked familiar enough—mismatched tents and tables, thrift-store scales and baskets of gleaming produce—except for the people, all of whom appeared to be (a) in their twenties and (b) crunchy as fuck. The lot teemed with ponchos and tie-dye, Hacky Sacks and antiwar bumper stickers, hand-drawn signs advertising artisanal soaps and precious stones and made-to-order waffles with local maple syrup. This was not the Wisconsin I'd grown up with.

We leaned our bikes against a gnarled pine and walked through the market, looking for Jennifer Sauter Sargent, the friend Donn had called that morning. Based on his description, I guessed she was the dark-haired, smiling woman presiding over a table full of summer squash and purple peppers. We walked up to introduce ourselves, but she spoke first.

"You must be the bikers! I was wondering when you'd get in."

I opened my mouth to ask how she knew, then looked down at my clunky shoes and sweat-stained shirt. My cheeks flushed.

Jennifer told us she needed to stay at the market for another hour or so, but that we should feel free to head to her house, just a couple of miles up the road. She pointed to the east. Right where we'd come from, at the top of the hill we had just bombed down. I threw a silent tantrum, then smiled and thanked her.

Climbing that hill seemed like a lot of work, so we loitered awhile at the market, then headed over to the four-block strip that constituted downtown Corny. At the south end of the strip, across from Fish Lipps Bar and Restaurant and a tiny shake-sided shack that, I shit you not, boasted of being "Wisconsin's northernmost post office," was the local general store. From the street, it seemed ordinary enough—the piles of seasoned wood, the obligatory ice chest—but once we stepped inside, I wondered if it might have been airlifted from one of Madison's hippie enclaves. Among the standard groceries were "natural" hygienic products, jars of locally made honey, herbal extracts, and copious usage of the word "organic." Corny and Conover were about the same size, but my hometown general store had been a gas station–cum–deli–cum–video rental depot known as Energy Mart. Now I wondered what a childhood in Corny might have looked like. What I might look like had I grown up here.

In the hour we spent exploring town, the afternoon's dose of endorphins and ibuprofen slowly wore off. By the time we got back on the bikes, I was feeling lousy and had the sinking feeling I was fighting something worse than a nasty cold. My lungs had shriveled into useless little raisins, my legs protested every pedal stroke, and pins and needles poked from under my skin. The Lump, for its part, seemed as healthy as ever.

We got back on the road. I tucked behind Rachel, kept my eyes on her shoulders, and focused on staying a few feet from her rear wheel. Up till this point, I'd only ridden beside or in front of her, and now, in her wake, I was noticing things: how the muscles of her back flexed and furrowed as she drove down the pedals, how her body blocked my view of the landscape, and how she was raising her head every few seconds, eyeing me in the rearview. Adjusting her speed, keeping me close. It felt at once comforting and patronizing, and I wondered if she'd noticed me doing the same thing on our ride from Park Falls to Washburn.

Soon enough, we reached the Sauter Sargents' driveway and followed it to the house, a rectangle wrapped in corrugated steel and adorned with Tibetan prayer flags and Technicolor hammocks. Andrew, Jennifer's husband, was out front, working on what appeared to be a chicken coop. With his snap-button shirt, khaki shorts, and sideburns peeking from a backward baseball cap, he looked like a dozen guys I'd known back in high school. Rachel and I laid down our bikes and walked up to introduce ourselves, and I felt a faint boost. I was done riding for the day, and that knowledge was its own kind of medicine.

Jennifer soon pulled up in an old white Ford, and after we helped her unload the market supplies, she and Andrew showed us through their handcrafted, solar-powered home, then walked us back outside to point out the property lines of their seventy-acre spread. It was a mix of forest and overworked farmland, and they were bringing the soil back, beginning with the flourishing fenced-in garden just west of the house. This, Jennifer said, was the beginnings of an organic farm, and they had big plans to grow tons of veggies, raise chickens, and produce their own lacto-fermented foods.

I had no idea what that meant. But I was feeling too spacey, not to mention proud, to ask.

Rachel wasn't. "Sounds exciting. I've heard the term, but what's lacto-fermentation?"

"It's the way people used to preserve things," Andrew said. "You just use salt and spices, and they bring out the lactic acid in whatever else you've got in the jar."

Jennifer said we could try one of their concoctions alongside the soup Rachel had offered to make with the dried lentil and bean mixture we had been hauling since we left my folks' place. We hadn't yet touched this mixture, let alone the pancake ingredients or granola or the pasta and quinoa we'd picked up in Ashland—it had proved a whole lot easier to subsist on snacks from small-town stores and leftovers packed by our hosts. Still, we kept the grains and powders, figuring we'd need them when the trip *really* started.

Jennifer and Rachel headed inside. I wanted to follow them, curl up on the couch, and sleep through the night. My head was pounding and I was exhausted. But Andrew was going to keep working, and I knew that I'd feel like a lazy, freeloading turd if I didn't help. I joined him in the yard, where he was putting up a fence around the coop. Despite my heavy lungs and snotty nose, it actually felt good to wrap my fingers around a shovel and drive its blade into the dirt—to leave a mark on the land, not just pass over it.

At dusk, we gathered inside for a dinner of lentil soup, pickled beets, and fresh-from-the-garden salad. It all looked delicious, but my tongue was bathed in bacteria. Everything tasted like Styrofoam. The soup did soothe my ragged throat, just enough that I was able to chime in when Rachel began the obligatory this-is-how-we-met-and-where-we're-going-and-why speech.

No matter how many times we told this story, it still felt like a romantic epic. Both of us far from home. A crowded bar, me in the shadows, Rachel on stage. Me swooning and chasing and eventually ending up on stage beside her. The slow evolution from bandmates to friends to lovers to partners. The months of distance we endured to embark on this adventure together.

Jennifer and Andrew then shared more of their story, and I found it to be every bit as romantic as the one we'd just told. They talked about how they had met in Door County and moved north and bought this land and built this house, how Andrew had read a book about salt and become obsessed with fermentation, how that had turned into building a certified kitchen and provided a business model for their burgeoning farm, how they had found a like-minded community of young progressives up here, and how they were trying to live their values while respecting the old-timers who wanted their town to stay the same and did *not* want to hear another goddamn thing about doulas or a community theater or bringing more organic food to the general store.

I wanted to know more about the town and their day-to-day life and whether they had any regrets about settling so early. But I was struggling—droopy-eyed and feverish and ready to crawl into bed. I began raking my fingers across the Lump.

"So, what's that all about?" Andrew asked, pointing a spoon toward my neck.

I snorted a laugh, feeling like Frodo with his ring. I had been probing the Lump because I was feeling weak, because I wanted to disappear. But I'd only drawn more attention to myself.

"A swollen lymph node. Donn looked at it this morning. He said it could be mono."

"Yikes," Jennifer said. "You know, there's a clinic just up the road, in Red Cliff. You could probably see someone tomorrow before you head out." She looked at Andrew, then at Rachel, then back at me. "Actually . . . Do you two feel like you're going to want to ride?"

Rachel looked at me and shrugged. "It's up to you."

I sat with this for a second, then released a baleful, would-that-I-could sigh. "I'm not sure I'll be able to do much tomorrow."

"Well, I ask because we're going to an old-time music festival tomorrow night," Jennifer continued, "and we haven't found anyone to feed the dog and the chickens. You could get some rest here, and it would be a big help to us. I'd say you two seem pretty trustworthy." She turned back to Andrew. "Right?"

He looked us over, pursing his lips and squinting, as if searching for evidence. Then he sat back and folded his arms. "Yep, they're clean."

Just like that, the place was ours. And as if the house wasn't enough, Jennifer offered to leave the keys to their truck, so I wouldn't have to bike to the clinic.

I was struck by their trust, by how easily they offered their space, by *how much* they had to offer. I marveled at the half-dozen guitars and banjos and mandolins, the jam-packed spice rack, the teeming bookshelves, the half-finished commercial kitchen where they'd do their lacto-ferma-fuck-if-I-could-remember. And then I looked out the window, where I could see our bikes, lonely and moonlit, lying on the lawn.

The Red Cliff Community Health Center's waiting room was pretty charming, as waiting rooms go: natural light streaming through the windows, stonework on the south wall, friendly receptionists. Rachel sat beside me, paging through magazines, as I moved through a stack of intake forms. On the first, I confirmed my personal information. On the second, I detailed all the ways I was uninsured and signed on the yes-I-know-this-might-mean-I-am-totally-fucked line. And on the third, I provided my medical history and checked off my symptoms. I'd always liked this part of the process, a personality test of sorts. If I checked the right combo, the doctor might feel compelled to tell me I was an intuiting, feeling, perceiving introvert.

I'd been a bit apprehensive about scheduling an appointment at this tiny clinic on an Ojibwa reservation, even though Jennifer had assured me they accepted any and all patients. I was a well-off white guy, after all. Every door in the world was open to me, and now I was walking through this one, into a clinic that was probably overwhelmed with *real* problems, just because I felt sleepy and had a bump on my neck?

If my body was 60 percent water, the other 40 percent was guilt, principally of the white, class, male, and Jewish varieties. And so while I felt relieved to be treated cordially when I entered the clinic, I only felt it for a second before realizing how fucked-up it was that I needed affirmation from an Ojibwa woman to feel comfortable, and even now I was considering—

"Brian Benson?"

A short, smiling woman was standing by the reception desk, holding open a door. We headed back to an exam room, and I went through the motions: stepped on the scale, rolled up my shirtsleeve to make way for the comforting python grip of the blood-pressure cuff, cringed when she inspected the Lump, breathed in, breathed out, said aaaah.

The nurse slid back from the table I was seated on and looked me in the eye.

"You don't have mono."

"What? Really?"

"Well, I can't say for certain, but it seems like you just have a really nasty cold. The doctor can run some lab tests, of course, but that's just going to cost you a bunch more money."

I choked out a laugh. I had never heard these words at any other clinic, and haven't since. "Thank you for your honesty," I said. "Should I still rest up for a bit? I don't want to overdo it and get even sicker. And what about this?" I pointed at the Lump.

"Lymph nodes can swell for dozens of reasons," she said, standing from her chair. "It'll probably be there for another week. Just pay attention to your body. If you end up having mono, you'll know. But if you wake up tomorrow and feel all right, I'd say you'll be fine on the bike."

"Wow," I said. "I really wasn't expecting to hear that." I paused, waiting for her to add more advice or qualifications. Silence. "So, I can leave?"

"Yes," she said. "You can leave."

Later that night, Rachel and I lay together on the couch, our feet tangled under a mess of blankets. She was scribbling in her journal, and I was trying to do the same. But I couldn't focus. I was paying attention to my body, just like the nurse had said I should.

All morning, and during our drive to the clinic, I'd been struggling, disease-ridden, dying. But now, after a few magic words from a straight-talking nurse, I felt like a different person. Though I still had the headache, the face full of snot, the goopy weight in my chest, these discomforts were no longer harbingers of impending doom—just garden-variety cold symptoms.

"You can leave," the nurse had said, and I'd believed her. I could leave. Now I just had to decide if I really wanted to.

After returning from the clinic, Rachel and I had huddled up in the den, playing rummy and listening to an Etta Baker CD I found under the coffee table. "One Dime Blues" came on just as we were finishing a game, and I dropped my cards, closed my eyes, and listened. When it ended, I got up and played it again. And again. I loved that song. Wasn't sure what Etta had in mind when she wrote the music, but something about it—the delicate arpeggios climbing upward, damn near sliding off the neck of the guitar, then sinking back into the sweet, sure melody—always made me think of coming home.

At dusk, we prepared a stir-fry, again using vegetables from the garden, then, midmeal, burst outside to fight off whatever snarling predator had suddenly stirred the chickens into a frenzy. Turned out it was the black lab puppy, who had somehow broken into the run. He thought he was playing—didn't understand why the chickens were shitting all over themselves and squawking bloody murder. Rachel pulled the dog inside, then returned to snap pictures as I bumbled around, herding the birds into their coop. By the time I coaxed the last one inside, a full twenty minutes later, Rachel and I were cracking up, tears in our eyes.

After we finished dinner, Rachel had put down the bowl she was drying and said she was kind of glad I'd gotten sick. She'd really enjoyed our day here, and she almost didn't want to leave. Now, as I stared down at my journal, I wondered what she was writing in hers—if she'd meant it when she said she didn't want to leave. I mean, I knew she didn't actually want to stay here, in

Andrew and Jennifer's living room, and neither did I. But being with her, alone in this space, had given me a taste of what we might have if we made up our minds to stay somewhere. It seemed brilliant, full of potential. Coops to build, gardens to grow, ideas to follow through on. Supposedly, we were going to do all that after the trip. But I knew there was no guarantee we'd make it to "after."

I walked to the kitchen and put on some water for tea. As I waited, I stared at the kitchen island, the cards from our rummy game scattered across its surface. I was reminded of yet another visit to *el lago*, when Rachel and I had spent an entire day playing cards and drinking wine by the water. Every few hours one of us would tug the other into our rented room, where we would tear off our clothes and attack each other as if we'd been apart for years. That day together, and every one that had followed, had only been possible because I'd ventured into the big unknown. Because both of us had. That's what made our story *so fucking romantic*, right? We'd found each other far from the places we called home, and found a new, shared place. And that's what we were doing, again, with this trip. I had no guarantees when I loaded up that backpack, but I'd let myself wander and stumble and second-guess, and if I hadn't, I wouldn't be here with Rachel, seeing Wisconsin as I'd never seen it before.

I looked over at Rachel, who appeared to be nodding off, her journal spread open on her chest. Then I walked to the front window. The bikes were still lying on the lawn, right where we'd left them. Patiently waiting to take us home.

PART III

THE IN-BETWEEN

CHAPTER 7

What Awaited Us

This day, our tenth on the road, would be a day of firsts.
For starters, day ten would mark our (1) first Minnesotan miles. We'd arrived in Duluth three days earlier, only to stall out again. This time, at least, it wasn't on my account. The morning after my clinic visit, I'd woken feeling good, and by the time we finished our seventy-mile, Corny-to-Duluth journey I had shaken my symptoms . . . and given them to Rachel. While she battled a lumpless version of my not-mono, we holed up in another comfy home, this one owned by Tonia Simeone—daughter of Bob and Terry—and her fiancé, Mike. Tonia, a grade-A midwestern sweetheart I'd known since my diaper days, was happy to host while Rachel recuperated, and it was great catching up with her and Mike. But after three nights, I got restless. Impatient. I mean, it helped hearing that Galen, now in western Ohio, had taken a little spill and banged his knee and stopped to heal up for a few days. But still, I felt like Rachel and I were somehow falling behind—not behind Galen, or really anyone in particular, just behind. And so when Rachel announced, on our fourth morning in Duluth, that she was officially healthy, I was

beyond ready to get back on the bike—and ride the wrong direction.

Indeed, on day ten we would take (2) our first due-west-is-for-suckers detour. Neither Rachel nor I had seen Lake Superior's North Shore, and dozens of people—Mike and Tonia, especially—had insisted that we *had* to check it out or we'd die miserable and regretful deaths. Mike recommended we ride as far as Illgen Falls, apparently the best cliff-diving spot in the universe. This would entail heading sixty miles east-northeast. Quite different from west-west. A big detour, but why not? This was the reason we'd shunned the Adventure Cycling maps. We were individuals. And sometimes being individuals meant riding sixty miles in the wrong direction.

On that note, day ten would also be (3) our first foray outside Simeoneland. Up to this point, Bob and Terry had hooked us up with places to stay every night. At their cabin, then with Donn and Ann—who in turn pointed us toward Jennifer and Andrew—and finally, with Tonia and Mike in Duluth. I was grateful for their help but ready to step away from the safety nets and into uncharted, unknown territory. And we were about to do exactly that.

Rachel bit into a carrot, her eyes fixed on the lake, and said, "I wasn't expecting this to look so much like the South Shore."

"Well," I replied, "that's because you're a bad listener. Tonia and Mike said it wouldn't get all big and dramatic until Gooseberry Falls."

She threw a chunk of carrot at me. It bounced off my cheek. I picked it up and ate it.

"I know *that*," she said. "It's just, we're in a new state. I guess I thought it'd be different."

"Yeah. Me too."

All morning, we'd been riding north on a series of lake-hugging side roads, and I had to admit the North Shore looked an awful lot like the South Shore: the same infinity-plus-one-mile views, the same puny waves lapping onto pebble-strewn beaches. It felt like a final embrace with Wisconsin, a long kiss good-bye. Too long perhaps. I loved the South Shore, but I was ready to leave it behind, to explode out into the big unknown. The Lump, after all, was deflated. Dead. It had softened from Ping-Pong ball to matzo ball and now merely resembled a healthy zit. I was at full strength, eager to see what I was capable of, incredulous that, after nine days, I *still* didn't know. Thanks to the spokes and the Lump, we hadn't been able to push ourselves—hadn't banged out any big-mileage days, hadn't so much as touched our beer-can stove, hadn't gotten sunburned or battle scarred or built up baseball-size calves or *T. rex* quadriceps.

And, well, no time like the present, right? I was ready, as was Rachel—the color had come back to her cheeks, and she was really *wearing* that grease-inked, chain-link calf tattoo. Even the Fuji looked poised. Its spokes were in fine fettle, chain oiled, tires topped off, down tube newly adorned with a neat oval sticker I'd bought at a Duluth brewery. I planned to pick up many such stickers along the way, to both personalize and uglify the bike. Soon the corporate logo would be hidden, the frame festooned with enough hideous fonts and clashing colors that even the most desperate of thieves would be like, uh, no thanks.

Rachel had attached the same brewhouse sticker to her bike. At first I whined, because *I* had seen it first. But then Rachel reminded me that *she* had first shown interest in the Fuji I now loved so dearly, and so hadn't she perhaps made the bigger compromise here? I relented. She had. And really, given the ridiculousness of our matching bikes and bags, it did kind of make sense to just ham up this barfy his-and-hers thing.

We were all ready, then. Me and Rachel, Fuji and Fuji.

The four of us now rode the final quiet miles into Two Harbors. Here, Old Highway 61 unceremoniously dumped us onto new Highway 61, which, like all (new) highways, was designed for big-ass vehicles to go stupidly fast. Logging trucks and tourist-toting SUVs and rusty old junkers clogged both lanes, burying the minty-fresh breath of the lake under the sulfurous reek of the tailpipe. To make matters worse, the highway now veered from the coast and into second- or third- or fifteenth-growth forest. Our "view" was reduced to scrubby pine, airborne chunks of gravel, and, depending on who was riding out front, each other's butt cheeks.

I was eager to get these miles over with, and so I mashed the pedals, all the while eyeing the speedometer, watching the numbers climb. Once I hit fourteen miles an hour, I checked the rearview. Rachel was right there, her jaw set, brow furrowed, shoulders rocking side to side. She was hugging my rear wheel, just begging me to speed up, so I dug harder, until my heart was racing, my legs screaming, my lungs begging for oxygen. I gulped greedily, not caring that the air tasted like rotten eggs, suddenly loving this highway. After so many days of blown spokes and Lump rubbing—of being held back—it felt amazing to actually work for something.

Now I looked to the rearview. Rachel was gone. In her place, a tiny, wavering figurine. She must have been five hundred feet back, but I'd fallen so profoundly into a three-cheers-for-me reverie that I hadn't noticed the gap I was opening. My first impulse was to feel annoyed that I *had* to notice, to check my speed, to abandon my reckless abandon just because Rachel couldn't fucking keep up. Then, a tsunami of guilt. A familiar voice telling me I hadn't earned my speed or muscle structure, hadn't earned a goddamn thing, ever, and that this wasn't about Rachel, or anyone else, keeping up. It was about me recognizing why I found it so easy to pull ahead.

I was usually quite attuned to all this. But after a year of following—no, chasing—Rachel, I had begun to lose focus on the whole male privilege thing.

Not knowing what else to do, I downshifted, spun the pedals, discreetly checked the mirror. Once Rachel caught up, I kept my eyes on the rearview, carefully adjusting my speed, trying to match hers without seeming like I was trying to match hers. We continued this way for five miles, still sandwiched between traffic and yawn-inducing, scrubby forest, until at last we rounded a bend and saw a bike trail, the one Tonia had told us about, the one that would carry us straight to Illgen Falls. It was called the Gitchi-Gami State Trail, its name a bastardized version of the word the Ojibwa had long used to describe the lake: *gichigami*, "big water."

We climbed the trail up to the top of a pine-Mohawked dome of granite, dropped our bikes, and gawked at big water. From this vantage point, it looked bigger than ever. The lake now seemed to extend forever, a shimmering sheet of blue uninterrupted by ships or seagulls, by islands or driftwood or even a lonely whitecap. And to the north, chiseled cliffs rose high above the blue, proudly bearing their age-old scabs and scars. Here we were, at last, at the beginning of the *real* North Shore. Now we could look forward to miles of peaceful riding on the Gitchi-Gami, a dip in the cool waters below Gooseberry Falls, the jagged splendor of Split Rock Lighthouse, and, of course, twilight cliff dives at Illgen Falls.

As if reading my thoughts, Rachel nodded at the shoreline before us and said, "This is going to be amazing."

"Yes," I replied. "Yes, it is."

It wasn't.

Just north of the dome, the Gitchi-Gami State Trail disappeared. Bewildered, we backtracked, asked a guy in a wayside parking lot if we'd missed a turn or something. He grinned, said this was a teaser of sorts, that the continuous, fourteen-mile section began at Gooseberry Falls, nine miles to the north. We'd have to hop back on (new) 61, with its flying rocks and farting tailpipes.

These were not my favorite miles of the trip. Still, I wanted to love them—had been daydreaming about them for days—and so I mustered up a midwestern dose of excessive enthusiasm. As I rode, taking pains to go neither too fast nor too slow, I kept yelling over my shoulder about the boat I could barely see through the trees, or the roadkill on the shoulder, or the fact that it was only four—wait, sorry, five!—miles to Gooseberry Falls. Rachel, maybe because she couldn't hear me over the traffic, maybe because she was tired and needed to focus on moving forward, didn't respond. At best, she offered a tight-lipped grin and kept riding.

At three o'clock, after riding nine miles in just under an hour, we arrived at Gooseberry Falls. As I locked the bikes to a dented guardrail, I peered into the canyon. River water the color of iced tea was spinning in upstream pools, dribbling through tiny grooves and channels, free-falling from cliffs. This was *it*, the North Shore I'd been waiting for, and I wanted to tell Rachel how happy I was to be here with her. But she was frowning, glassy-eyed. It was like she was barely even seeing the falls.

"What a spot," I said. I kept my eyes on Rachel, looking for signs of life. "Wanna head down to the water? Maybe have a snack and take a swim?"

She looked at me and shrugged. "I guess so."

We'd been waiting for this all day, and that's all she could muster? *I guess so?* I dropped my head, trying to find the right words. Then I opened my mouth, and this came out: "Could you be a little more boring?"

These were not the right words.

Rachel's eyes froze over. Silently, she got off the bike, pulled out some snacks and her journal, and started walking down to the water. I waited a few seconds, then followed. She settled on a ledge overlooking the falls, and I sat beside her, apologized, and said what I had meant to say: that I just wanted to find a way to share these moments with her.

"It's okay," she replied. "And I'm sorry for being so . . . I don't know." She looked to the opposite bank of the river, where a giggling toddler was dipping his toes into the water. "It's just hard. You're stronger and . . . It's just hard sometimes."

I nodded, unsure of how to respond. Usually, I was the one being all pissy and vulnerable.

"Well," I started, "regardless of speed, I think it's awesome that you're . . . that we're doing this." I hesitated, then added, "It's hard for me too." This was true. In a sense.

Rachel accepted these words, or at least pretended to, and we made the first of many promises to be open and communicative and such from here on out.

We wandered downstream, stripped off shoes and shirts, and waded into an armpit-deep pool between two falls. The river was too cold to stay in for long, so we climbed out and lay on the rocks. The water soothed my sunbaked skin, and the rapids trickled and crashed, drowning out the hum of highway traffic. For a few minutes, I slept.

North of Gooseberry Falls, the Gitchi-Gami started behaving like that well-intentioned host who shows you every homemade quilt, every inherited-from-Grandpa bookcase, every photo of Jeffrey when he was a baby, when all you're looking for is the fridge. As the trail headed north, it plunged into valleys, climbed heaps of granite, chased birch groves and lake vistas, so that every highway mile seemed to require two trail miles. This might have been fun on an afternoon joyride. But we were hauling freight, had been all day, and no longer needed a roller coaster. We needed to get to Illgen Falls, fast. It was pushing six, and the sky was clouding up, and my butt hurt, and this meant that Rachel's butt probably hurt too, and her butt hurt might cause her to get cranky again, and then I'd probably end up saying something stupid, and then she'd call this whole thing off and leave me out here, alone.

So we barely even stopped at Split Rock Lighthouse, just gave it the obligatory, two-minute ponderous gaze; chugged right through Beaver Bay, which was less the quaint town I'd been expecting and more a collection of gas stations; and suffered through the final miles on 61, which was getting downright ominous. The pavement dipped and dove, wind tumbled off the water, and cauliflower clouds rolled in overhead. My legs were burning, my neck and back stiffening up, but I ignored all the aches, focused only on the rearview, on Rachel, who was struggling too. I did my best to find a speed that neither patronized nor exhausted her.

It was dusk when we pulled up to the barely marked trail that led to Illgen Falls. The path was narrow and brambly, and we walked it gingerly, steering the bikes around roots and ducking under branches, until we emerged at the basin Mike had described. Before us, river water shot from a sheer face, falling forty feet into an inky lagoon. I dropped the bike, walked to the edge, and focused on the spot where falling water hit waiting water. It was all blue and black and mist and foam. I tore off my clothes, and before I could cool down, before I could get squeamish and second-guess, I took three steps back, two bounds forward, and flung myself over the edge.

Forty feet is a long way to fall, long enough to ask yourself why the hell you just decided to step off firm ground and launch yourself into the void. Then your feet slap the water, and you plunge through the black, and everything becomes a seething, swirling mess, and for a nanosecond you believe you'll never stop falling, never be able to claw your way back to the surface. But then you do.

Hours later, after our first cooked-on-the-beer-can dinner, after some making-up-for-the-fight-we-almost-had sex, after Rachel fell asleep, I crawled out of the tent. Listening to the roar of the water, pulling sweet mist through my nostrils, I thought about the day, our first without the safety nets. I had to admit it hadn't really been that enjoyable in the moment. It was only now that I could smile about the ugly highway and the meandering trail and my own idiocy, only now that I could construct the stories I'd eventually tell others. The stories I'd tell myself.

I wondered if this was what awaited us. Thousands of miles that would only make sense in retrospect.

Breakfast was cowboy coffee, bananas, and pancakes topped with the Simeones' syrup. On the lip of the falls, Rachel and I ate while looking over a glossy threefold pamphlet she'd been handed at the visitor center in Two Harbors. The cover showed a pretty, hilly forest bisected by an arcing strip of pavement: the Superior National Forest Scenic Byway. Didn't exactly roll off the tongue, but the route looked fantastic, a westward-winding path from the North Shore to the "historic Iron Range." I had never heard of the "historic Iron Range," but it sounded big and chunky and vaguely communist. Sold.

I turned to the inside cover, read aloud a section we'd already laughed at a half-dozen times. "Although not an everyday occurrence," I said in my best instructional-video voice, "black bear and moose have been sighted hanging out along the byway."

"Just hanging out," Rachel said, her words muffled by pancake. "Puttin' out the vibe."

I folded the brochure and set it atop our Minnesota State map, a freebie Rachel had found in a gas station. We had barely used it, just like we had barely used the super-map in Wisconsin. After 334 miles of riding, we had almost exclusively followed handwritten directions provided by our hosts. This, we'd decided, was the way to travel. Listening to locals, choosing routes day by day, avoiding any decisions we couldn't bail on by nightfall.

By the time we cleaned up and packed, it was hot. Nasty Midwest-summer hot. It's-already-eight-o'clock-and-my-knee-pits-are-sweating hot. I wanted to get back in the water, and I convinced Rachel to join me. While I dove from the highest spots I could find, she climbed down to the lagoon, grasping a rope hung from a big oak on the rim. Tiptoeing from boulder to boulder, she made her way to a rock ten feet above the water. And there she sat for quite some time, giggling and grimacing and looking up every few seconds as if to ask, "Do I *have* to?"

I sat at the top of the falls, laughing with her. It was a sort of relief, seeing this Rachel: the Rachel who wasn't in control, who couldn't quite keep up. From the day we met, she'd been perpetually out front, keeping me in pursuit, but now, out on the road, there were more and more moments like this one, where she was trying to keep up with me.

Now at last she plunged in, half-jumping, half-falling from her perch. She disappeared for a second, and then an arm shot out of the water, arcing upward and plunging back down. Just like that she was speeding across the surface, her form perfect, doubts dismissed.

We packed our things, pulled on the Lycra and the hide-the-Lycra, and started to walk the bikes back to the road. I'd been out of the river maybe ten minutes, but already I felt beads of sweat on my forehead, a tingling ache on my tongue. I reached for a water bottle.

"Shit." I looked up at Rachel. "Do you have any water?"

"No, I used the last of mine for the coffee. Remember? I thought you had some left."

"I did. But then I used it for dishes." By which I meant I drank it while doing dishes.

"Well, then," Rachel said over her shoulder. "This should be fun."

It was not fun. And it wasn't the heat—wasn't even the humidity—that really got me, or rather, it was, but only because I was working so goddamn hard. West of Illgen Falls, it was all hills. I imagined a chummy group of highway engineers challenging themselves to design a route that never—not even for one measly foot—flattened out. By the five-mile mark, my eyes were sweat stung, my temples pounding, my gums raw. I felt like I'd spent all morning gargling fiberglass insulation. Rachel, I could only assume, was feeling the same way; she'd quickly fallen silent and was now staring at the pavement, gamely pushing the pedals.

According to our map, the next town, Finland, was just ten miles away. A ten-mile ride, I'd thought, was nothing. I was wrong. Absent water, and present the scorching sun, a ten-miler was murder, and for that matter, so was an eight-miler, or a six-miler, or whatever paltry distance we'd ridden by the time we saw that heaven-sent, roadside bait shop. We crash-parked the bikes and burst inside, and before I knew it, we were sitting in a gravel lot, our backs against a propane-cooled ice chest, our water bottles refilled but untouched, both of us bloated from the king-size Snickers bars and liter bottles of Mountain Dew we'd just inhaled, at 9:42 in the morning.

I closed my eyes and smiled and said, "I'm not sure anything has ever tasted that good."

"I know," Rachel said. "I kind of want more candy."

"So let's get more candy."

We got more candy.

Also, soda.

Also, a kind of weird look from the lady at the counter.

That morning we might have learned a boring lesson about foresight and preparation. We did not learn such a lesson. We did not so much learn anything, actually. But we did remember, both of us, having long ago imagined that the best thing about growing up would be getting to eat candy whenever we wanted. And now, we agreed, we'd been so, so right.

The Superior National Forest Scenic Byway was huge, a forty-foot-wide strip of smoother-than-smooth pavement, and it was utterly empty. As we rode, Rachel and I guessed at why it even existed. It was pretty and all, but no more so than a million other areas in the Northwoods. Maybe it was a pork-barrel project trumpeted by a politician who owed some highway contractors a favor? Or maybe the 1,763 residents of Aurora and Beaver Bay, the towns at either end, were important people, let's-build-an-expressway-between-them people? Whatever the case, we felt lucky to have found the byway. It was our own private theme park, full of attractions: a centuries-old Finnish schoolhouse here, a trail there, and always a lake, stream, or bog beyond the roadside trees. The miles passed easily, and by early afternoon we were halfway to Hoyt Lakes, the town where we were thinking of camping that night.

We pulled off and took a break at Sullivan Lake, attraction no. 11 in our brochure. We were the only ones at the lake, despite the huge campground on its banks, and so we stripped naked and ran into the water. Rachel took off toward the opposite shore, practically hydroplaning across the surface, and I followed for a bit, then gave up and headed to the shallows to practice underwater handstands. It was pushing ninety, and the water felt perfect. Well, almost. It was cool enough to cut the heat, warm enough to stay in for hours. But it was also orange enough to pass for Kool-Aid. There was quite a bit of sulfur and rust in northern Wisconsin water, but nothing like this. It tasted like melted pennies.

I waded out of the lake and starfished on a picnic table, trying to recall the last time my pasty white ass had seen sunlight. After a few minutes, Rachel nudged me over, started situating herself, squealed. A leech was stuck to her calf. A big, fat, slimy one.

I smiled. Rachel pretty much never played damsel-in-distress. This was going to be fun.

"That there's a keeper," I said, still on my stomach. "We should get it taxidermied."

"Get it off!" she shrieked, between hiccups of laughter.

"I just wish I'd brought a bigger knife." I sat up and reached toward a pannier. "Oh, and do you have the lighter? We'll need to cauterize the wound."

"Brian!"

Generally, I was not a man who knew how to do manly things. I could not change my oil or differentiate between a planer and a router or tie a bowline knot or carve a turkey or stoically repress my emotions. But I had spent half my youth in and around lakes, and I knew how to deal with leeches. Now I leaned over Rachel's knee, slid a conveniently untrimmed fingernail up her leg, and pressed it to the leech's sucker. Slow and careful, I forced it free, raised my hand up, and made a big show of flicking the little booger back into the water.

Somehow this was foreplay.

And somehow, fifteen minutes later, when a forest service truck rumbled by, its driver waving through the open window, we had washed away the evidence and pulled our clothes back on, just in time, just as we had our second day out on the road. I was really starting to feel like other people were only appearing to remind us that no one, not them nor anyone else on the planet, had any idea what we were really up to.

It was dusk by the time we reached Hoyt Lakes, and we were both weary and hungry and wondering where exactly we were going to sleep. For the first time, we wouldn't be staying under a roof, wouldn't be camping in a yard or a recommended campsite. We were on our own.

After splurging on greasy pizza at a greasy spoon, we cruised town, checking out the parks and the lakeshore, looking for somewhere discreet. The park bordering Colby Lake, just north of town, was wide open and well lit, with abundant "No Camping" signs, so we headed west and turned off on a random back road. After a mile or so, we found what appeared to be a snowmobile trail. It was poorly lit and flat. Perfect. We set up the tent, pulled our bags into a pile near the door, and climbed inside. Then I caught a whiff of our leftover pizza, climbed right back out, and carried it a hundred yards away. This was, after all, a place where bears hung out.

Rachel and I tucked into our bags and pulled out books. She was still reading *Still Life With Woodpecker*, and I was halfway through *The God of Small Things*. I knew the story by heart, which was good, because I wasn't actually reading it, was too wrapped up in reviewing the events of the day. It felt amazing to be moving, truly moving, away from the familiar and into the unknown. I kept returning to the thought I'd had back at Sullivan Lake: Nobody knows where we are right now. What we're doing. Nobody.

We soon turned off our headlamps, rolled away from each other, began drifting into sleep.

Outside, something snapped.

And another something snorted.

"What was that?" Rachel's hand was on my shoulder.

I rolled onto my stomach, propped myself up on my elbows. "I don't know," I whispered.

More snapping, more snorting. Whatever the something was, it was close. The tent fly was almost opaque, and through it I could see only the fluorescent glow from a lamplight at a nearby resort. "Did you notice if there were horses at that place?" I nodded toward the light. As a kid, I had spent a good deal of time at some nearby stables. I had heard horses snort.

Rachel shook her head. She looked terrified. I realized I probably did too.

The something was moving. It snapped and crunched and snorted, getting closer and closer, until it sounded like it was right outside the tent. I wanted to comfort Rachel, not to mention myself, wanted to say it might just be a deer or a porcupine, and that even if it was a bear, I would wrestle it to the ground, choke it with one hand, flick its ears with the other. But I couldn't say any of that, couldn't even do what I knew I was supposed to do: make a bunch of noise, brandish makeshift weapons, appear threatening. I was frozen, afraid to even whisper.

For what felt like an hour, the something moved around us. It would pad away, stay quiet for a time, then shatter the silence with a snort. It was fucking with us, I was sure of it.

Eventually the snaps became more distant, the snorts less frequent. Then, silence. Finally able to speak, I said it had probably just been a whitetail. I tried to sound confident, authoritative. Rachel didn't reply, didn't need to. She just tucked up against me, and there we lay, quiet and motionless, imagining the something, knowing what nobody knew.

CHAPTER 8

Riding Blind

Loose gravel to the right. A caravan of cars to the left. And straight ahead, a strip of torn tire spanning the shoulder. Shit. I leaned left and pulled the bike just inside the white line, barely missing the mound of rubber, then checked the rearview to see if Rachel had followed. But I didn't see Rachel. I saw a big fucking truck. And now I felt it, blasting air up my back. I gripped the brake hoods and leaned from the lane, against the wind shear, but overcompensated and slid off the shoulder into soupy dirt. I fishtailed and fought back onto the pavement, just in time to swerve around a twinkling heap of broken glass.

All morning with this shit. We were heading west from Hoyt Lakes, away from the scene of the something. Pretty scenery abounded—a mess of silver-blue lakes, spires of balsam fir and white pine, too-small-for-stoplight towns with names like Biwabik and Pineville—but I'd only glimpsed the surroundings. Highway 135, just like 61, was full of vehicles, and the shoulder was puny and peppered with debris, and so if my eyes weren't on the pavement, hunting for hazards, they were fixed on the rearview, monitoring Rachel's speed and adjusting my own.

I was doing my best to feign optimism but was starting to

wonder if this was what the trip was going to be about. The rearview and the road ahead.

Behind me, Rachel yelled something. A passing car muffled her voice, but I thought I heard "bike." I looked down, assuming I had a flat or another blown spoke. More yelling. I checked the rearview, saw she was pointing at a sign, a black bicycle silhouetted against a yellow diamond. We rolled up, and just beyond the sign was an eight-foot-wide tar ribbon snaking through tall grass, running parallel to 135. A bike trail. I looked back to the east, saw the trail hugging the stretch we'd just ridden. I hadn't even noticed it.

"You think we should take it?" Rachel was already back in the saddle, her right foot clipped in, her left ready to push off. This was one of those rhetorical questions.

"Yep," I replied. "Looks like it's headed the right way now."

We had seen another sign for this trail, the Mesabi Trail, a few towns back. Despite the snappy, traveling-through-the-trees logo—the trail had a logo—we had assumed it was your standard small-town path, the kind that takes you a mile in the wrong direction, then deposits you in a Shopko parking lot. But here it was again. Still heading west.

We pulled off the highway and onto the trail. The change was immediate, glorious. Sure, we could still see the cars, could hear their whining engines and smell their putrid exhaust, but now they were merely annoying neighbors. And annoying neighbors were better than battering rams.

After a few miles, the trail veered into the trees, wiggled between jagged towers of dynamited rock, and deposited us at the edge of a sheer cliff, where we stopped to take in the sort of panorama I'd never thought existed in the Midwest. To the north, a placid emerald river cut through a someone-must-have-stolen-this-from-Arizona canyon. It was hundreds of feet deep, its striated red-orange walls softened by evergreen carpet.

We stepped to the scenic overlook, read the interpretive sign. "The Rouchleau Mine." Well, that explained it. This was not a canyon but a crater; not a river but a man-made lake. The red cliff walls were taconite and hematite, two types of iron-bearing sedimentary rock. So this was the Iron Range.

A rumble from the west. Some purple, anvil-shaped clouds were rolling in, and there was a hint of distant mud in the air. After twelve days on the road, we hadn't yet seen a drop of rain, but that streak was about to end. Time to move.

Past the mine, the trail plunged into a series of sidewinders, whipping us left and right and up and down, a bring-your-own-cart roller coaster. I pedaled hard and tucked low, topping thirty in seconds. Now I was giggling. Squealing. If I could have taken both hands from the bars, I'd have clapped them and barked like a seal. The trail gradually flattened, and as I coasted, waiting for Rachel to catch up, the trees split like curtains and the macadam widened into a residential street. I figured this was it, the end of the trail. But then I noticed another sign and, beside it, a thin strip of pavement tucking into the trees, continuing onward.

Rachel pulled up next to me, said what I'd been thinking. "More!"

Above, a crack of thunder. More would have to wait.

We turned onto Chestnut Street and rode into Virginia, a pretty little mining town with worn brick storefronts and triple-globe streetlamps and businesses with names like Jim's and Stacy's and Frank's. At the end of Chestnut, we found a food co-op. Perfect. Now we could stock up on snackies, and those hippies would surely know how far the trail went. We locked the bikes, pulled lime-green waterproof covers over our panniers, and ducked inside just as the rain began.

I'd never really shopped in co-ops. There were none where I grew up, and though Madison had a great one, I'd only been

inside once, as my college cuisine had consisted mainly of
Eggo waffles, pretzels, and Busch Light. But Rachel? She was a
Portlandia native, a greens-and-grains-please healthy eater, an
amateur herbalist who could make (and spell) tinctures. She
was at home in this co-op, and she navigated the aisles with
ease, grabbing miso soup mix, premade palak paneer, bulk
almonds, and a handful of Emergen-C packets. As she stole
her fourth yogurt-covered pretzel from a bulk bin, a forty-
something man, decked out in three shades of beige, walked up
and introduced himself as Jim. He'd noticed the bikes, pegged
us as the riders. When we told him we were headed west, he lit
up. His work, apparently, took him all over Minnesota and
North Dakota.

"What do you know about the Mesabi Trail?" Rachel asked,
her enunciation slightly muddled by the stolen pretzel.

He turned to a rack and lifted a brochure, opened it wide
and placed it in Rachel's hands. There it was again, the
somebody-got-*paid*-to-design-this logo. Beneath it, a detailed
map with close-ups of the twenty-three "downtowns" the trail
passed through over its—two jaws dropped in unison—eighty-
two miles. This wasn't just a bike trail. It was a goddamn insti-
tution. Though we'd somehow missed the trailhead back in
Aurora, we still had 64.3 miles ahead of us.

"They've been building this for a decade," Jim said. "Some
of it follows old rail lines, but mostly it was designed to take
you through the prettiest parts of the Mesabi Range." He
pointed at the close-up of Virginia. "Through downtowns
too. Supposed to inspire tourism, but it always seems empty.
Actually, it being Thursday, you'll probably have it all to your-
selves."

We thanked Jim for the info, then headed to a table to pore
over the map. We'd be riding by dozens of lakes, through towns
with names like Mountain Iron and Marble, past a slew of mining-
related attractions. It looked like there were campgrounds, but if

Jim was right, we could probably just throw up the tent wherever we wanted. I bounced in my chair. This was why we had done almost no route research, why we had shunned those Adventure Cycling maps. Okay, also because they were fucking expensive. But, mainly, this.

I'd seen my share of bike trails over the years, and most were rail-to-trail conversions. Graded for the steam engine, these paths were straight and flat, peaceful but monotonous, and all too often routed through the most drearily industrial sections of the cities in their right-of-way. Rail-to-trail paths always clung to the smoke-smeared factories, teeming junkyards, white-walled corporate compounds, and (one of these things is not like the others) boxy Section 8 housing complexes. The "blemishes" cities invariably zoned into oblivion.

The Mesabi Trail was different. It had been designed not to facilitate the unfettered transport of freight but to maximize interaction between people and place, and the fourteen-mile stretch west of Virginia felt like an interpretive tour of the Northwoods. The pavement—pitch-black, unblemished, something-to-call-home-about pavement—rolled over sudden hills, bent from ragged rock to cobalt mine-pit-crater lakes to birch-filled bogs, all the while tucked into hushed boreal forest. When it did emerge from the woods and hug the highway, the trail dipped and dove, following lazy S curves that wound around nothing at all, as if the pavement had been poured that way because, hey, it's a bike trail, why the fuck not?

Upon reaching an "urban" area, the trail would dump us onto Main Street or take us through the town park, as it did in Mountain Iron, the Taconite capital of the world. Its little park was a veritable mining museum. Had I seen it at age six, I'd have had a brain aneurysm. There was a gargantuan tire, its treads as thick as my thighs; a nine-foot-high shovel bucket; and a tar-black steam engine that had once hauled ore from the open-pit Mountain Iron Mine, visible from the park. It was just past seven when we arrived, and despite our rumbling bellies and the waning light, we lingered, eating almonds atop the train car, then snapping I-bet-we're-the-millionth-people-to-do-this-but-I-don't-care photos: Rachel in the tire, doing her best La-Z-Boy lounge; me inside the shovel bucket, arms overhead, barely able to reach the upper lip.

At dusk we rolled up to Stubler Beach, a taupe-sand crescent hugging a glassy little goose egg of a lake. Nearby was a campground tucked into shoreline pine. Sold. We got off the bikes and stretched. Quads, calves, hamstrings, hip flexors. No amount of stretching could soothe my bruised butt, but otherwise I felt great. My legs were buzzing pleasantly. They felt tender. Succulent. Like choice cuts of slow-cooked beef.

We were planning to sneak into a campsite under cover of darkness, hoping to avoid the outrageous five-bucks-apiece fee. So we jumped in the lake, washed grit and grime from our bodies, then pulled out the beer can and prepared palak paneer. At sunset we tiptoed into the campground, past a heaping pile of firewood, which, according to a filthy cardboard sign, was "FREE!!!" So much for stealth; how could we pass up a campfire?

We lingered by the flames for some time, gushing about how lucky we were to be where we were: beside a fire, under a star-speckled sky, on this trail, this adventure. Together. We were covering ground and getting surprised and rolling with whatever the world threw at us, and it wasn't killing us. We were killing *it*—day by day, mile by mile, killing the ridiculous notion that our grand adventure, the very idea of which had kept our relationship alive, would end us. When the flames began to fade, Rachel kissed me good-night and headed for the tent. I crouched by the fire awhile longer, watched the embers flicker and fade, listened to their snap, crackle, pop. Rachel was still awake when I slid in next to her, and before I could crawl into my bag, she unzipped hers and pulled me inside. We were alone in the campground, but still we moved slow and silent, our fingers feathering cheekbones and eyelids, both of us exhaling slowly, reluctantly, then pulling the same air back inside. Savoring it. Preserving it.

For the thirteenth straight morning we woke to sunny skies, and by eight we were on the bikes, following the trail as it darted around like a tail-wagging puppy, arcing north to sniff wildflowers, shooting south to peer into abandoned mine pits. We didn't encounter a soul for ten miles, not until we reached Chisholm, where we saw both man and *Iron Man*, the latter the third-largest freestanding statue in the States, a cast-iron, pick-and-shovel-toting miner perched atop two criss-crossing circles bisected by an artfully flared I beam. I loved this beacon of small-town pride, this hint of the big story behind the Mesabi Range. I still knew few of the details, but that almost made it better. Mile by mile, I was discovering this place.

Just up the trail was Hibbing, birthplace of two American icons—Bobby Zimmerman and Greyhound Bus—and home to a pair of obligatory, icon-worshipping museums. We visited neither. I have no idea why we skipped the free Dylan shrine, and honestly I don't want to talk about it, but I will say that we at least tried to check out the Greyhound exhibit. Unfortunately, the guy at the gate said admission was five dollars, and since five dollars was equivalent to twenty Nutty Bars, we just loitered in the lobby, paged through pamphlets and picture books, and eventually decided the place had nothing we couldn't find on Wikipedia.

We continued into Hibbing proper and stayed a full four hours, writing and sending off stacks of postcards, checking e-mail at the library, hitting up the town's hundred-year-old bakery for fresh éclairs and day-old muffins, and napping off our sugar-crash comas in the town park. This was quickly becoming our in-town routine (coma very much included), and I was really beginning to appreciate the structure it brought to our otherwise formless days.

Just before leaving town, we visited the local bike shop. Rachel was still having trouble with her wrists and knees, and she said as much to the head mechanic, a clean-cut guy named Pete. He nodded and said, "Not surprising. You've got a men's frame there."

"I know," Rachel said. "I couldn't find any women's bikes that worked for me."

"Pretty common, unfortunately. There aren't a lot of good women's touring frames on the market. The geometry of most bikes, yours included, is better suited to riders with longer torsos and arms. Men, generally."

Geometry. Yeah, I liked that. I was going to use it in a sentence as soon as possible.

I glanced at Rachel, who looked like she couldn't give a flying fuck about expanding her bike vocabulary. Her eyes were fixed on Pete, her face falling into a frown.

He noticed and changed his tack. "We can, of course, make some adjustments."

He had Rachel stand over the bike, sit on the saddle, grip the bars in various places. He shifted the saddle, lowered the seat post. Tilted the bars and raised the stem. Rachel tried a lap around the block and returned smiling. Pete had done good. We chatted awhile longer, and he asked if we'd checked out the Hull-Rust mine. When we said we actually hadn't done any of the things one was supposed to do in Hibbing, he pointed and mouthed, "Go," and when we both hesitated, he added, "It's free."

It was a quick ride to the mine, which, according to a sign in the rim-top museum, was known as the "Grand Canyon of the North." I could see why. The pit was mind-boggling. Three miles long, two miles wide, 535 feet deep. I peered down below, pressing my forehead against the chain-link fence, and marveled at the microscopic bodies, the corduroy striations on the pit's sheer walls, the convoy of mustard-yellow Tonka trucks buzzing back and forth. One of the trucks was on display up in the lot, to give visitors a sense of scale. Its tires were twice my height, its dump bucket bigger than any room I'd ever rented. I kind of wanted to move in—to Hibbing, if not the dump bucket itself. Though I knew so little about the place, or maybe because I knew so little, it seemed perfect.

We reached Grand Rapids, and the end of the Mesabi Trail, by early evening. As I coasted down the trail's final hill, my head was pounding, not from the helmet, which I'd removed when we left the highway, but from the tug-of-war match raging inside my skull. Past, present, and future were yanking at my brain, stretching it like taffy, and though I was doing my very best to both soak up these final moments and indulge some fuzzy nostalgia, it wasn't going so well, because up ahead, through the trees, I could hear music, and not just any music, but earsplitting, shit-kicking country music, and, look, I dare you to try and be mindful while listening to that.

I rounded a bend and found myself in a sprawling county park. Tim McGraw's voice blasted through the loudspeakers overhanging a mess of tents and RVs and oversize pickups and people, so many people, all of them here, according to an enormous vinyl banner, for the Itasca Vintage Car Club's 36th

Annual Northern Minnesota Car Show and Swap Meet. I stared, slack-jawed, at the scene, unsure if I was more bewildered by the bursting of our bike bubble or the fact that northern Minnesotans had, for thirty-six years, put up with saying and reading and writing "Itasca Vintage Car Club's Annual Northern Minnesota Car Show and Swap Meet" (and, I hoped, even if it only happened once, using the initialism IVCCANMCSSM).

Rachel, who I'd outpaced on the long hill that dropped into the park, now pulled up beside me, and together we took in the IVCCANMCSSM. There must have been a hundred RVs, with names like *Cougar* and *Conquest* and *Avenger* and, my personal favorite, *Bounty Hunter*. The air was thick enough to eat with a fork, a summery soup of fry oil and charcoal, singed meat and sunscreen. McGraw's voice reigned supreme, but I could make out a dozen others—Toby Keith, Deana Carter, Sammy Hagar—floating from boom boxes and car stereos.

We tracked down a couple of bratwurst and a bag of kettle corn, and wandered through the meet. I usually loved small-town festivals, and wanted to want to stay, but I was already missing the solitude, the we-own-this-place feel of the trail, and so when Rachel suggested that maybe we head back to the woods for the night, I agreed. Soon enough, we'd be sharing the road with these RVs and anonymous throngs. But we didn't have to share a campsite.

As we were finishing breakfast at our trailside campsite, the phone rang. Rachel picked it up, held her hand over the receiver. "It's Galen!" She started pacing, the phone pressed to her ear. For a few minutes, I scrubbed plates and packed panniers, but soon I was pattering behind her, eavesdropping.

"Are you kidding?" Rachel stopped walking and spun

toward me, wearing an expression that fell somewhere between ecstatic and desperate. Not unlike the face she made while having an orgasm. She gasped. "Gaaaaaaalen!"

"What?" I mouthed, leaning toward her, needing to know.

Rachel spun on her heel and went back to pacing. She was wearing only her hide-the-Lycra shorts and a sports bra, and I let my eyes wander over her toned, tanned legs, the dimple in the small of her back, the curve of her ass against the fab—

Galen. I caught up, circled in front of her, jumped and waved my arms like a rodeo clown. She turned and kept walking. I flicked her ears. Poked her kidneys. Goosed her. At this she shrieked, pulled the phone from her ear and mouthed two words: "Kill you."

"Galen, I get the impression Brian wants to talk to you," she said, then paused, her smile widening. "Yep. Let's talk again soon."

She handed Galen over. Turned out he was in Chicago, and Rachel had been squealing about the trip that had taken him there. The previous morning he'd woken in eastern Indiana and decided he wanted to be in Chicago. So he rode all day, past sunset, into darkness. By the time he reached the outermost circle of suburban hell, it was past midnight. Traffic was light, so he rode the Chicago Skyway—a twelve-lane, megamonster freeway—into the city, finally arriving at a friend's place around three in the morning. By the end of his odyssey, he had ridden 132 miles. In the past two days combined, Rachel and I had barely broken 100.

"Whoa," I said, unable to come up with anything else. I wanted to be happy for Galen. But I wasn't. I was jealous. Angry. First at Galen, for having pulled off such a spectacular ride. Then at Rachel, for riding too slow and holding me back from doing the same thing. And finally at myself, for being such a petulant, self-absorbed dickbag.

I spoke to Galen for a few more minutes, then hung up. It was time to get moving, to prove to myself, and Galen, that while I had enjoyed the trail, I sure as shit didn't need it.

Rachel seemed to be on the same page. After breakfast at a café in Grand Rapids, we rode fifty miles in four hours, stopping only twice, first in the charming town of Remer, to grab sandwiches and Gatorade and Grandma's cookies, then at Mabel Lake, for a quick swim in tepid water, and now, in front of me—*in front* of me—Rachel was charging uphill, legs pumping, torso bobbing metronomically. A frisky tailwind was shoving us forward, and we were riding hard, twenty-miles-an-hour hard, damn near flying through the Chippewa National Forest.

This highway, Highway 200, was a gift—smooth blacktop, scarce traffic, and lake after lake after lake. We'd stumbled upon this road, just like we'd stumbled upon the trail, and I was now feeling like the luckiest ignoramus in the world. And wondering if that made Rachel and me ignorami. And, come to think of it, whether that band name was still available.

I mashed the pedals, took in greedy gulps of breeze blowing off the city-size lake to my right. This world was so gorgeous and inviting, so superlatively superlative, and I was feeling exceptional, a peak-life-experience kind of joy, and so I pushed harder, still on an incline but accelerating, catching up to share this moment with Rachel, who now turned her head and opened her mouth and just completely out of nowhere said, "I want us to live in Portland." And because I was feeling peak-life joyful, because I was accelerating uphill, because I loved Rachel more than ever and was at the moment ready to say yes to anything and everything, I said yes to this—said, "I think I actually want that too"—and then as quickly as I'd said the words I forgot them and dropped my head and rode, because for the foreseeable future, wherever we were was where we were going, and we were here, riding blind through uncharted Northwoods, together, and it was even better than—

Ping! Ping!

I kept riding. It couldn't be. I was still going so fast, and the road was still empty, the breeze candy sweet.

Now I took a deep breath, looked down. With every revolution, my rear wheel was wobbling left and right, as if navigating a slalom course. I pulled onto a side road, waved Rachel over, and together we investigated. I had three blown spokes. For a few minutes, I shuffled around and kicked pebbles and spat out every profanity I knew, finally landing on a gem I'd picked up from Steve, a rough-and-tumble farmer who was foreman on my old landscaping crew.

"Fuck me with a football."

"Do you think that'll help?" Rachel asked.

I stuck my tongue out, then dug for the cassette-removal tool I'd picked up in Ashland. I began to reacquaint myself with the instructions, but it was hard to focus. My brain was soaked in expired adrenaline, and I was aware of something like regret nosing up from the murk. Also I was being eaten alive. So many mosquitoes, biting and pinching and sucking my flesh.

Minnesota, like Wisconsin and Michigan and probably every other state besides maybe Utah, was full of T-shirts and postcards sporting pictures of hairy, scuzzy insects and this groaner of a slogan: "Minnesota State Bird: the Mosquito." Well, here on the shores of Leech Lake, there was a state bird convention. A reunion. It wasn't yet dusk, but a huge crowd had assembled for cocktails, loosening up before the main event. Rachel danced around, slapping herself and swearing, and I tried to maintain a mind-over-matter Zen state, to will the bugs away from me. After about fourteen seconds, I jumped up from my bike, screaming and kicking.

A station wagon turned onto the road and stopped beside us. A pretty woman with wavy black hair dropped her window, poked her head out, and swatted at a cloud of mosquitoes. "Can I help you?" She nodded at the gravel road ahead of her. "This is a private drive."

"Oh, um, sorry?" Our first run-in with the this-land-is-my-land property police. Great.

Her eyes softened. "This road doesn't really head anywhere. Do you know where you're going?"

"Nowhere, for a bit," Rachel said.

We told her about our trip, becoming more harmless with every detail about how far we'd come (480 miles), how far we had to go (no idea), how immobile we were at the moment (very). The woman introduced herself as Sherry and said her family lived a half mile down the drive. She looked around our gravel-strewn, sun-beaten, mosquito-besieged base of operations. "Why don't you come and work in our yard? It's shady, and we'll feed you when you're done."

It was a quick walk to their home, a honey-colored log cabin tucked into the trees. Somehow there were no mosquitoes in the front yard, so Rachel and I set to working on the wheel. I played surgeon, Rachel the surgical assistant. As I tinkered, she read instructions, passed me tire levers and spoke wrench, monitored the vital signs of bike and biker. All the while, we remarked on the record that Sherry had put on. It was a solo fingerstyle performance, the melodies shimmering and sliding, one of those major-key songs that still sounded bittersweet.

The music stopped abruptly. I heard a man talking to Sherry, and under his voice the sound of plucked strings. He was speaking in halting bursts—the same way I did whenever I tried to talk while playing guitar—and then he wasn't speaking at all; he was walking through the house and out the door, shaking our hands, and introducing himself as Paul, Sherry's husband. He said he had been playing a Dobro, that he also played mandolin, banjo, and a dozen other instruments, played them well enough to make a living doing session work in Nashville with big-name bluegrass players. He and Sherry and their two daughters lived in the Cities, but they tried to make it to the cabin often, hoped to eventually live here full time.

They invited us in for a spaghetti dinner, then served up heaping bowls of ice cream, then invited us to camp in the yard and do laundry and take showers and hang out inside as long as we wanted. We thanked them repeatedly and clumsily, then took them up on every offer. And just as we were about to bid them good-night, Paul hauled out an old nylon-string and played a medley of Celtic ballads, which I still recall as one of the most stunning performances I've ever heard.

Eventually, reluctantly, we headed to the tent.

"I wonder if the whole trip will be like this." Rachel was propped up on her elbows, considering the Minnesota map.

"Like what?"

"Every person we've met has offered something," Rachel said. "It's been, what, two weeks? We've barely even had to look for campsites. And every time something remotely bad happens, a guardian angel swoops in."

"I know. I kind of expected it to be harder. Or lonelier. Or something."

I looked at the map. The part of Minnesota we'd just ridden—up the North Shore, across the Mesabi Range, into the Chippewa National Forest—even looked pretty on paper. Expansive chunks of forest and thousands of sky blue blobs and tendrils. We had maybe one more day of *that* Minnesota. I traced our route to Detroit Lakes, a sizable city that lay about seventy miles away. It too was surrounded by tiny blue splotches. But to the west the splotches ended. And North Dakota began.

I didn't know if Dakota was going to be lonelier, or harder, or something else. I just knew that once we crossed that border, it was going to be different.

I looked up from the map to find Rachel looking at the house.

"It was so fun hearing Paul play tonight," she said. "I miss making music. We should find people to play with when we get to Portland."

Now that the mania had subsided, I was back to feeling like Portland maybe wasn't such a swell idea. For now, I decided to leave it alone.

"Yeah," I said. "I was thinking the same thing."

By midmorning, after breakfast and photo snapping and good-bye hugging, Rachel and I were on our way, heading west on the Heartland State Trail. We'd been thrilled to learn that yet another trail, this one twenty-eight miles long, lay directly in our path. Later we'd learn that these "lucky" encounters were anything but. Minnesota has been recognized as the "Best Trails State" in America, boasting over twenty-five thousand miles of paved rail-to-trail bikeways, and one would be hard pressed to ride east–west without running into one. But at the time, we didn't know this. It felt like every trail we encountered had been built just for us.

The Heartland was empty and well paved, and though it steered us through more charming small towns, it was hard riding. With every mile, the forest thinned, opening up more space for the westerly winds we'd heard so much about. I kept looking down, checking for blown spokes or flat tires. Nothing. Just the low, almost imperceptible breeze, its fingers on my forehead. By the time we arrived in Park Rapids, Rachel and I were both exhausted, and we headed to the town park and passed out on picnic tables.

It was dusk when we pulled into the barely there town of Osage. We had no idea where we were going to sleep, and prospects were looking dim. The land was nearly treeless, the park too open to properly hide in. As we sat on the shoulder, considering options, Rachel noticed a woman in the front yard of a nearby house.

"What do you think?" she said.

I shrugged. The woman, who appeared to be in her sixties, was watering plants. The house was modest, with a large, well-groomed yard sloping down toward a creek bed. Yeah, she might be another angel, but I was feeling queasy. This wasn't just accepting generosity but actively seeking it out. I pondered. Considered. Ruminated. And as I did so, Rachel walked her bike toward the house. I followed a few steps behind, close enough to be associated with her if the conversation went well, far enough that I could feign disapproval if the woman was put off.

"Hello!" Rachel's voice was chipper. The woman looked up, hesitated, then walked over. Rachel quickly explained who we were and where we were coming from and going. "We're trying to find a good spot to sleep tonight. Do you have any suggestions?" Now I played along, looking back and forth, playing the part of lost little puppy.

The woman looked at the highway, then toward the river, then back at us. "I guess you could just set up here in our yard. We've certainly got the space. Let me ask my husband."

Rachel did a little dance. A minute later, the woman, Nancy, came out with her husband, Bill, and they showed us a nice spot by the river. Their son, they said, was our age, and he had once taken a long trip of his own and had stayed with several strangers. They were happy to help.

After setting up the tent, Rachel and I biked to the town park, on the south shores of Straight Lake. In the cool water, we bathed and washed away the day's dirt. I'd grown accustomed to this ritual, the nightly cleanse, the moment when we scrubbed off everything that had stuck, so we could start the next day fresh. I had the feeling we were about to lose our little ritual. From here on out, we'd get dirty, and we'd stay that way.

CHAPTER 9

Slightly Mangled but Still Intact

'd somehow been expecting the Northwoods to melt away like a slow-fade outro, the lakes and forests shrinking slowly and sweetly, easing us into the silence of the prairie. And so as we rode west from Osage, still buried in boreal forest, still marking miles with sun-sparkled lakes and streams, I did not pay proper homage, did not swim at that pristine beach or rest under this roadside pine bough, because I thought there would be more ahead, because I was waiting for the hush, the sign that it was time to be attentive and nod reverentially and say good-bye.

But there was no hush. No sign. One moment, Rachel and I were lazing in lukewarm shallows. The next, we were riding west, and I was blinking once, twice, thrice, and *poof*, plains, period. Suddenly the land was treeless, save for rows of oak planted to block wind or protect property, and waterless, excepting the brackish sludge that sat in irrigation trenches and ponds.

By noon it was ninety. Sweat escaped from pores I never knew existed, stinging my eyes, soaking my shirt, pooling in my shorts. Clouds of grain dust blew off fields and into our faces, mixing into sweat streams, streaking Rachel's cheeks with what looked like gravy. All the while the wind lashed us, variably: ten miles of I can't believe we chose to ride into prevailing headwinds (fifteen miles per hour), another five of I think I have a flat (eight miles per hour), and an all-too-brief lull of it's perfectly calm but I still feel like my arteries are filled with Velveeta (three miles per hour).

Thirty miles of this felt reasonable. Forty, even. But ninety-two? Not so much.

And yet. We had made plans to stay with some Fargonian friends of Rachel's folks, and said friends had promised us a meal and a bed and a shower, and so even though Fargo was ninety-two miles from Osage, we were going get there by nightfall, goddammit.

For forty, fifty, sixty miles, I pretty well sustained this can-do bluster. But by the time we hit seventy, I was standing more than sitting and newly sympathetic to the term "ass hatchet." My legs were noodles, my neck no longer interested in supporting my head, my head no longer interested in much at all. Save for a verse of "Home on the Range," I hadn't strung together anything like a continuous, coherent thought for hours. Also, the air must have phase-shifted at some point, because, well, I now seemed to be underwater. Or in space. That would certainly explain the stars. And maybe the cotton mouth? I wasn't sure if space gave you cotton mouth.

I coasted into the lane, and Rachel pulled beside me. Her face was crimson, her right cheek smudged with grease. I wondered if I looked like that. I hoped so.

"It's awful out here," she said. "If we don't find water soon, I'm drinking that chain lube."

"I think we're almost to Downer," I replied. "But by all means help yourself to the lube."

We had failed to refill water bottles in Detroit Lakes, the last town we'd seen. For miles, we'd been nursing the final drops, but now the bottles were bone dry. Thus the twinklevision, the cotton mouth. Our plan was to rehydrate in Downer, an intersection town that, according to the map, should be appearing anytime. Should, as a matter of fact, be just past this bend in the—

"Civilization!" Rachel pointed at a distant silo, a cluster of beige buildings.

We rolled into downtown Downer. Dropped the bikes. Wandered. Peeked. Knocked. Sighed. The town had zero open businesses, zero accessible spigots, zero residents willing or able to answer their doors. Downer, we agreed, was a total fucking downer. And so we continued on, bound for the equally sexy-sounding town of Dilworth. For a short while, we were laughing, about Downer and Dilworth, sunburn and sweat gravy, but soon the laughter stopped, and the headaches started, so we just hunched over the bars and sucked on saliva and endured eighteen miles of gusting wind and beastly hot sun and, once we merged with Highway 10, poison-spewing rush hour traffic.

Given certain anatomical realities, whenever I forgot to monitor the rearview I ended up leaving Rachel a hundred yards behind. Every time this happened, I'd feel a stab of guilt, and then I'd coast, or hop off the bike and check the tire pressure, or come up with another ruse to let her catch up without seeming like I was letting her catch up. Maybe she felt I was rushing her, and maybe I felt she was holding me back, but neither of us said a word. We were a team. If we opened our mouths, it was only to complain about the wind and heat. To rally against a common enemy.

After we'd at last hit Dilworth and found a spigot and filled our bottles and drunk them down and filled them again, after we'd promised to never again be so careless about staying hydrated, we spotted an ice cream drive-in and, recalling a certain candy-and-soda-in-the-morning splurge, decided to treat ourselves to one carton of cheese curds and two extra-large milk shakes. This seemed like a truly stupendous idea until I got back on the bike and realized I now had to ride seven more miles with a helium balloon in my colon.

It was half past seven by the time we pulled up to the Levitts' home. We'd been on the road for ten hours. A bruise pulsed between my legs. My left pinky was numb, my joints frozen solid. I could barely bend my knee, so the only way to dismount was to lean onto the bars and swing my right leg over the frame—a slo-mo, off-balance roundhouse kick. Rachel leaned her bike beside mine and pulled off her helmet. Back in Dilworth, she'd tugged her hair into a ponytail, but by now a few locks had slimed out and cemented themselves to her forehead. She removed them one by one, as if peeling an ear of corn.

I felt I should say something profound. We had just ridden ninety-two miles in hellish conditions, had moved beyond the cozy Northwoods into the brutal Plains, and we were still standing. Together. I stared at my feet, tried to find the right turn of phrase. Rachel beat me to it.

"I feel like shit," she said. "But I'm proud we did that." She gritted her teeth and dropped into a squat and did her best full-body flex.

"Rach," I said, "we discussed this. Even though the chamois *feels* like a diaper, it's . . . "

Now she exploded up into a sort of airborne curtsey. She stuck the landing, raised her arms high, and started laughing that delirious staccato laugh.

I stood, smiling, watching. Here she was, doubled over beside a bike-tank in some stranger's driveway, covered head-to-toe in Lycra and plastic and polyester, wind blasted and sunburned, sweat soaked and filthy, and she was not just game but happy, not just happy but delirious, and now she looked up, saw me seeing her, and right when it was about to get real schmoopy, Helen Levitt opened the front door and beckoned us inside.

The next day, I went to a bike shop and talked to a mechanic, who recommended I pay him several dozens of dollars to relace my wheel with double-butted spokes. I wasn't quite clear on what "double-butted" meant, but I knew the guy had kind eyes, and that "double" sounded sturdier than "single," and that I needed sturdy. Adept as I was at flustered roadside fixes, I was feeling pretty done with blown spokes and did not want any surprises in the coming weeks. Ahead loomed North Dakota and Montana, vast tracts of sparsely populated territory, the next known bike shop nearly a thousand miles away.

As we left the shop, Rachel said, "I wish something would go wrong with *my* bike. I figured I'd have learned so much about maintenance by now, but I haven't even had a flat."

"You want to trade?" I asked. "I think you'll like my bike's pedagogy."

She shrugged. "I kind of do."

I kept walking, smiling now. I hadn't thought of it this way. The Fuji didn't hate me. It merely wanted to help me build character.

We spent that afternoon walking around town. Sort of. I couldn't get much more than fifty degrees of flexion from my knee and hip joints, and, really, that was probably for the best. I felt like I'd spent the previous day sitting on a cheese grater, and my nether nerves screamed at the slightest brush of boxers against skin. Rachel was no better off, shuffling alongside me. But we both found that a slow, straight-legged gait largely protected our tender taints from the caresses of well-intentioned undergarments.

We'd wanted to explore Fargo, but it was ruthless out there. The temperature flirted with triple digits, and at the slightest movement drops of water materialized from the air, landed fatly on foreheads and forearms. After a ten-minute waddle around the surprisingly charming downtown—an ornately restored theater here, a straight-from-the Old West hotel there, a diverse array of small businesses in between—we holed up at Juano's Mexican Restaurant, bought happy-hour margaritas and indulged in the free chips and air-conditioning.

By five the shop had built me a bombproof wheel, and we returned to the house for dinner with Helen, a petite, frenetically friendly nurse, and Ralph, a doctor who was doing a way better job wearing those blocky, black-framed glasses than his legions of hipster imitators. As we ate, I tried to come up with something nice to say about Fargo. I hadn't, of course, really seen it, but Helen and Ralph had been so generous with their space, letting us stay two nights, inviting us to raid their refrigerator, and so I figured the least I could do was douse their city with midwestern effusiveness. I began commenting on all I'd seen, and then, at a loss, I brought up the Coen brothers' movie named after their city. I did so with the same silly grasp for connection that compels people to talk about their favorite character on *The Wire* whenever they meet someone who is from, has been to, or has heard of Baltimore.

"It must have been really cool for you guys when *Fargo* came out."

"Uh . . . sort of," Helen said. "It sure got us a lot of attention. I'm just not sure it was the right kind of attention."

I backpedaled the same way I always do, lapsing into convoluted, pseudoacademic jargon. "Well, yes, I guess it was a highly subjective perspective on a place few had previously sought to understand."

Rachel was smiling. She'd heard this crap before.

"And I'm sure," I continued, "that people internalized it as this supposedly authentic—"

"Steve Buscemi got put in a wood chipper," Ralph interjected.

"Yes. Right."

I sat with this for a moment, considered the fact that the vast majority of Americans most likely associated the name Fargo with a man being fed into a wood chipper. I could think of no other place, save for Casablanca, whose identity was so completely wrapped up in a piece of cinema, and none with such unfortunate results.

Later I lay in bed, thinking about Fargo. I knew all about banal regional stereotypes and damn near lost my mind every time some jackass boiled Wisconsin down to cows and cheeseheads, both of which were far better connotations than—not to belabor the point—a man being fed into a wood chipper. Anyway. Now I had new images of Fargo. My own images.

The next day, the wind was vicious, the forecast calling for triple digits, and so we decided to linger until late afternoon and wait out the worst of it. We dropped the drapes, cranked the air-conditioning, and for much of the morning, mapped our route through North Dakota, by which I mean that Rachel pretty much instantly suggested we take Highway 200 border to border, then curled up on the couch to enjoy her novel, while I spent hours in front of the computer, gorging on options, frozen by indecision, before eventually, inevitably, agreeing.

We spent the afternoon taking care of chores. We washed our crusty socks and shirts—I'd begun wearing the gray T-shirt almost exclusively, and a dinosaur-egg-shaped, salt-rimmed sweat stain now splotched the back—then headed out to the garage to tune up the bikes. Together we lubed the chains, aired the tires, even wiped road grime from the frames. It felt good, taking care of the Fujis—knowing how to take care of them. Sort of.

Finally we repaired to the kitchen, pulled stools to the counter, and tried to decide what to do about those two quart-size bags of Cheerios and M&M's—the "trail mix" Helen had whipped up for us. We had no qualms about the contents, but the volume was worrisome. Each bag easily weighed a pound and a half, which meant three pounds of food (good), but also three pounds of luggage (bad). Eventually we balanced our gluttony against a fastidious aerodynamic sensibility, and took one bag, leaving the other with an appreciative and explanatory note.

Four o'clock came, and we loaded the bikes, scoured the house to make sure we weren't leaving anything behind. We were. Two king-size chocolate bars, final gifts from Helen. Rachel picked them up and packed them, and we locked the door behind us and returned to the road.

Several weeks earlier, my hometown mechanic had warned us about westerly winds. When we'd mentioned our potential route, he'd nodded and looked back and forth between us. "East to west through Dakota, huh? Gonna be a battle. Be prepared to pedal as hard as you can just to keep moving. It'll probably take you a couple of weeks."

These words echoed in my head as we rode from Fargo. Wind was licking around buildings and over gas pumps. Treetops were shivering, American flags popping and locking. We stuck to quiet side streets as long as we could, but then we hit the city limit and turned onto a country road that paralleled the interstate. The horizon opened up. And the battle began.

After all the buildup, what surprised me wasn't the force of the wind but its deafening roar. Had we been facing downwind, I bet it would have seemed like a placid late afternoon, but now, facing the current, I felt as if I'd stepped onto a crowded airport tarmac. I mean, it wasn't like we hadn't experienced wind before—"Honey, the air, it's . . . it's *moving*!"—but this was in a class of its own. The howl rendered conversation impossible, which was actually kind of nice, as it forced me to keep my mouth shut and watch the wind assail the wheat. The latter performed a languid dance, lilting southward here, easing northward there, like a field of terrestrial seaweed.

I'd thought the Osage to Fargo ride was our first day in the Plains, but that, I now realized, had been nothing. Here the land was religiously flat. There were no curves or crevasses to greet the wind, whose ghost was everywhere. Lonely trees tucked tattered branches to their trunks. Granules of sand perched atop tractors, reluctantly nomadic.

If all along I'd known we were crossing the country, now I could feel it. The land unfurled before us, allowing no confusion about just how far we had to go.

We'd ridden twenty-some miles when the sun began to drop, the wind with it. We pulled over, plopped down in a roadside ditch, and prepared dinner—two PB&J sandwiches and a pound and a half of trail mix—and as we ate, Rachel, her mouth half-full, began to sing, "My baloney has a first name: it's O-s-c-a-r. My—"

"Please stop."

"Baloney has a second name: it's—"

I yanked a handful of grass and made to shove it in her mouth.

She ducked away, sang the final words into her armpit. Her performance complete, she looked up and said, "All fucking day. I haven't been able to get it out of my head for hours."

"Yeah?" I said. "I'm stuck with 'Home on the Range.' But I only know the first verse."

We both tried to remember the second but came up blank, which, really, was maybe for the better. Rachel pulled out her book, and I my journal, and there we sat for some time, just reading and writing, the ditch like a den. *This* is home now, I thought, and wrote.

Eventually the bugs found us, and so we got back on the bikes and rode toward the setting sun, kept on even when it slipped from sight. Soon it was black all around. I could make out the glow of distant farmhouses, could see the faint flicker of headlights and watch them twinkle like stars until, five minutes later, they finally whooshed by. I kept stealing glances at Rachel as she pedaled beside me, her headlight painting the pavement. Riding with her through this hushed landscape, utterly alone, felt like a secret. We were in a world all our own.

Eventually the horizon surrendered a dull glow, which grew and sharpened into the lights of a town called Page. We stole into the park, set up behind a pavilion. I said I wanted the chocolate. Rachel said it had only been an hour or two since our roadside dinner. I said *chocolate*. She rolled her eyes, began digging around in her bags.

"I know they're here somewhere," she said. "Can we just wait until tomorrow? I'm full." I shrugged. I didn't really want to wait, but I rationalized that I was already feeling pretty nourished, having faced down those headwinds, having discovered this forbidden, starlit spot. And I was sure tomorrow would be another tough day. It would be easier to endure if we knew it would end with some hard-earned sweetness.

The next morning the air was angry. I started out in front, tucking my head to my chest and fighting for every turn of the cranks, and Rachel hugged my rear tire, trying to find that sweet spot where my frame blocked the breeze. We wordlessly switched every few miles, the drafter chugging past the leader to take lashes from the current. Progress was painstaking. We may as well have been pedaling through pudding.

A few miles out of Page, we turned west on Highway 200, which we'd now be riding for, well, we weren't sure, but it was somewhere between a long-ass time and forever. Immediately we saw two tiny ants on the horizon. They grew into pine beetles, then pinecones, until, at five hundred yards, they became people. On bikes. I was wondering when this would happen. By chance (and only, mind you, by chance), we'd stumbled onto an Adventure Cycling route, and now, for the first time, we were encountering another pair of cross-country cyclists. Maybe I should have been excited to see them, but I wasn't. I hated them. They appeared to be traveling at 943 mph, driven forward by the same wind that was pressing against us.

There were no cars, so the four of us coasted toward the center stripe. They were two guys, probably in their twenties, long and lanky, just like me. We eyed each other's panniers and judged outfits, stopping just short of sniffing asses.

"Looks like you guys are riding the right direction," Rachel said, holding a hand up against the wind. I caught a slight hint of malice in her voice.

One of them snorted. "For the moment. We've had awful headwinds for three days."

I perked up. So prevailing didn't mean "permanent." This was encouraging.

Turned out that, throughout North Dakota, they'd only encountered west-bearing winds, and many locals had commented on how odd this was. How rare. I cursed the Lump, the trail, the spokes. If Rachel and I had gotten here just three days earlier, we'd be flying. We chatted for a few more minutes, covered the wheres and whens of our respective trips, none of us interested in delving into the whys, and then we wished each other well and moved on.

The prevailing winds continued to prevail. After twenty miles, we stopped off in Cooperstown, a sleepy town whose ornate theater, wide streets, and plentiful-but-vacant storefronts spoke to a prosperity come and gone. We settled in the park, spent a few hours reading, sleeping, and baking cookies whose only redeeming quality was being prepared on a stove made from a beer can. Again I thought of asking Rachel to pull out the Fargonian chocolate. But we still had many miles to ride. I mustered up more patience.

Once the wind had dropped, we returned to the road, again riding past sunset, alone under starry skies, basking in prairie quiet. We'd been riding for two hours when the town of Glenview appeared on the horizon. We rolled into its park, set up the tent, lit up the beer can. Rachel told me, in an accent best described as drunken Queen's English, that she was "properly famished." I replied that she was in luck, as we'd soon be feasting upon quinoa with mixed vegetables paired with a side of string cheese and a 2007 bottle of Gatorade.

We feasted, and it was good, and as I began to clean up the dishes, Rachel stood and began rooting around in her panniers, rooting around for what seemed like an awful long time, which, I mean, I guess I didn't really care how long it took, so long as she found—

"I can't find it," she said.

"What?" My mouth gaped. My eyes bugged.

"The chocolate. I can't find it."

"Did you look in all the bags?"

"Brian. Yes. You just watched me."

"Okay," I said, sounding more desperate than intended. "Maybe look again?"

She looked again: unearthed her pink jersey and orange camp towel and flip-flops and loose change, pulled out a heavily creased North Dakota map, three ballpoint pens, a book of stamps, two unsent postcards, and a bottle of sunscreen. But no chocolate.

"I'm really sorry," she said. "I wish I had it. But I don't."

I avoided eye contact and rubbed two stones together. "It's all right."

We both sat there for a moment, silent. Then Rachel stood and walked to the bathroom, crouched beside a water spigot and began scrubbing the chamois of her spare shorts. She did this every night, without fail.

Without fail.

The rage was sudden, disorienting. I rose from the table and set off across the park, let the venom course through my gut, into my bloodstream, up toward my brain, where it cohered into the sobering realization that this was no mistake, that Rachel, queen of routine, did not make mistakes, that, in losing this chocolate, she had revealed herself to be precise about the wrong things and careless about the right ones, and as such, had not just lost chocolate but rather had become—or perhaps had always been—the *kind of person* who lost chocolate, and, okay, fine, I admittedly wasn't sure what this meant, exactly, but I knew it was important, was in fact vastly fucking important, and so I stewed on it, all night and for much of the next morning, right up until the moment when Rachel, who had for five minutes been digging through panniers in search of her wallet, suddenly yipped and did a little dance and held up two slightly mangled but still intact chocolate bars.

CHAPTER 10

An Answer to All My Questions

On a town park picnic table in Carrington, North Dakota, I sat beside Rachel, puffing my bare chest against the sun. After weeks of exposure, and despite a daily slathering of sunscreen, my skin now felt like fruit leather. Filthy fruit leather. Since leaving Fargo, we'd seen no lakes, no rivers, no showers—no water of any kind, save for the rusty sludge that flowed from gas station sinks and the snot-colored, algae-coated, agro-chemical gravy that pooled between amber waves of monoculture—and so we were covered in grease and grain dust, redolent of synthetic coconut and organic armpit, submerged face-deep in a world defined by wind-whipped wheat and heat-rippled pavement and a steamrolled horizon that never . . . fucking . . . changed.

And yet. At the moment, the sun felt warm but not hot. The breeze like fingers through my hair. I was pleasantly groggy and full, having just napped off my well-rounded breakfast of one sub sandwich, twenty ounces of soda, twelve fistfuls of trail mix, and that melted chunk of found chocolate. I was happy. I wanted nothing and nowhere else.

I propped myself on my elbows, plucked a few blades of grass, and tossed them aloft. They floated to the ground, landing just west of their point of origin.

"Check it out," I said to Rachel. "I think the wind is gonna be behind us today."

She smiled politely, as if I'd said I was going to be an astronaut when I grew up. She was getting used to these proclamations.

"Rach? Can you feel it? We're going to have a tailwind."

"Maybe." She squirted out a dollop of Chamois Butt'r and stuck her hand in her shorts. "Or maybe you flicked your wrist a teeny bit, in a westerly direction, when you 'dropped' the grass."

This was exactly what I had done. But it was for a good cause. A tiny lie told in service to our sense of momentum.

I shrugged. "We'll see about that."

I pulled on shirt and shoes and helmet and followed Rachel across the grass. We got on the bikes and started pedaling, and as we rode out of town, past cloud-colored grain silos and pole barns, I swore I felt a breeze tickling the back of my neck. I began nodding and pointing vaguely up at the sky, and just as I was twisting around to gloat, the wind stutter-stepped and feigned a wild starboard gust. I bit the fake—bit hard—and as I leaned into the current, the air abruptly about-faced and knocked me to the gravel. I fought back to the pavement, only to find that the wind had shifted again and was now slap boxing me back to Carrington.

This was not a headwind, not a tailwind, not even a crosswind. Just an asshole wind.

Now Rachel pulled up beside me, smirking, and said, "Some tailwind we got here."

"Very funny."

"I mean, this almost feels *too* easy."

"Right, okay, you win. But I still think—"

A horn blew. We were taking up the entire lane, and what with the wind's roar, we hadn't heard the truck approaching from behind. As it blasted on by, the driver gave us the finger.

"I'm sorry," I muttered, to no one in particular.

I pulled back in front of Rachel, dropped my head, drove the pedals. The wind was now roaring, worming into my ears and eyes and nostrils, making me feel not so very happy, and so I began casting about for something to appreciate. But the roadside grasses were convulsing in tight, violent spasms, as if being electrocuted. And the sunflowers off to the south—which, hours earlier, under flattering dawn light, had rolled their big beautiful heads in lazy little circles, calling to mind a lost scene from *Fantasia*—now leaned uncomfortably close, their faces bulbous and leering in the high-noon sun, looking less *Fantasia* and more *The Day the Plants Attacked*.

I shifted my gaze to the northern wheat fields. Much better. There the stalks swayed elegantly, swaths of gold rolling and rising in unison, rippled by the ever-changing current. As I watched the wheat dive toward me, then felt a gust barrel into my kidney, I realized: I could *see* the wind. Nostalgia surged. I'd grown up sailing tiny boats on tiny lakes and had loved scanning the water, searching for telltale shivers. Out here it was the same deal. If I kept my eyes on the wheat, I could rob the wind of its element of surprise, could lean into south-bearing crosswinds before they hit, duck into gusting headwinds, sit back and savor short-lived bursts from behind.

I didn't get it right every time, but that wasn't the point. Soon I was absorbed, engaged with the world, having myself a moment. And when, an hour or three later, we rolled up to the hold-your-breath town of Sykeston and slid into a window booth at the Country Cafe, I felt like I'd earned my slice of cherry pie, my cup of coffee, my sense of momentum.

The instant we got back on the road, I knew something had changed. I could feel it, could smell it, and I *couldn't* hear it, couldn't really hear anything at all, save for those super-subtle sounds usually buried under the wind's howl: tires humming on pavement, chain links whirring over steel teeth. Also, I was suddenly feeling like a superhero: barely working but damn near flying. I eyed the speedometer. We were going twenty, on flat ground, without breaking a sweat. I whipped into a U-turn and faced up to the eastern horizon. The wind was surging. Ferocious. It blasted back my eyelids, tore the skin from my forearms, bored a hole in my chest. I spun around again and rocketed forward, as if fired from a giant slingshot.

We finally, indisputably, had a tailwind.

For one, two, four miles, I rode in rapture, the cranks all but spinning themselves, my legs merely along for the ride. I tilted my head back, and I hoovered down the glorious prairie air, and it tasted so saturated, so sweet. I wanted to kiss it. Lick it. Marry it.

I mean, I must have on some level understood that I was tasting more than the moment. That the sweetness had something to do with those muscular clouds creeping over the northern horizon. Thunderheads of a purple so deep and dark they seemed capable of raining ink. But the wind was blowing from the east, and the clouds were so far north, right? Right.

We were about five miles west of Sykeston when I felt the first gust. It came in low and fast, drove straight into my rib cage. I shrugged it off as an anomaly, a sort of airborne eddy, the wind curling upon itself before continuing downstream. But more bursts followed, and then a steady push. By this point the northern horizon—not just the clouds but the horizon itself—appeared to be closing in, and above its bushy purple eyebrow I noticed a yellow smudge. Maybe I was an adrenaline junkie, a risk taker, but I was also a midwesterner, and midwesterners know that when you see a yellow smudge on the sky, you get the fuck inside.

I yelled to Rachel and pointed to the conveniently located rest stop on our right. We pulled in and discussed. We considered holing up at the wayside, but it only had a three-walled enclosure, and that wasn't going to cut it. There was nothing to do but head back to Sykeston.

I took the lead, and Rachel tucked in close behind. The wind was fighting dirty now—tossing dust in eyes, hitting below the belt. And that doomsday eyebrow was getting awfully close. Soon a taproot of lightning lit the sky. Seconds later, an ovation of thunder. The heavens flashed brighter and brighter, and the thunder followed ever more closely, until it was rumbling along with the lightning, rumbling right overhead.

We skidded up to the Country Cafe just as the rains began. There was no drip-trickle upswell. The heavens just shrugged and kicked over a Dakota-size bucket of water. It took us two seconds to reach the café door, but already we were soaked. We smiled sheepish smiles at the deeply dimpled proprietor, ordered cups of cocoa, and slid into a window booth.

The rain was now falling in sheets. Blankets. Shag carpets. The gravel lot was already flooded, and falling drops sprayed standing water like machine-gun fire. We played some rummy, waiting for the storm to wear itself out, as all prairie storms do. Except this one didn't. It was feeding upon itself, and by five thirty it looked nastier than ever. The café was to close at six, and we didn't have a plan for how we were going to achieve not going back out there. But we knew it was not going to happen. It couldn't. "I say we just look as pitiful as possible,"

Rachel whispered, nodding toward the woman behind the counter. "What's she going to do? Boot us out and watch us die?"

Five minutes before closing, some headlights cut through the wall of water. A blurry form scampered in front of them, then burst through the café door. A woman in her midforties, her soaking wet hair dripping onto a sweatshirt and mom jeans.

"Hi, Kim," the owner said, smiling. She pulled a couple of paper bags onto the counter. "You're right on time."

Kim smiled, mopped her brow with a sleeve, and pulled a couple of bills from her pocket. "This is some storm," she said. "There must be three inches of water in your lot." She turned toward us. "Are those your bikes out there?"

We nodded as if we'd been asked to identify bodies.

"Yeesh," she said. "Where are you sleeping?"

Four shoulders shrugged.

"The storm kind of caught us off guard," I said. "We're not really sure what to do."

Kim hesitated for a second, as if conceding a point in an argument only she could hear. Then she took a breath, smiled, and told us she had a camper parked outside her house. We could sleep there. We *would* sleep there. I managed a, "We don't want to impose . . . ," but she cut me off with a head shake, freeing me from going through the whole we-couldn't, okay-maybe-we-could, actually-we'd-fucking-love-to charade.

A half hour later, we were sitting in a warm living room with Kim and her husband, Chris, listening to our clothes tumble in the dryer and eating a too-midwestern-to-be-true dinner of ham and scalloped potatoes and cola. While Chris, a short, muscled guy with crazy hair and crazier eyes, watched TV and yelled at their two whirling-dervish kids, Kim talked about her little town, about commuting to Carrington and juggling jobs, about running for mayor of Sykeston. She was in the midst of her campaign and was, at that point, the sole candidate.

As soon as we cleared our plates, Kim snatched them up. She refused to let us help with the dishes, filled our arms with linens, and showed us to the trailer, one of those tiny models in which each thing was actually many things. A couch folded into a bed. A table became a box spring. A toilet stall was also a shower. It resembled, I thought, the Scamp my uncle had bought a few years back. I'd fallen in love with that trailer, or at least the idea of it, had dreamed of taking it on a road trip. And now, here I was, with Rachel, in a Scamp-like trailer, on a road trip of sorts, all because of the rain that even now was pounding onto the roof.

We tucked ourselves under moth-eaten wool blankets. I leaned in to give Rachel a this-has-been-a-great-day-and-I'm-exhausted-so-let's-go-to-sleep kiss, and she responded with a maybe-we-could-stay-awake-a-little-longer earlobe nibble, and so I came right back with a fuck-it-we're-in-a-lightning-lit-trailer-and-I-want-you caress that began at her neck and found its way to the skin that, even after a thousand miles of Lycra imprisonment, had surrendered no softness.

We had barely kicked away the covers when the tornado hit.

A deep, syrupy bass note pulsed through the air, as if someone had hit the lowest black key on the world's biggest keyboard. Gradually it rose in pitch and volume, hitting its crescendo at an earsplitting high C. Back in my hometown, a siren like this meant one of two things: either it was lunchtime at the lumber mill or the sky was about to shatter. Sykeston didn't have a lumber mill, and it sure as hell wasn't lunchtime. We needed to get out of this trailer.

We ducked into the rain, ran through the yard, and burst into the house. Kim and Chris were sitting in the living room, watching the nightly news. "Um," I said, wondering how I hadn't yet noticed our hosts were *fucking insane*, "shouldn't we get downstairs or something?"

They both looked at me blankly, as if I were speaking a foreign language.

I pointed dumbly toward the sky. "Doesn't that mean there's a tornado?"

Kim frowned, then chuckled. "Oh no, honey. That's just the ten o'clock siren." She turned back to the TV.

I wish, so much, that I'd had the wherewithal to ask what she meant by a "ten o'clock siren." But I was too baffled to speak, and apparently so was Rachel. We scurried back through the rain, to the trailer, into bed, under the covers.

I lay silent for a moment, then asked, "Did that just happen?"

"Yep," Rachel replied. "And I love the way she answered you. 'Just the ten o'clock siren.' Let's make sure to not act surprised when she sounds the eight o'clock breakfast gong."

I wondered whether there might be an eight o'clock breakfast gong. I kind of hoped so.

At dawn, pre-gong, we rolled back onto Highway 200. The storm had left its mark. The sky was still overcast, but the purple-puff anvils had disappeared, leaving a gray, deflated cloud-carpet that was as flat and dull as the landscape below it. Floodwaters buried farmland, and wheat stalks rose from the murk like marshland cattails. Brown-blue puddles filled potholes and pavement cracks, and the asphalt itself looked revived, like a Zamboni-polished strip of ice. Unblemished. Slick. Ready to be attacked.

And attack we did. From the first pedal stroke, riding felt easy. Yes, we had been riding for three weeks and had barely broken thirty miles the previous day. We had strong legs, revived legs. But this was a different kind of easy: a meteorologically explicable kind of easy. Wind was whipping the wheat, the world was hushed, and moving forward felt less like riding than falling.

"I know this is your line," Rachel said, "but I'm pretty sure we have a tailwind."

We *did* have a tailwind. An absolute monster of a tailwind. Even better, there were no distant thunderheads, no signs the current would shift anytime soon. And it didn't. All day it stuck with us, carried us past that rest stop, through the tinier-than-Sykeston town of Chaseley, and over what appeared to be hills, the first we'd seen since Minnesota. The speedometer told me I was going eighteen and twenty and twenty-two miles per hour, and I pushed harder and harder, laughing aloud. A gap began to open between Rachel and me, but I didn't let up. These miles were easy for both of us, and for once I didn't feel obligated to do anything but move forward.

After thirty miles, we stopped in Goodrich and prepared lunch on the lawn of a graying church. While fixing sandwiches and beer-can cooking some soup, we blubbered—both of us, Rachel just as excited as I was—about the wind. By now I was feeling guilty about having left her behind. I asked if she minded me taking some stretches at my own pace.

"Brian," she said, "I would be thrilled if you did that more often."

I nearly spat out my soup.

"You think I can't see you checking the rearview every three seconds?"

I raised an I-have-no-idea-what-you're-talking-about eyebrow.

She replied with a give-me-a-fucking-break snort.

"You're like fifteen feet taller than me. Which makes you faster. I get it. It's fine."

I blinked.

"And I appreciate that you try to ride my speed. But sometimes I just want to ride how I want to ride and not worry about slowing you down."

I blinked.

"How about this? If you want to ride ahead, you don't need to stop and hug me and tell me you love me. Just go. Maybe try to stay within sight. But really, if you wanna go, go."

I nodded and, unsure of what to say, took a jaw-distending bite from my sandwich.

Rachel smiled and squeezed my arm. "I'm glad we had this talk."

Back on 200 the wind was still tumbling westward, and within seconds, I was floating along at eighteen miles an hour. I dropped a hand from the bars, grabbed the top tube, and suddenly felt like a cowboy racing across the open plain, one hand on my saddle horn, the other working the reins. I took a deep pull of prairie air and swept my eyes up from the road to the distant hills to the big open sky. Blue-gray clouds lay over me like blankets, and I felt tucked in. Cozy and contained. Alone.

I found myself thinking of Galen, wondering if this was his every day—if he always felt so free, so powerful, so . . .

I shook off the thought. This was *my* moment. I wasn't going to spend it worrying over Galen or Rachel or anyone else, wasn't going to pay attention to that rhythmic click in my pedal or the gritty whine of my unoiled chain, wasn't going to question Wisconsin behind or Portland beyond. No, I was just going to be here, alone, doing what I was doing because I wanted to do it.

And so I rode, aware only of the pavement below and the hills ahead and those wind-tickled wheat stalks that were so pretty when pointed not at my face but at my horizon. For four miles, or maybe forty, I moved through this landscape, utterly alone, floating far ahead of Rachel and into a sort of trance. My legs kept a steady beat and my breath slowed and I felt like I was focusing not on any one thing but on all of it at once. I took in the plentiful-if-polluted ponds and the distant tractors and the grayscale skyscape and the charcoal tongue of the highway, and they became one thing. They became where I am.

Late afternoon we rolled up to Turtle Lake. Population 510. A Dakotan metropolis. The town sat to the north, tucked behind a grove of oak, and its main street, which looked more like a farmhouse driveway, cut through the trees to meet 200. At the intersection was a skyscraping pole that displayed the American flag I'd seen from a mile away, and beneath it a bus-size, solid-bronze turtle. "Rusty the Turtle," according to the plaque. I climbed atop his shell, hugged his head, rode him like a stallion. Rachel snapped a photo of me straddling his neck, waving an imaginary lasso. It was a great shot, this ridiculous reptile sitting in the prairie, and me on top of it, the wind whipping my hair so hard it actually appeared that Rusty and I were moving.

And that's exactly what I wanted to do. Keep moving. We'd already covered seventy-eight miles that day, but with the tailwind, I felt like we'd just started. I could ride all night, and I told Rachel as much. She nodded but said nothing.

"It's only twenty-eight more miles to Riverdale," I said.

No response.

"We can probably make it there by dusk," I continued. "What do you think?"

She looked past Rusty, toward town. "I don't know. I'm kind of ready to be done."

Something like anger rose to my throat. I was feeling invincible, and now I was going to have to sit around and twiddle my thumbs during the prettiest part of the day, all because Rachel didn't want to push herself? I took a breath, managed to remind myself that I had no idea whether she had, in fact, been pushing herself all day; that I was, as she'd put it, like fifteen feet taller;

that she'd given me the green light to cowboy up all afternoon; and that since I'd done exactly that, maybe a little compromise was in order.

"Yeah," I said. "I guess I could stop too. This does look like a cute town."

We set up in the tiny, tree-lined park and cooked up some couscous and veggies, then strolled downtown and headed into Betty Boops, the local watering hole. As we sipped pints of watery pilsner, the bartender, Tina, a pretty blonde with a gravelly voice and a seen-it-all-thirteen-times perma-smirk, told us all about Rusty. Apparently, a few years before, the town had optioned a cash reserve and given residents the choice between a community pool and Rusty. Families wanted the pool. Old folks wanted Rusty. The old folks won, and now, on ninety-degree summer days, Tina found herself wanting to murder an inanimate reptile.

She invited us to join in the nine o'clock bingo game. Rachel and I went in together on four cards and lost terribly. When the game wrapped up, some old-timers shuffled over to a table in the corner, and I asked Tina what was happening. "Blackjack," she replied. "Blackjack?" I asked. "Blackjack," she repeated. Apparently, gambling in bars, not just video poker but actual card games, was legal in North Dakota. Rachel wasn't into it, but I sat down, rationalizing that I'd been really good about sticking to my ten-dollar daily budget and could afford to have some fun, and that playing cards for money in a bar was a fleeting experience, to be seized and savored.

To my surprise, I'd won thirty bucks by the end of the first shoe. And to my deeper surprise, I actually stood up and left, rather than gambling my winnings away.

It was almost midnight when we left Betty Boops. Rachel grabbed my hand, and as we strode through side streets, back toward the park, I felt like the king of North Dakota. Like I was being rewarded, over and again. The gods had discovered where I was, and what I was doing, and why, and how, and they had been pleased, had showered me with tailwinds and table winnings and the admiration of this strong, proud, ass-kicking woman, and now we were standing together at the gates to a magical new world, a world where life was and would always be getting better, where each new mile would build upon the one before it, would be richer and sweeter and simpler, until the final mile was not a mile but an answer to all my—

Rachel squeezed my hand. "Hey," she said. "What are you thinking?"

I wasn't sure I could get all that to come out right, so I squeezed back and nodded up at the night sky and said, "Just that I'm so happy we're here."

"Me too," she said. "This is always my favorite part of the day."

"And which part is that?"

"The not-riding part. Being in these small towns. Being done."

"Oh," I said. "Well, yeah, you know I love small towns, but I more meant the whole—"

"I know." She traced her fingers up my arm, around my back, and kept walking.

I opened my mouth to say more, to try to convince her that *every* part was the best part, that mine was the right kind of happiness. But I thought better of it. Happiness was happiness, and we'd both found it in this moment, and that, I thought, was enough.

CHAPTER 11

The Photographer

At half past dawn in a well-treed park in a town called Hazen, I sat up and yawned and nudged Rachel awake. With sleep-swollen eyes and rumbling tummies, we dragged ourselves out of the tent and over to the Cenex station, where we holed up at one of the faux-fir booth tables by the window, and for the better part of an hour, we sat and sipped coffee and ate oatmeal and read the paper and pocketed butter packets and, whenever the clerk was distracted, which was often—the place was teeming with carpenters and ranchers and truck drivers, few of them paying for gas, most just nursing coffee and talking about the weather, the jobs they'd lined up for the week, the fish they'd caught that weekend—we tiptoed over to the airpots and topped off our cups.

After her third refill, Rachel slid back into the booth and crossed her arms on the table and said, "So, don't get me wrong, I love cooking over a beer can and having ants in my sandwich and all . . . but how the hell have we never done this before?"

I spooned the last bit of oatmeal from my tin bowl. "I don't know. But I say we plan to sleep within sight of a Cenex from here on out."

"Why don't we just sleep *at* Cenex? We won't even have to set up the tent, what with the canopies, and we can huff gas right from our sleeping bags."

I laughed, and shook my head, and said, "You're ridiculous."

Whenever I found myself unable to keep up with Rachel—with her wit, her intellect, her decisive clarity—I'd say those words. I didn't, of course, find her the least bit ridiculous. But it was a way less vulnerable thing to say than "I am in awe of you."

Now she stood and announced her plan to have a sponge bath in the gas station bathroom. I decided to follow suit. My skin hadn't seen soap since Sykeston, but it had seen a whole lot of dirt and sun and grain dust. My torso in particular felt like it was covered in Velcro. I headed to the bathroom and locked the door and pulled off my shirt, and as I washed away the stink, I considered myself in the mirror. Weeks ago, in Duluth, I'd trimmed my beard back using a pair of kitchen shears, and now that it had grown out, I could see I'd done a particularly shitty job. The beard was bushy in a very literal sense: there were several little hair shrubs with their own shape and structure, and they only appeared to be one composite thing—one beard—when viewed from afar. The oldest shrubs, the ones I must have missed in Duluth, had taken on a rusty red that, I thought, contrasted nicely with the ruddy bronze of my cheeks. Add in the bloodshot eyes and Kramer hair and candy-cane-contrast farmer's tan, and I looked like a hardened bike tourist. Or maybe a militia member. Either way, I was proud of myself.

I put on my shirt, slipped a roll of toilet paper inside it, and walked out to the lot, where Rachel was loading butter packets and jam tubs into our spice kit. I smiled, and she smiled back as I flashed the toilet paper, and then, in plain sight of a half-dozen men shooting gas into their tanks, we applied our sunscreen and our palmfuls of Chamois Butt'r. I was not embarrassed. Nor, it seemed, was Rachel, who was staring off at the western horizon, one hand on her hip, the other in her shorts. We were both just doing what we needed to do to be where we belonged. And if it bothered the bystanders, well, that couldn't be helped.

I stuffed the Butt'r back into the bag. I put on my helmet and swung my leg over the bike and clipped into the pedals, and Rachel did the same, and I followed her out of the parking lot and onto the highway and into whatever came next.

Hazen was a border town, the gateway from farmland to ranchland. It was an instant shift, just like the forest-to-plains transition in Minnesota, and as we rode west, I marveled at our new surroundings: craggy buttes peeking through prairie grass, beef cattle behind barbed wire. Also, hills. I could see why people always called this place rugged. The earth before us seemed to have been riven and raised up like some kind of ranchland drawbridge. Rocks and livestock stood in for manhole covers and streetlamps, jutting toward us at gravity-defying angles.

Rachel and I looked at each other, took dramatic deep breaths, and hit the hill. The grade was initially modest, in the neighborhood of your average ADA-accessible ramp, but slowly it steepened, until pedaling felt less like spinning than like weight training. By my thirtieth rep, the speedometer told me I was moving at 3.2 mph, and for a minute there I thought I might have to—God forbid—get off the bike and walk. But I kept at it, one pedal stroke at a time, and as I chugged along, I found I actually kind of enjoyed this pace. It forced me to pick my head up and inhale the cow-dung hay-dust breeze and feel this rugged new world.

We were in the West, all right. Weathered rocks were everywhere: here, sprawled out under a frayed blanket of high grass; there, stacked four high, a giant's cairn. And the grass, which through some trick of lighting or sentiment appeared gold and green and blue all at once, was speckled with what must have been a hundred tar-black steer. A hundred rigidly attentive steer. Every last one of them, I realized, was staring at us with dopey intensity.

"Do you see this?" I asked, pointing toward the cattle. Some were standing, some lying down. One was spraying piss with the pressure of a fire hose, and another had frozen midmeal, a mouthful of grass hanging from its face. All of them were possessed by our presence.

"Makes me feel self-conscious," I said. "Do I have a cold sore or something?"

Rachel didn't respond. She was breathing hard, and her cheeks were flushed, and she seemed to be deliberately avoiding eye contact. And, well, what the hell? She'd been downright effusive back at the Cenex, not twenty minutes earlier. What had I done?

"Is something wrong?" I asked.

She kept riding for a moment, then turned and said, "I'm just getting tired of this."

I nodded, relieved. "Yeah. This is quite a hill, right? But I think we're almost to the top."

She gave me a well-you-just-missed-the-entire-fucking-point stare.

I looked down at the pavement, trying to find the I-do-too-get-the-point words. But I did not get the point, did not quite grasp what she was tired of, and so finally I just pulled back in front of her and shrugged at my bovine spectators and rode.

Soon the grade flattened out, and we began picking up speed, riding what I swore was a faint tailwind. At the Cenex, a pleasant fifty-something woman had told us to expect "a really tough day" of hills and headwinds, and the local paper had similarly predicted westerlies gusting up to thirty-some miles per hour, but now I set to rewriting the forecast. The winds would shift, and the hills would lay prostrate before us, and we'd have ourselves another glorious tailwind romp.

About that. For ten miles, or perhaps six—okay, maybe it was only four, but definitely no less than four—the air stayed gentle, and I stayed silent, and Rachel stayed right on my tail. But then we came around a little bend in the road and—surprise!—here was that west wind. At first it was playful, tickling my ribs and whispering in my ear, but soon the whispers became curses, and the rib tickles gave way to cheek slaps and eyeball pokes, and finally the wind just planted its feet and gave me a yes-I'm-picking-a-fight-with-you shoulder shove.

I swore under my breath and hunched over the bars and pushed, my attention split between the grasses, which telegraphed nothing I couldn't feel, and the rearview, where I could see Rachel's head bobbing, her eyes like ticking time bombs. I decided to ignore both, just dropped my eyes to the speedometer and fought for double digits. It was a slog, but I held strong at nine or ten miles an hour, for nearly an hour, and just when I felt like we were getting used to the wind, like we'd established something approaching momentum, we came up over a little hump in the road and the wind just fucking ambushed us.

The air attacked so suddenly, and with such force, that I honestly wondered if it might be a prank, the most elaborate *Candid Camera* gag of all time. Maybe the horizon was actually a mile-long canvas, and said canvas would now roll up to reveal a wall of industrial-strength fans, an array of cameras, a gaggle of friends laughing and backslapping. But this was no gag. It was a humorless, soulless wind. It knocked my rearview out of position, burned my eyeballs, burrowed into my nostrils. And that howl. Never had a landscape sounded so angry.

I was now going four miles an hour. Barely. I was amazed at how difficult it was to keep myself moving—not moving quickly, merely moving—but I was not about to be defeated by a bunch of bullshit molecules, and so I sunk as low as I could and squeezed the bars and just plain Godzilla-stomped the pedals, and, well, now we were getting somewhere. I even hit seven miles per hour for a couple of seconds. I pushed harder and harder, until I could almost feel the veins worming out from my forehead, could almost taste the sweat soaking my shirt, and soon I was feeling pretty triumphant, because here I was, in the unforgiving West, and the world was assaulting me with the worst it had, and (cue strings) I wasn't backing down.

At a certain point I remembered I had a girlfriend. Who was riding her bike cross-country. With me. Since my mirror was now aimed at a power line, I couldn't see her, and I had to actually spin around and look over my shoulder, and, of course, just as I did, the jerk-off wind surged and sent me swerving into the lane. I righted myself, and looked again, and saw that I'd left Rachel a good fifty yards back, so I slowed up and tried hard to hold a draftable speed. But the wind kept launching sucker punches every time I glanced back, and it was hard enough just to keep moving, so I looked less and less, outpaced her more and more.

Nine miles of this nonsense. Nine miles that took almost two hours. By the time we arrived in the not-quite-a-town of Halliday, my eyeballs were acid soaked, my entire body was aching, and I wanted nothing more than to drink a liter of corn syrup and pass out on a picnic table. I said so to Rachel. She nodded and said—her voice just above a whisper, her eyes all but empty—that she was just going to head to the park. A few minutes later, I found her there, slumped against an oak, speaking with quiet intensity into her phone. I started to lean my bike beside hers, but she put a hand over the receiver and looked up and said, "I'm on the phone." She kept looking until I got the hint and wheeled my bike to the other side of the park.

An hour passed. Then two. I kept expecting Rachel to come over and talk, but every time I looked up, she was still in her corner, leaned against the tree, one hand holding the phone, the other ripping up patches of grass. I wanted to join her over there, but I didn't know what I'd say. And so I kept myself busy—wrote in my journal, scribbled out a couple of postcards, even pulled out the ukulele. I'd barely played it thus far, but now I studied the chord chart, got comfortable with a few progressions, and set to figuring out a uke version of a song I'd written in Xela. As I played, I found myself thinking about the months we'd spent there. I thought about *el lago*, and the beachside path where this whole thing had begun, and it all seemed very far away.

The sun was kissing the horizon when Rachel at last came out of her corner.

"I'm sorry," she said.

"For what?"

"For being such a brat."

"You're not being a brat."

"Yes. I am. And I wanted to tell you that it's not about you."

"Everything is about me."

She gave my shoulder a shove. "I'm serious, okay?"

"Okay."

She pushed her hair out of her eyes and looked down at the grass and said, "It's just hard. I guess I knew I'd be tired and dirty. But I thought I'd like it. And sometimes, most of the time, I do. But there are days, like today, when I just feel totally bored and discouraged. And then I ask myself why I'm even out here. You know?"

I did not know. But I nodded.

"And it's not even about my butt being sore or my fingers being numb or whatever. Really, it's just that sometimes—and, again, today especially—I just get caught on the thought that I really don't want to do this. That I could be doing *anything* else right now."

What I said was, "I know what you mean."

What I did not say was that what she meant was the opposite of what I felt: that I loved this trip precisely because it closed off anything—everything—else, and I thought this thing we were doing was pure and true and glorious, and I felt like I could—

"Hey."

I looked up. "Sorry. I was just thinking about what you said."

"Well, I was saying I'm done talking now. I just wanted you to know that I do want to finish this trip, and I know this is all in my head, and I'm going to try to be more positive."

"And I'm going to try to be more supportive," I said. "But can you help me out a little? I'm having trouble finding that sweet spot between ignoring you and annoying you."

She said she'd try to do that, and I grabbed her hands and said, "Help me help you," and then she kicked me in the shins, and I came right back with a Lycra wedgie, and we agreed that it was maybe time to get back on the road.

That night we rode twenty-five miles. The wind sank with the sun, a deep quiet settled with the night sky, and by the time we saw the distant twinkle of civilization, from the town of Killdeer, it was past ten and the temperature had dipped into the forties. Even I, the winter-loving northerner, was shivering as we rolled into the town park, which meant that Rachel, who wore multiple layers in seventy-degree apartments, was freezing.

When we learned the park had heated bathrooms, with *show-ers*, Rachel was jumping-up-and-down ecstatic. I offered to set up the tent on my own, and my offer seemed to land right in that sweet spot we'd been talking about. She headed to the showers, and after some tent erecting and self-congratulating, I did the same. For some time, I lingered under steaming water, my skin tingling, my mind sweeping over all the miles that had made this cramped, funky shower stall feel downright posh.

The next day we laid over in Killdeer. All morning we loi-tered at a nearby Cenex, and come afternoon we headed back to the park to write postcards and read books and call friends. One of those friends was Galen. He was now in eastern South Dakota, apparently battling some equally fierce headwinds. His last three days, he said, had been "pretty hellish."

When I hung up, I told Rachel what Galen had said, how discouraged he'd sounded.

She smiled and said, "I'm embarrassed to admit how happy I am to hear that."

The rest of the day passed slow and lazy. We had a little uke sing-along, played a dozen games of rummy, strolled every street in town. Every hour or so, one of us would say something about how good it felt to take a break, to step out of the day-to-day. To just, you know, enjoy each other's company.

When thunderheads rolled in, around five, we took refuge in the town bar. It ended up being a four-pints-of-pilsner storm, and when the skies finally cleared, we walked back to the tent and had some four-pints-of-pilsner sex. Eager and clumsy and over before we knew it.

By morning the rains had resumed, so we shuffled back to the Cenex to eat breakfast and drown our four-pints-of-pilsner hang-overs in cheap coffee. Rachel pored over newspaper horoscopes. I

began, and quickly gave up on, a crossword. And then we headed
back to the park for shamefully long showers. Sure, in a couple of
days we'd be staying in a proper home—Kim from Sykeston had
set us up with friends in a town just past the Montana border—
but we'd learned that in our time-space continuum, two days
could feel like two months.

North of Killdeer, Highway 200 was mercifully flat, and it
wound gently around weathered old barns and postage-stamp
horse pastures. Though the forecast had called for more life-
ruining winds, I could barely detect a current. The air was
calm, the sun obscured by a slate cloud pillow, the highway, as
ever, nearly free of cars. For twenty-some miles, Rachel and I
rode side by side, stopping frequently for pictures and pee
breaks, wondering aloud why every day couldn't be like this,
and discussing which route to take through Montana. It was
hard to believe we might be there, might at last escape North
Dakota, by the following evening.

Slowly, almost imperceptibly, the flats gave way to gentle
rollers, and then not-so-gentle rollers, until we found ourselves
perched on the edge of a river valley, its western banks rising
toward what appeared to be mountains. Oddly familiar mountains.

"I thought these were in South Dakota," Rachel said.

"Me too."

Back in Fargo, I'd pored over pictures of this exact landscape, had briefly gotten obsessed with the idea of veering down
to South Dakota. To the Badlands. We'd decided against doing
so, had even steered clear of Theodore Roosevelt National
Park, which I understood to be the poor man's Badlands. And
when we'd made these decisions, a little part of me, the part
that believed the secret to happiness might be perched atop one
of those buttes, had died. But here we were, amid the white
space, the place between places, a place that, according to our

map, was merely an amorphous blob defined by all it was not: Not lake nor stream, not park nor forest, not reservation land nor county seat. Not the Badlands. And yet. It was.

The land before us rose in a mess of massive humps, some knobby and wrinkled like an old man's knuckles, others jagged as shark's teeth. This, of course, was not how I described it at the time. No, I took in the Badlands and, echoing every other human who has ever gazed upon a stark and unfamiliar landscape, I said, "It looks like the moon."

I turned to Rachel. "I want to get a picture of you on the moon." As I dug out the camera, she waddled forward with her bike. I pulled back to a wide angle, fitting in the rippled horizon, the sloping pavement, some foreground buttes and, off to the side, Rachel, who was still waddling. I called her name, and when she turned to look over her shoulder, I snapped the shot.

I've looked at that photo many times over the years, enough that I don't need to see it to tell you that Rachel, with her sucked-in cheeks and her narrowed eyes and her mouth twisted into a tight half smile, was trying to look tough. Rachel always exuded toughness, but there, in deep Dakota, she was straining to project what had once come naturally.

And I definitely don't need to see the photo to tell you about the photographer. He was positioning the camera, fussing over the framing, trying to capture the big picture—so consumed by the composition that he'd lost sight of its subject.

CHAPTER 12

A Single Whisper

I tilted my head skyward and raised up the bottle and squeezed it with both hands. A shy tablespoon of lukewarm water wet my tongue. I squeezed harder, and the plastic made that pathetic wheezing-donkey sound, and here came a drop, and another, and another, and . . .

My eyes still on the bottle, I asked, "So, hey, how much water do—"

"I don't want to talk about it," Rachel said.

"Right. Well, then I guess I'll just have to drink these here Cheetos."

"You do that." She looked off to the west, over the barbwire and apple-bobbing oil derricks and dirt—so much dirt—and said, "How far did you say it was? To Wilford Brimley?"

"Watford City," I said. "About thirty miles."

She picked up a rock, tossed it from hand to hand. "We're not very good at this, are we?"

"No," I said. "No, we are not."

Despite having spent the morning shuttling between Killdeer's well-equipped town park and its downright deluxe Cenex, we'd forgotten to fill our Camelbaks. Again. And now, barely halfway into this ride through high plains heat, we'd emptied our bottles.

Rachel stood and stretched her arms high overhead, shielding her eyes from afternoon sun. "Well?" she said. "Wilford ho?"

I nodded. "Wilford ho."

We saddled up and pushed back into the blast-furnace heat, and after a mile I already felt like I was sucking a salt lollipop. I tried to distract myself, to think of anything else, but there was only this. Only thirst. When I closed my eyes, I saw a montage of plump, juicy oranges and rain-forest waterfalls. When I opened them, I saw dirt. And dirt. And dirt.

The Badlands weren't so romantic when viewed up close. Those velvety wrinkles, the ones that from afar had made the mountains look as cuddly as sleeping shar-peis, were just a bunch of eroding canyons. And the peaks themselves? Those blue-brown, pastel-chalked domes? Piles of dirt. This was just a bone-dry, brown-scale dust bowl peppered with sagebrush and dead grass and the most decrepit little shrubs I'd ever seen. They looked as thirsty as I felt.

So, for that matter, did Rachel. Her skin was slick with sweat, her face a hangdog droop. I wanted to say something, anything, to help her forget the heat and thirst and dirt, but my mind was blank. I couldn't put together words, much less sentences. All I could do was ride. And count—pedal strokes and eye blinks, miles and minutes, fence posts and passing cars. I'd had a mild sleep disorder as a kid, and now I was thinking of those long hours when I'd lain in the dark, counting sheep or, more often, puppies. I'd keep my eyes shut as long as possible, would finally check the clock to find that nine minutes had passed since I last looked. It was the same shit out here. Only now my clock had this speedometer, this oscillating reminder that time was moving so slow only because I was too weak to speed it up.

For somewhere between an hour and a decade, Rachel and I rode, silent and separate, suffering from cotton mouth and twinklevision, until at last we came upon a splotchy white ranch house sitting just north of the road. We dropped the bikes in the gravel driveway, climbed the steps, and knocked on the door. No answer. I walked to the side of the house, hopped the chain-link fence and cased the backyard. Sure enough, over there by the deck was a spigot. I popped around the house and told Rachel to toss over the bottles, and she did, and I filled them, and I came back over the fence, beaming with pride, like some kind of returning war hero, and we both closed our eyes and put the bottles to our lips and took in that sweet . . .

Poison. Fucking *poison*.

I spat onto my shoes, Rachel onto the dirt between us.

"You've got to be kidding me." She spat again.

The water, if you could call it that, was hot enough to bathe in. And rotten. I'd had some nasty, sulfur-saturated sludge in my day, but nothing like this. It tasted like a sewer smelled.

Rachel dug out the toothpaste, and we both started finger-brushing our teeth and tongues and gums, and soon we were laughing, because boiling-hot sulfur-lava, because heatstroke delirium, because here was this truck speeding on by, the driver watching two sweaty idiots standing over two crash-parked bike-tanks, before a house they obviously did not own, with fingers in their mouths. And now I was laughing even harder, because I'd somehow forgotten that there were people in the passing cars, that they could help us if things really got dire, and that, anyway, I'd chosen this, had even secretly hoped I'd find myself in absurd situations just like this one, and so why not stop pouting and just appreciate it for a second? I mounted my bike-tank, and Rachel mounted hers, and with some poison in our bottles, some toothpaste close at hand, we rode on.

There was a park on the outskirts of Watford City, and we pulled in and drank cramp-inducing quantities of water and sat for a while on the swing set. Once my body temperature dropped below the boiling point, I stood up and started pulling the tent from the rack. But Rachel stopped me, suggested we maybe take a spin through town first, see what was going on.

And so now we were riding past the Dakota West Credit Union, the Do-It Best hardware store, Mike's SuperValu grocery. Stars and stripes billowed from every lamppost, and the only cars in sight were clustered near the bar, the steakhouse, the American Legion. This all felt very familiar, a slight variation on what we'd seen in so many other Dakotan towns, and really the only exception was that . . . actually, what *was* that? Over on the south side of the street, across from the puny pharmacy and even punier insurance office, was a grotesquely large, brand-new building, with a rainbow of earth tones on its sandblasted walls, a block-long parade of spotless windows, a gaudy sign for businesses like Six Shooters Showhall and Outlaws' Bar and Grill.

We pulled up to the curb. "Well," Rachel said, "can't say I was expecting this."

"Um, no. Definitely not."

"It's like an art exhibit." She gestured grandly at the building. "Presenting . . . North Dakota! As imagined by suburban Chicago."

"Maybe I should call my aunt in Buffalo Grove," I said. "See if someone's reported a stolen mini-mall."

"Wait." Rachel was now peering through the doors. "Is that a movie theater?"

It was. Six Shooters Showhall was a cinema, a huge, spotless cinema with giant tubs of popcorn and cushy seats and surround sound. And in forty-one minutes, it would be showing a big-budget action film that both of us actually wanted to see. We asked no further questions about what this was doing in Watford City, just sprinted back to the park, threw up the tent, lit up the beer can and shoveled in some undercooked pasta and tepid marinara, not caring how crappy dinner was, because *movie*. We rushed back through the theater doors, loaded up on soda and candy and popcorn, and slid into our seats just in time to catch the final preview.

The next two hours were embarrassingly good ones. After a week of wheat and wind and the subtlest subtleties, I wanted to be beaten over the head. And this film delivered. Car chases! Roundhouse kicks! Snappy dialogue and booms and crashes and bright, flashing colors! My whole being was awash in caffeine and adrenaline, my heart rate less human than hummingbird, my mouth frozen into a kid-at-a-candy-store smile, and when I looked over at Rachel, I saw she was wearing the same bewildered grin. Both of us were laughing at all the wrong times, which is to say at all times, because this film was not in any way comedic, but it was taking us for a ride, and we were both so happy to be taken for a ride by something, anything, other than ourselves.

It was barely noon, and we'd ridden not thirty miles, and already I was broken. My lips were cracked, my skin flaking off. Legs soupy, butt ravaged. All morning, I'd been doing what I could to democratize the pain—sliding left and right and forward and backward, standing from the saddle until the quad burn was worse than the taint ache—but it wasn't working. Nothing was. Not on my body, not in my brain. I mean, I was trying to think happy thoughts, trying to remind myself that if the previous day's ride had transmuted Hollywood brain candy into sacred treasure, then tonight's arrival in Montana—a place that embodied the West, a place that was very close to wherever the hell we were going—should feel like some kind of existential orgasm. But those were some complicated happy thoughts, and, at the moment, I couldn't do complicated. In fact, the only thing I could do was: *Hooooooome, home on the range, where the deer and the—*

"I want it to be over."

Rachel had pulled up alongside me. She looked like hell. Bleary eyes and blotchy skin, loose strands of hair stuck to her forehead.

I nodded tentatively. I wasn't quite sure what she meant by "it."

"Everything is starting to look the same out here," she said. "I want Montana."

Now I smiled, and said, "Me too. I mean, I know it's just an imaginary line, but it's got to be at least a little bit different over there."

"I hope so. I need a break from this." She nodded vaguely at everything.

I nodded back but could think of nothing more to say. Rachel again dropped behind me, and we rode for five, ten, fifteen miles, deeper and deeper into the harsh high afternoon, until the temperature was pushing one hundred, the wind pummeling our chests. Still I was empty of words, as was Rachel, and soon enough I began doing what one inevitably does with an overabundance of silence and self-pity. I blamed.

In a whiny, nasal, and—thankfully—internal voice, I reflected on how incredibly unfair it was that at a moment like this, when I just wanted to push myself and get this over with and make Montana, I had to putter around and wait for Rachel, who was holding steady at eleven miles an hour, while I wanted to go more like fourteen and, okay, so maybe she *had* told me many times to just fucking go fourteen already, but come on now, I could not do that, I would not do that, because I was a noble man, and I would do the noble thing, would silently and resentfully sacrifice for Rachel, even if she didn't want me to, because—

"I'm bored." Rachel had snuck up beside me again. "Wanna play twenty questions?"

"Okay," I heard myself say.

It took me a moment to get into it, and out of my head, but soon enough I was thinking not of eleven or fourteen but of "is it edible?" I pretty quickly guessed Rachel's subject—Nutty Bars—and she in turn got my Lake Superior with a few questions to spare, and after a few more rounds, we switched to this game where one of us would name a city and the other would come back with another city whose name started with the last letter of the one just named. This kept us busy for the better part of an hour, and when we found ourselves running out of new cities, we moved on to countries, and then bodies of water, and then nineties bands, and then I was picking my head up and squinting at a distant sign and realizing it said "Montana."

We'd arranged to spend a night in Sidney with Kelly and Forest Markle, friends of Kim from Sykeston. For the first time in almost a week, we'd have a home, a bed, a break from the road. And we needed it. I needed it. On top of the now-familiar biking-related aches, I was feeling the effects of sleeping, day after day, on an inch-thick mat, with a dirty-clothes pillow. My body felt not just sore but sharp. Angular. And Rachel looked just as jagged. After we crossed the Montana border, she'd taken the lead for a bit, and I'd noticed for the first time how muscular her calves had gotten. It was kind of gross. I was hoping a couple of days of comfort food and armchairs and blankies might soften up the both of us.

Forest and Kelly were already outside when we pulled into their driveway. From the moment I saw the pair, I felt I knew what to expect. Kelly, with her warm eyes and wild hair, would be spunky and inquisitive. And Forest, a closed-mouth smile crinkling his cheeks, his hand wrapped around a pint glass of clear liquid I correctly assumed was not water, would be self-contained but sweet, possessed of a downright midwestern sort of stoic generosity.

Over a spaghetti and salad feast made with garden-grown produce, each of them played to type. Kelly peppered us with the frequently asked questions—the where and when and for Pete's sake why?—then steered talk toward other topics: her knitting, Forest's love of cooking, their thoughts on small-town living. Forest, throughout, smiled and sipped, from time to time sharing a spare but fully formed thought. At some point I mentioned our beer-can stove, which led to a bit of show-and-tell, which led Kelly to demand we stay a second day and help her build one. We agreed to both proposals—the stove building and, especially, the second day.

After the meal, Forest actually let us help with dishes, and once we finished, Kelly showed us to our room, a little cave with an enormous bed. Though it wasn't yet eight, she and Forest were bidding us good-night. This was apparently their custom, heading to bed before sunset and waking up at what-the-fuck o'clock to sip coffee, skim headlines, and start the day. I couldn't imagine keeping that schedule. But at the moment, it felt perfect. Rachel and I were beat, so we too stuffed a blanket in front of our room's tiny window and slid into bed.

The next day was gloriously lazy. Our hosts spoiled us rotten. Football-size omelets at sunrise, an afternoon snack of peaches and cream, another food-coma-inducing dinner. It was clear that Forest and Kelly didn't have a lot of money, and yet they were sharing so much, so freely and joyfully, with two strangers. Beyond the food, they were simply great hosts. Hosts who understood balance. For every minute they spent with us, they took two more to do their own thing, leaving us to do ours. Even better, they actually requested our help. I'd always felt weird staying with people who insisted on doing everything—"Oh, I'll flush that, you just *relax*"—so I was glad to be not just allowed but asked to wash dishes, was thrilled to help Kelly build her stove, to know I'd leave behind something more permanent than tire tracks and dirty sheets.

Building the stove felt great, and when it was finished, I suggested to Rachel that we give the Fujis some long-overdue attention. Lubing the chains, for starters. Mechanic Jeff had told us to do so every hundred miles, and until Fargo we had, mainly because my blown spokes had forced me to think about maintenance every freaking day. But since Fargo, we'd traveled over four hundred miles and hadn't yet pulled out the lube. Not once. Day after day, I'd listened to the squeaks and gnashes, the telltale cries of a thirsty chain. Had worried, but had done nothing. It wasn't that I didn't know how. Lubing a chain was easy, even for a novice. I'd avoided the task because I was afraid that if I looked close I'd find something worse than a dry chain. Something I couldn't fix. And Rachel, maybe with the same self-sabotaging rationale, had been just as negligent.

So now we were side by side, kneeling in the gravel, shaking our heads. Both chains were dirt choked and grimy. Same for the cogs and derailleurs. Also the rims and brake pads and cables and hubs and, well, every other part that was responsible for propelling us forward or keeping us from crashing. And the myriad bolts, the ones that held on the racks and fenders and water bottle cages, the ones we'd been advised to tighten regularly, were all loose. All of them.

Rachel sat back and rested her arms on her knees. "Whoops," she said.

I shook my head. "I can't believe these things are still running. We're morons."

"Yes," she said. "Yes, we are."

It took us quite a while to wipe off the gunk, snug the bolts, oil and polish and pump. Somehow nothing seemed broken or overly worn. We realized we were lucky, and we both made promises, to the Fujis and each other, that from here on out we'd be more attentive. We'd be better. We said these things while sitting in a private driveway, in front of a cozy home, our bellies full and our bodies rested. And we believed them.

After washing up, Rachel and I headed to the bedroom, telling Forest and Kelly that we needed naps, but just intending to lie down together. To cuddle. Out on the road, we didn't get to do a whole lot of cuddling. We were always filthy or hot or caged in Lycra, and since neither of us was inclined to lie in the grass in a town park, limbs intertwined, fingers in each other's hair, while a family of four played on a nearby swing set, the tent was our sole source of privacy. But the tent was stinky and cramped, and when we tried to lie together, one of us would inevitably slide between the two Therm-a-Rests and onto the cold, hard ground. Not exactly cuddle-time central. Sure, we had our fair share of sex in there, but sex didn't require comfort. Cuddling did.

Now we sunk into the bed. Limbs intertwined. Fingers in each other's hair. We murmured things like "this is nice" and "I wish we could stay here all day." Rachel took my hand, rolled toward the wall, tucked my palm to her chest, and for an hour we lay like that, drifting in and out of sleep, my face in her hair, her warm skin on mine. Eventually she moved to get up. I grabbed her arm, and we did exactly what you hope to do when you pull someone back to bed. We could hear our hosts in the kitchen, talking about vegetables and where-are-the-measuring-cups, so we burrowed under the blankets, made hardly a sound, moved slowly, finished quickly. Maybe that doesn't sound sexy. But understand, we'd been together, incessantly, for four weeks. We'd just finished a nine-day Dakotan odyssey, an experience by turns deafening and disorienting, tedious and endless. At the moment, sexy was not a Hollywood blockbuster. Sexy was a single whisper.

When we left that room to join Forest in the kitchen, we were smiling secret smiles. And as I stood beside Rachel, chopping onions and garlic for another sure-to-be-spectacular meal, I felt something that had been missing of late. Tenderness. Overwhelming tenderness. I shook my head, let out a little snort-laugh. Forest looked at me, so I blinked and grimaced and said something about spicy onions. Rachel looked too, and she smiled, as if she knew what I was thinking, as if she was thinking the same thing.

Just past Sidney, 200 broke due west, into another expanse of drab, dry grassland. A brutal crosswind tumbled over the northern horizon and assaulted us at an angle of exactly ninety degrees. I had to lean hard into the current just to stay upright. It was an odd sensation, spinning my legs forward while pressing my shoulders sideways. Kind of like the rubbing-tummy-while-patting-head game, except that in this game, messing up wouldn't lead to a fit of giggles—it would lead to getting pancaked by a big fucking truck.

Soon enough, I was enjoying myself in the same masochistic way I'd enjoyed our battle with that *Candid Camera* headwind. These miles were so perfectly difficult, so uncomplicated, so very much mine.

I looked back to the rearview. Rachel was clenching the bars, and I could practically see the numbness settling into her fingers. The wind was shoving her, sending her into mini-swerves and not-so-mini-swerves, and her eyes were squinted against the rushing air, focused on the pavement. For the hundredth time, I reminded myself that I wasn't alone out here. These miles weren't mine to own. They were ours.

For thirty miles I pushed into the wind, hard enough to keep us moving but not so hard that I'd accidentally open a gap between us, until at last we came upon some hay bales sitting just off the shoulder. Rachel suggested we pull over, and for some time we huddled behind the hay, our noses buried in books. She was in the final pages of *Still Life With Woodpecker*, and I'd made it halfway through DeLillo's *White Noise*. I wasn't really getting it, the big message buried in the prose, nor was I getting the irony that my poor comprehension likely had more than a little to do with the ever-distracting, not-so-white noise of roaring winds and whining engines.

Soon I dropped my book and walked to the shoulder. The wind had been blowing from due north, but now I could swear it was shifting, was becoming more northeasterly. I turned to mention this to Rachel, then caught myself. Days earlier, she had forbidden me to talk about the wind. It was her opinion that while I did have great enthusiasm for the work I performed in my capacity as self-appointed crew meteorologist, I did not have access to current weather reports or knowledge of locally prevailing winds or anything beyond the most basic understanding of meteorology. She had, as delicately as possible, said it would be easier for her to endure the wind if I'd stop repeatedly, and baselessly, trying to raise her expectations.

I wanted to honor this simple rule. No wind talk. But I also wanted to make her, and myself, and us, feel happy, and I'd studied the map enough to know that four miles up the road, just before Richey, Highway 200 would bend forty-five degrees to the southwest. Once we made that turn, the crosswind would transform into something tailwindish, whereupon life would become just swell. And when you know something like that, even if you've been specifically asked not to share it, aren't you kind of obligated to share it?

I shared it.

Rachel looked up from her book, sunk her eyes into me, said a single word. "Brian." Through some magic of vocal tone and body language, she had turned my name into a weapon.

I left it alone and, unsure what else to say, suggested we get back on the bikes. We fought through four violent miles, reached that bend in the road and followed its southwestern arc, at which point, lo and fucking behold, the wind was with us. It wasn't precisely a tailwind—was more of a right-haunch wind— but it was clearly doing more good than harm. Rachel, quite gracefully, acknowledged that I'd gotten it right for once. And I, quite shamelessly, celebrated my clairvoyance. We rode the haunch wind to Richey, stopped to buy and inhale some food-like products, and then we eased into the day's final miles.

Southwest of Richey, we descended into a valley, moving from yawn-inducing plains into a mess of blue-brown badlands, and these badlands, unlike the ones we'd encountered in North Dakota, didn't seem to surrender their magic when viewed up close, or, rather, they did but it didn't matter, because for every fore-grounded dirt pile, there was another hump on the horizon, still distant enough to appear inviting, forgiving, uncomplicated. And then there was the asphalt itself—tucking between buttes, rolling over rises in the earth, whispering words of encouragement. "You can go here," it told me. "Matter of fact, you have to."

A few miles on, the asphalt disappeared, then reappeared, shooting skyward for what appeared to be a solid quarter mile. So much for gentle rollers. I could see that for miles and miles to come, we'd be rising, falling, rising, falling. A Wild West roller-coaster ride. I looked back at Rachel, trying to affect a grimace that said, "Jeez, this looks rough," in the hopes that it might distract her from my eyes, which were clearly gushing, "Ohboyohboyohboyohboy."

I hit the hill hard, driving the cranks, and then I tucked under the wind, cackling and wild-eyed. I was flying, didn't need the speedometer to tell me I was going thirty, forty, fifty, ninety-nine miles an hour. The road flattened and arced upward, and I was ready, pedaling again, keeping my momentum. The haunch wind gave me some help, and I made it halfway up the grade without even shifting, and when I did need to gear down, I did so downright expertly, not breaking my cadence for a second, storming to the crest. Then I did it all over again. By the time I finished the second climb, I was breathless, choking on adrenaline, and so I stopped and looked over my shoulder. I couldn't see Rachel. Anywhere.

I waited. After a few seconds, she appeared atop the initial hill, descended at a downright reasonable speed, coasted through the flats. She slowed to a near stop on the uphill, then began pushing herself up the slope. When she reached the top, I puffed up my cheeks and blew out a cartoonish breath. "It's like a roller coaster out here, huh?"

She gave a tight-lipped nod, kept right on riding.

Which, I guess, was not so surprising. These hills weren't much different from the crosswind—meaning this was harder for her, meaning I needed to be good. So for the next few miles, I took advantage of the low traffic and rode beside her. I kept bombing the downhills, but then I'd coast until she'd caught up, so we could climb together. Still a silence grew between us. My vocabulary had been reduced to rhapsody, Rachel's to updates on how much more tired she was than the last time I'd asked how tired she was. We were struggling to speak the same language. And soon enough, as the sun dropped to blister the horizon, we just stopped trying.

CHAPTER 13

Tomorrow

Day twenty-nine. I hunched over a picnic table, chin on crossed arms, eyes on my journal. I'd filled half its pages by this point—hadn't missed a day—but hadn't reread any entries since we'd left Fargo, ten days before. This was just massively out of character. I'd always spent more time poring over journals than writing in them, operating on the belief that within, say, twelve hours, I'd have gained perspective on the previous day's naïveté. But on the road every day had felt so full. I'd barely had the energy to produce new content, much less peruse the archives.

I glanced up at Rachel. She was standing where the tent had been, until I'd pulled it down, thirty-six minutes before. She was finally packing her sleeping bag. Most mornings, I'd have been pacing circles around her by now, muttering about beating the heat and how the early bird gets the tailwind. But at the moment, I was fine with the delay. I was reading a good book.

Thus far, I'd filled thirty-eight pages, in teeny handwriting. Each entry began with a boxed-out header that included, left to right: the date, a list of towns visited, and an accounting of miles traveled, average miles per hour, and total time in saddle. Now I skimmed the entries, comparing numbers, looking for trends. There was something comforting about this quantitative account of daily life, something comforting about stats. Because the moments weren't adding up to anything obvious.

And there were so many moments. Every entry packed with headwinds and tornado threats and sex and blown spokes and selfless strangers and stunning scenery and sex. I'd done a good job recording these moments—and, inevitably, burying them in masturbatory adjectives and shitty landscape metaphors—but the play-by-play had left me too spent to write about much else. About, for example, my anxiety over the horizon. Or my frustrations with Rachel.

I flipped back to Fargo, skimmed forward. Wow. Over that ten-day stretch, I'd managed a grand total of three sentences about said frustrations. All of them vague as hell. Example: "I have been finding myself more irritated with Rach than I would like." No analysis, no reflection. Just a banal platitude sandwiched between big accomplishments. My entries, I thought, were not unlike presidential press releases: self-congratulatory, baselessly optimistic, relentlessly on-message. Propaganda pieces aimed at maintaining the lie that Rachel and I were still living our big romantic story. And this didn't have a thing to do with exhaustion. I'd simply been avoiding the subject, hoping it'd go away, so I could pick up the journal in two days or ten weeks or thirty years and understand it all as steady progress toward Dream Life with Rachel.

But not this morning. No. It was time for some honesty. I picked up the pen, lined out the day's header, and got started. Warmed up with the previous day's events—by the time we'd pulled into Circle, I truly had been too tired to write much more than stats—and then I dove in:

> If this seems out of nowhere, I just haven't had time
> or energy to write it. But I've been thinking about
> it for awhile. It's hard, being with her 24/7, riding
> long days every day, trying (w/o success) to not be

frustrated with her for riding slower and in general
moving a bit slower, and in turn, feeling less attracted
to her. I don't want this at all, and feel selfish & in-
flexible for being annoyed about things that are sim-
ple, obvious products of the way our bodies are built.
And I know I still love her, definitely, it's just that I
currently lack the patience to always see that feeling
through the current haze of exhaustion/stress . . .

I stared back at the last sentence, wished I'd written it in pen-
cil. Because, first off, "see that feeling"? Yep. That was there to
stay. Also, I'd basically just written that I was questioning whether
I still loved Rachel. And because of what? Wind? Differential in
average speed? I shook this off as a poor choice of words and
launched Operation Backpedal. I qualified the living shit out of
my words and cheesed it all up with this triumphant closing:

At any rate, I'm still overwhelmingly happy with
what we're doing, and for the ever-approaching day
we hit the Rockies!

Right.
I distinctly remember sitting at that table, scribbling every
word. I remember looking up to make sure Rachel was still
packing or flossing or quad stretching—wasn't peering over my
shoulder, into my thoughts. And I remember shutting the journal, staring at its cover, asking myself if, in finally admitting
these feelings, I'd just stepped closer to some kind of reckoning.
If this *was* the reckoning. I didn't know.

I licked my finger and held it aloft. I wasn't really sure if or how
a moistened fingertip improved one's ability to assess weather,

but I knew this was what people did right before they turned to their girlfriend and said, "I think we're gonna have a tailwind."

Rachel smiled but didn't reply, just grabbed her bike, started walking across the park, toward the road.

We were aiming for Jordan, sixty miles west. The night before, we'd loaded up on food and water, because between Circle and Jordan there would be no towns, no shelter, no water. Just white space. According to our Montana map, this would be the case for the foreseeable future. Over on the map's left-hand side, clinging to the Idaho border, was an artful mess of sea green and powder blue, mustard and periwinkle—the Montana I'd always imagined, a land of forests and lakes and parks and mountain towns. But that Montana was no wider than my palm, and the rest of the state, which stretched from elbow pit to dirty fingernail, was white space. Sure, there were a few splashes of color—a wildlife refuge (purple) here, a mountain range (silver) there—but 200 skirted them all. And so for several hundred miles, it would be sagebrush and barbwire. Flatbed pickups and gusting wind.

We set off, and pretty much instantly I was forced to admit (silently) that we didn't have a tailwind. Not even close. This was pure, uncut crosswind. Angry air whipped across the flats, sending sheets of dust over convulsing grass. Its grabby hands were all over me, shoving and poking, blowing my shirt up to my armpits, packing my nostrils with handfuls of high desert.

Out of the corner of my eye, I saw something darting around fence posts and shrubs. A tumbleweed. Till then, I'd only seen tumbleweeds in crappy westerns. I'd assumed they always moved in lazy hops. But this tumbleweed was flying. It skipped across the pavement, hurdled an embankment, and shot toward the northern horizon, as if fleeing some kind of awful monster. I watched it grow smaller and smaller, so mesmerized that I stopped looking at the road and didn't notice the oncoming semi until it was nearly upon us.

The semi's wind shear joined forces with the already-hellish crosswind, creating this sort of mutant super wind, and said mutant super wind hit me head-on, hit me so confusingly hard that I had the urge to hit back. And maybe I would have, if the blast hadn't sent me swerving to the shoulder. I jammed the brakes, fishtailed to a stop, and before I could even turn around, Rachel was beside me, shaking her head, saying, "I don't think we should be out here right now."

In retrospect, I can say she was 100 percent right. But in the moment, I couldn't conceive of being anywhere but "out here." Going anywhere but forward. So I shrugged and suggested, "I don't know. I bet it'll be easier up around that bend."

Rachel blinked.

"Really," I said, nodding toward that bend. Up ahead of us, the road did arc northward. Windward. Just as it had back by Richey. "I bet it'll be just like yesterday. How about you hang out here, and I'll go and check? If it's still awful, we'll head back to Circle. Cool?"

Rachel didn't answer. Or maybe she did and I didn't hear, because I'd already pushed off and headed into the wind. It took me ten breath-stealing minutes to reach that bend, and when the road began to curve, I leaned, craned my head, twisted my torso, eager for the sweet hush, the gentle fingers on my back. But when I finished the turn, the howl was louder than ever, the air a swirling mess. It was coming from everywhere, converging on my forehead. The wind's version of a personal rain cloud. I pulled to a stop and felt the first hazy symptoms of an adrenaline hangover. There was no point in fighting this. We'd have to head back to Circle.

I looked to the east. Rachel was awfully far away, but I could see she was now off her bike, standing near two other ant-size figures. Behind them, a boxy little Micro Machine, some kind of SUV. Shit. What was wrong with me? What if they were bad people? Even worse, what if they were good people? People who had greeted Rachel, heard her reasonable words about wanting to stop, then looked to the horizon, where her dumbfuck boyfriend was pushing onward and . . . well . . . what, exactly, was he doing? I saddled up and pushed off and rode as hard as I could, hoping all the while they were neither bad people nor good people. Just dumb, unobservant people.

They were good people. In fact, they were good Wisconsin people. A woodworker and a teacher headed out for a week of hiking and biking in the Beartooths. And these disarmingly sweet, obviously experienced outdoorspeople were clearly baffled by our being out on such a violent day. "We'll give you a ride to Jordan," said Rick, the woodworker, who had a movie-star jawline and kind eyes and bulging calves and this general aura of competence. A hard guy to disagree with. Toni, a brunette who appeared as ripped as her husband, was already popping the trunk, rearranging gear, making space for the bikes.

I stared down at my bike, considering. It didn't feel right, catching this ride. We didn't really need the help, not like we had when I'd blown all those spokes. This was just cheating. I mean, there was no way in hell Galen would take this ride, right? No, he'd wait it out in Circle and ride by night, or he'd just push into the wind, or . . .

I blinked, took in a lungful of sage-scented air. I was being an ass. I was not Galen. And I was not alone. I was with Rachel, and Rachel was saying, at least with her eyes, "I need this."

I helped strip the bikes and fit them into the trunk, and once the bikes were loaded, we slid into the backseat, got situated just in time to see a hellish gust of wind slam the driver's side door on a kneecap belonging to Rick, who had been reattaching a bungee on the roof rack. Like a proper *slam*. Metal on bone. Horrendous. He cursed and clutched, hobbled from the car, and Rachel and I, after a few "are you okays," sunk into that special silence that arises when a stranger hurts themselves not quite badly enough to require your help.

Rick slid into the passenger seat, wincing and rubbing his knee, and Toni took the wheel. She wasn't kidding around. By the time we reached the spot I'd ridden to, we were going seventy and still accelerating. Seventy felt absurd. Impossibly fast. Out the window, my life was flashing before my eyes. Ice-cream-scoop hills and weather-beaten barns, appearing and disappearing.

Forty-five minutes. Fifty-five miles. We had time-traveled to Jordan. The pair dropped us in the town park, helped us unload, handed me a business card with their contact info. "Just send a postcard," Rick said, for the tenth time. "That's all we ask in return. To hear how it ends."

We watched them drive away, and I turned and started walking toward a corner of the park, and when Rachel made to follow me, I said, "I think I'm gonna hang out alone for a bit, if that's okay." She held my gaze for a moment, then wheeled her bike away. I headed the other direction, pulled on my fleece, and climbed onto a picnic table. I hadn't realized how tired I was, but now I felt the windburn on my eyeballs, the melt in my muscles. I slept for some time, and when I woke, I walked to Rachel's table. She pulled out some granola bars, and I pulled out the map, and we ate our food and talked about the coming miles, and then we went and rode them.

Eight o'clock. The golden hour. Low light washed over the world, softening edges, turning glare into glow. Even the barb-wire was looking sexy.

The wind had died down around six, and we'd pushed on, had ridden twenty-five hilly miles before stopping for a snack, at which point Rachel had surprised the hell out of me by saying, "I'd be up for riding awhile past dark." I'd been very much on board with that idea, especially because my mom, when I'd called her from Jordan, had reminded me that this mid-August night was to be the peak of the annual meteor shower, the one I'd watched from dock chairs and beach blankets in my youth. Perfect. We'd ride deep into the night, would take in the stars from our saddles and eventually slink into a secret campsite, just as we had on those charmed nights in eastern North Dakota. A brilliant end to a disappointing day.

But now there was this. A yellowing, rust-scarred beater, kind of skidding onto the shoulder before us. The driver door was opening, and a guy was getting out and muttering and holding up his hand like to signal "stop," and we were stopping. Now the guy walked up, stepped uncomfortably close. He looked at me, then Rachel, then back at me. There was something going on with his eyes. Blood bolts and dime-size pupils. They were sort of doing that googly Muppet thing, but in a decidedly bad way. Cookie Monster on methamphetamine.

"You two," he said, "best get off the road."

So much for hello, I thought. I didn't know how to respond, so I just cocked my head and asked, "Yeah?"

"Yeah. You know there's a rodeo tonight? Done anytime now. There's about to be a bunch of drunks on the road."

"Huh." Pretty reasonable advice, I had to admit. Back home I'd have never dreamed of riding busy roads in the wake of, say, a Monday-night Packers game. Still, this guy didn't seem like a super reliable messenger.

"Where you headed?" he asked. He was speaking only to me, had barely acknowledged Rachel. Now I looked at her. Total poker face, but there was alarm in her eyes.

I turned back to the guy. "West," I said.

He snorted. "Nothing west of here, not for miles."

"There's Sand Springs," I replied, instantly regretting it.

Rachel and I had talked about maybe bandit-camping in Sand Springs, which was some fifteen miles away and which we'd heard was basically a smattering of shuttered buildings. And now I'd just told this asshole.

"Pretty much a ghost town," he said. "Can't sleep there."

"Well, maybe farther, then," I replied.

"Not tonight." He was swaying a bit, listing toward port. "It ain't safe out here."

"I don't know. We've ridden at night a bunch and it's been fine. I mean, we've got lights." I pressed the button on the red orb that hung from my saddle. It pulsed weakly.

He grunted. "That little blinky thing? I'll tell you what that is. A fuckin' target. It'll just make it easier for the drunks to aim for you."

I had no idea how to respond to that. I glanced at Rachel. Usually, with strangers, she was doing just as much of the talking, often more. But now she was just staring at me.

"I know a place you could sleep," the guy continued. He gave a sharp nod to the west. "Safe spot. Just a few miles up the road. Hop in the car, I'll take you up there. Your girlfriend can wait here. If it looks all right, we'll come back, pick her up."

"We're fine," Rachel said. We both turned toward her. She held the poker face, but her eyes were screaming.

"Yeah," I seconded, still looking at her. "We'll be all right. Thanks, though."

The guy bored into me with those bloodshot, black-hole, devil-Muppet eyes. And then he did this kind of jittery shrug, like he'd just caught a chill. Without another word, he turned heel and headed to his car. Slammed the door and leaned out the window. "It's a couple of miles up, on the left," he said. "You should stop there. You *don't* wanna be out here once the sun drops." And then he hit the gas, spun a U-turn, and sped away. Back toward wherever he'd come from.

Rachel spoke first. "What . . . the . . . fuck?"

"I know." I strained to sound more amused than terrified. "*That* guy was warning us about drunks on the road?"

She didn't seem to hear me. She'd turned her back, was staring off to the east, watching his car climb a distant hill. "Why did he turn around? Did you notice that? He came up behind us, and now he's . . ." She trailed off, nodded at the receding taillights.

Somehow, this hadn't struck me as odd. But she was right. It was very fucking odd.

We needed to get to wherever we were sleeping. Soon. Because maybe the road would indeed be teeming with rodeo drunks. And either way, that guy was out there, and he could at any point turn around and find us and . . . We stopped hypothesizing and just rode. Chattering nervously, checking rearview mirrors. After a couple of miles we came upon a cluster of buildings sitting just south of the road. Collapsing roofs. Busted windows. Grayed, rotten siding. It looked like a set for a horror film. I kept riding, unable to face Rachel, to say what we were both thinking. Not a meth addict. A fucking serial killer.

Now she pulled up beside me. "Holy shit. He was going to bring you here."

I wanted to say something reassuring. There was nothing reassuring to say. So I just nodded, hunched over the bars, and pushed harder, until my legs were burning, my breath deepening. Rachel stayed right with me. Every time I looked to the rearview, she was there, so close she appeared to be riding my back. I scanned ditches and ravines, hoping to find a spot to throw up the tent, but this was bleak, exposed country. Boulders and shrubs, none big enough to hide behind. And anyway it was barbwire everywhere, hugging the highway, fencing us in.

The light was no longer soft or sexy. Just disappearing,

stretching fence-post shadows, sucking warmth from the air. And as the sun receded, traffic began to pick up, the distant headlights like death threats. I could feel it. He was coming for us. Adrenaline surged, and I found myself sliding into the lane, mumbling to Rachel that maybe she should set pace. She nodded, and I tucked behind her, drunk on testosterone. I'd protect us, somehow, back here. At the very least I'd get mowed down *first*, which seemed vaguely heroic.

Darkness sunk in. The headlights kept coming, rising sharp and torturous in the rearview, inching closer and closer, their piss-yellow glare spilling onto the pavement, climbing Rachel's back, reflecting from her helmet. A roaring engine, a rush of air, a terrible moment of knowing this was it. Of course the truck would just whoosh on by, and I'd feel a sweet melt of relief, but then I'd see, in the distance, another pair of probing headlights.

Ten miles of this. Ten hilly, black miles. Muscles tensing and releasing, jaw clenched so tight my teeth would be tender for days. I had no idea if Rachel was thinking the same thing. I just knew she was riding hard, and that I was staying as close as I could.

Now we crested a long hill, and Rachel pointed ahead, toward a distant cluster of lamplit buildings—Sand Springs. My relief lasted a half second. Because as we hit the top of the hill, a fierce, gusting wind blasted into us. I looked up. Stars twinkled above, but off to the west the sky was smudged. Clouds, maybe a storm front. So much for the meteor shower.

We pulled into the lot of Sand Springs' dingy little post office. The wind was now making this truly awful noise. Like the note you get from blowing across the lip of a glass bottle, but amplified through a bullhorn. I walked around the lot, which was lit by a single lamp. There was a small apartment adjacent to the post office, but nobody seemed to be home, and the only other building in "town" was this big house just to the east. All the lights were off, but its driveway was packed with cars. The one nearest us, a dented black Suburban, sported a bumper sticker with the words "Border Control, Not Gun Control."

We walked behind the post office. Beyond a small, unkempt lawn was what appeared to be pasture land. If we set up the tent right behind the building, it looked like we'd be hidden from the highway. This would have to work.

"We should check with the neighbors," Rachel said. "See if they mind."

I did not want to check with the neighbors. I wanted to dig a hole and crawl inside and tell no one. "Yeah," I replied, "we probably should."

We walked up to the house, stopped and stood before it. I was hoping Rachel might take the lead. She was good at this stuff. Rachel did not take the lead. So I climbed the concrete steps, up toward a door that led to a sort of screened-in mudroom. The wind was whipping the door open, slamming it shut. I looked over my shoulder at Rachel, who had stopped on the bottom step. She looked like she was going to puke, which was about how I felt. I turned back, pulled the handle, and the door creaked on its hinges. I forced out a little laugh.

I walked through the porch, to the main door. Took a breath, raised my hand, knocked. A stained, lacy drapelike thing covered most of the door's small, rectangular window, and where I could see inside, it was pitch-black. I knocked again, swore I heard something moving in there. I imagined sunken eyes under soaking-wet, jet-black hair. Or, worse yet, googly eyes under a receding hairline. Maybe he'd driven right past us, had been waiting for—

"Fuck this." I power walked through the porch, down the steps. "Nobody's home."

Rachel nodded, and we both pretended to believe my words.

We pulled the bikes behind the post office, set the tent up in record time. To make sure it was hidden, we walked 200, scoped it out from every angle, scampered out of sight whenever we saw headlights. Finally we crawled inside. We left the fly off, despite the clouds, because I wanted to be able to see through the mesh walls, and into one of the tent's pockets I stuffed my Cub Scout pocketknife. I wasn't sure what I'd do with this knife if our tormenter did show up—butter his bread? file his toenails?—but it made me feel safer, and I wasn't going to question that.

That night, the gaps between the Therm-a-Rests didn't matter. We cuddled. I lapped my bag over Rachel's and tucked up behind her. Neither of us said a word about the guy from the highway, or the maybe-vacant, maybe-not house I could still see, through the mesh, bathed in flickering light. We didn't have to. I could feel Rachel's fear, just as I'm sure she could feel mine. Both our bodies shuddered at every wind-slammed door, every snapped twig, every approaching car, and when we did speak, it was to murmur about how and when we'd leave this place, about waking before dawn and riding hard, for a hundred miles, clear to Lewistown. About tomorrow.

CHAPTER 14

We're Still Here

I bolted from the pillow like a little boy on Christmas morning, two perfect words in my head: it's tomorrow! But this wasn't Christmas morning. I wasn't tucked next to my sister in a room softened by string lights, wasn't thinking of Mommy and Daddy and ribbons and wrapping paper, wasn't thinking of the things I wanted. No, I was in a tent behind the Amityville house, lying beside a woman I recognized less every day, thinking only of the things I wanted to escape. The googly-eyed motorists and gun-toting neighbors. The barbwire fences and relentless winds. The ugliness that was seemingly everywhere, around and inside me.

And so now I was rubbing Rachel's shoulder, and she was blinking her eyes open and murmuring, "Well, I guess we're not dead," and I was nodding, was skipping "good morning" and "how did you sleep?" and simply talking about Lewistown.

Lewistown, Montana. The promised land. Back in Sidney, Forest and Kelly had said it would be a sort of milestone for us. It was a proper city, a five-thousand-person city, about four times bigger than anything we'd seen since Fargo, and we were both ready for a dose of urbanity, particularly Rachel, who had been talking for days, with real passion, about a sixteen-ounce latte, a cozy armchair, and a book. To me, *what* was far less important than *where*. Lewistown seemed like the gateway to western splendor. Yeah, we'd still face a bit more high desert after leaving town, but basically this was the line between the Plains and the Rockies, between the in-between and the un-complicated place where everything would be fine.

We decided we'd try to make Lewiston by nightfall. This would be no small feat. The city sat 102 miles west of Sand Springs, and we had never ridden that far in a single day.

"So," Rachel said, "if we make it there tonight, we should probably get a hotel room."

"You think so?"

"I do."

I stopped packing and looked up at her, considering whether this violated my moral code.

"Also," Rachel said, "haven't we been on the road for exactly a month?"

I continued staring, did some math. Shit. We had.

"Kind of calls for an anniversary party, don't you think?"

Rachel smiled. She'd just laid a trump card. We both knew my integrity didn't stand a chance against my raging sentimentality.

By seven we were on the road, riding through sagebrush flats, the sun warming our backs. For a few miles, we talked about our big plans for the big city, but soon enough we fell silent. This was becoming the norm. Rachel wasn't yelling CB or BFTB, I wasn't updating her on the latest news from the speedometer, and neither of us was mentioning Portland, which now felt so far away I doubted whether it even existed. I mean, I still wanted to talk, but there wasn't a whole lot to say. We were rarely encountering anything new, around us or between us, and, of late, the few breaks in the monotony had only pushed us apart or made us feel weak and small.

This was what novelty now looked like. Arguing over a hitched ride or huddling together in terror. I shuddered just thinking of that guy. That house. The raw fear had subsided, but there was a lingering queasiness in my gut. A fear hangover.

We'd ridden almost twenty miles when some fuzzy little warts appeared on the horizon. If I hadn't known better, I'd have said they were trees. We kept riding. They were trees. Real trees. For weeks, we'd seen little more than windbreak rows of oak, but now there was this sea of luscious evergreen cascading into a river basin. I hadn't quite realized how much I'd been missing trees, but seeing them now, I felt this warm buzz, as if I'd just opened an old journal.

At the lip of the basin was a big modern building behind a sprawling parking lot. This was what remained of Mosby, an oil boomtown turned highway rest stop, one of the two spots of civilization between Sand Springs and Lewistown. We pulled in, paired vending-machine soda with beer-can-heated oatmeal and called it breakfast. And then we each holed up in a bathroom. I scrubbed away the two-day-old grease stamp on my right calf, washed the salt and dirt from my tacky skin. Aside from the beard, which was now a bit Unabombery, I thought I looked respectable. Clean. But I still felt filthy.

Rachel emerged a few minutes after me. Her hair, free of its omnipresent ponytail, was wavy and wild, bright against her ruddy cheeks. Watching her walk toward the table, I felt this twinge. Not an ache or a longing. Nothing tender like that. Just a twinge. I'd felt it before, enough to know that its domain was not the candlelit dinner but the job interview. The funeral. It was something to be ignored in the moment, examined in retrospect, acted on never.

I acted on it. Stood and tugged Rachel toward me. Kissed her. Grabbed her hips and pulled. She hesitated for a moment, then pressed back into me. I was already tugging at her shorts, and she was helping with one hand, reaching for me with the other. We were in plain view of the highway, but before I knew it I was bare assed on a lacquered bench, my back pressed against a glass-encased map of Montana. My hands were ripping at her shirt, searching for skin, my head banging against glass, and I squeezed my eyes shut and held my breath and disappeared.

I slumped against the glass and opened my eyes. Rachel was looking at me with this kind of bewildered smile. "Where the hell," she asked, "did that come from?"

I'd already sunk far enough into crystal-clear humiliation—more commonly known as the refractory period—to have a pretty good idea of where "that" had come from, to know that it had something to do with trees and high desert, nostalgia and shame. I decided not to share this. Instead I just ran my fingers up her back and said, "I was about to ask you the same thing."

We sat like that for a little while, until a truck barreled past. We both hid our faces, like little kids playing our first game of hide-and-seek. *If I can't see you, you can't see me.* Then we got up, cleaned up, and returned to the road.

West of the Musselshell—a parched river, a barely moving river, but a river nonetheless—Highway 200 refused to stay flat for more than a few feet. This was the sort of topography you might miss in a car, but on the bikes we felt every bit of it. By the time we pulled up to Winnett, forty-four miles into our ride, my legs were pumping magma, my eyelids heavy. I was feeling like a few hours of restless sleep and a midmorning orgasm might not have been the best prep for this century ride. And Rachel wasn't exactly killing it either. A few miles back, when I checked the rearview, she appeared to be falling asleep in the saddle.

But now we'd made it to Winnett, which, for the moment, was all that mattered. This was one of the best things, I thought, about bike touring. No matter how long and awful the day, we could break it up into manageable chunks. Sand Springs to Mosby. *Breathe*. Mosby to Winnett. *Breathe*. Winnett to . . . Well, we'd see about that in an hour or two.

Winnett was the sole town on this hundred-mile stretch and, we'd later learn, in the entire county. Petroleum County. Had we passed through a century earlier, we'd have also encountered Cat Creek, Roy, Teigen, and Flatwillow, but they'd disappeared long ago, in the way that towns tended to disappear in places with names like Petroleum County. Winnett itself was barely hanging on. Back in the twenties, the town had boasted a population of three thousand plus, but now it was down to a few hundred residents. As we pulled up, we were greeted by a wooden sign erected by the Lions Club. "GO AHEAD AND BLINK," it said, in black caps. "WE'RE STILL HERE."

Winnett appeared to have a one-to-one person-to-building ratio. Years back, I imagined, we'd have found rowdy saloons, bustling wool shops. Now it was just shuttered windows. The only fresh paint I could see was this crude anti-meth mural on the side of an empty building. We were both exhausted and hungry, so we visited the general store, bought sandwich fixings and candy and chips, and more candy. We feasted in the park, wrote postcards, explored a bit, and discovered that Winnett had a community pool. It was closed, but a woman who was sweeping and mopping told us to help ourselves to the showers. We did. And, on her suggestion, we headed over to a church turned thrift shop, which had a book exchange on a corner shelf. I swapped *White Noise* for Tom Wolfe's *A Man in Full*, and Rachel left the Robbins novel and picked up Allende's *House of the Spirits*. Then we were back on the road, well fed and smelling of lavender Dr. Bronner's and saying, "Well, that was a nice little town, wasn't it?"

The rest of the day bleeds together. A fifty-eight-mile montage of exhausting tedium. The soundtrack: first verse of "Home on the Range," running on loop. The scene: two slouching figures backdropped by absolutely nothing. The action: me getting on the bike after a two-minute snack break, wincing stoically; Rachel failing to hide behind a bush while peeing; several spirited conversations about what kind of ice cream might be purchased in Lewistown; and a montage within a montage of Rachel and me standing, then sitting, then standing, then sitting, unable to find a position that relieved both throbbing crotches and screaming quads.

Somewhere around mile ninety-two, a wall of evergreen-peppered earth rose up before us. The Judith Mountains. This was a proper range, one deserving of a silver splotch on our Montana map, and we'd have to climb it to reach Lewistown, which sat a thousand feet above Winnett. At the end of a hundred-mile day, this should have been excruciating. But I barely remember it. All I recall is being surrounded by pine and pasture and long-forgotten shades of green. Before I knew it, we were descending, fast, thirty-five-miles-an-hour fast, for one, two, six miles. The road was leveling out, and a big, beautiful "100" was appearing on the odometer, and Rachel was saying, "I can't believe we actually rode this far," and we were coasting into Lewistown.

We rode down Main Street, slack-jawed. Neon-lit saloons and Mexican restaurants and functioning stoplights and adorable diners and ornate brickwork and a used bookstore and people, so many people, everywhere: in their cars, behind the glass of every store, strolling the sidewalks. It was like watching that movie in Watford City, but now we were in it, were amid the flashing lights and bright colors, and our weeks of work had made this city more sacred than I'd believed a city could be. While Rachel began pointing out the places she'd visit the next day—we'd not yet discussed staying a second night, but clearly, yes, we would—I schemed about what we'd do now. It was only six, so I figured if we got a room right away, we could still go to a steak house and make out under streetlamps and get canned at a tavern and buy four-scoop ice cream cones and stay up all night having it's-our-anniversary-and-we're-superheroes sex.

Here's what actually happened. It took us an hour to find a hotel, and during the search we had to climb some nasty hills, which pretty much gobbled up all our available blood sugar, so that when we did decide on the Calvert Hotel—a handsome, brick-walled mansion run by Jehovah's Witnesses who could have charged much more than thirty dollars if the place weren't in such a state of disrepair—we were both too exhausted to do more than head to a grocery store for premade sandwiches and boxed wine and a tub of (mint chocolate chip) ice cream, which we ate in bed just before falling asleep to a few lazy kisses and face-in-pillow mumbles about let's-do-this-tomorrow.

I was hugging a tree: rubbing my nose into ridges in the bark, horseshoeing my arms around the trunk. And why not? Nobody was around. I was on a dead-end road, searching for a ghost town deep in the pine-drenched Judith Mountains, drunk on a cocktail of vitamin D and adrenaline and nostalgia and a mischievous awareness that nobody in the entire world had any idea where I was or what I was doing. So I was hugging a tree, because I fucking wanted to.

Rachel and I had woken that morning with different ideas about the day. She wanted to check out a museum, make calls, laze around at a coffee shop, and I wanted to do the same things, wanted to do everything that could be done by anyone anywhere, but from the moment I'd looked out the window and seen the mountains towering over town, I'd known I needed to dive in and submerge myself in pine. So I'd suggested we split up for the day, had said it like it was no big deal, though it had been a month since we'd spent over an hour apart.

The ride up was perfect. No panniers, no rearview mirror. Just me and the Fuji, the blacktop and blue sky and foothills so eye pleasing they appeared computer generated. The grade was steep, but I charged up it, feeling sleek and powerful, even after the previous day's hundred-mile ride. Ten miles north of town, I turned onto a dirt road, bound for the ruins of Maiden, an abandoned mining town I'd read about in a brochure. Halfway there, I decided I didn't care about seeing Maiden. I just wanted to be in the woods. I stopped, dropped the bike, and made my way toward a stand of pine.

So here I was, wrapped around a tree, laughing aloud. I hadn't, I realized, felt such pure joy for quite some time, maybe not since that tailwind ride to Turtle Lake, when I'd let myself forget life outside the mile, when I'd been free to enjoy the moments as I wanted, without the perverse conviction that Rachel and I had to enjoy the same things, the same way, always. And so now I found myself thinking of Galen. His trip, I imagined, was just one big orgy of freedom. Every day he and he alone got to decide how far to ride, where to take breaks, when to hug a tree. He got to wake up every morning and think, "This is mine." I mean, I had no idea if he really did or thought any of this. I'd only talked to him within earshot of Rachel, so I couldn't exactly ask, "Hey, could you tell me how awesome it is to not have to compromise with your girlfriend?" And even if I'd had the chance, I'd never have asked. I didn't really want to know.

But here I was in the woods, alone and happy, thinking *this is mine* and wondering if I couldn't learn something from Galen or, better said, from my idea of Galen. Maybe I could make more space for this kind of freedom, even amid all the compromise. Yes. Of course I could.

I met Rachel back at the Calvert. She'd had a good day too. Those were the words she used, at least. But then she explained what she'd done—phone calls to Portland friends, a nap, a book, a latte—and I thought her day sounded kind of ridiculous. Here we were, in the trees, on the cusp of the Rockies, and she was thinking about Portland? So I just nodded and said, "Cool," which is exactly what she said when I tried to impart what I'd found up there in the hills. I didn't have words for it, I realized, and it just sounded kind of silly, all the tree hugging and beauty of being alone. Soon we stopped talking about why we'd been happy, alone, all day and focused on how happy we would be, together, for the rest of the night.

We'd planned a romantic evening: dinner and drinks and a bottle of wine back at the hotel, where we'd be staying a second night. Thirty bucks was a lot of money, so the evening would have to be perfect, and with this in mind, at dinner I subbed wine for beer and forced myself not to overeat, because getting farty and falling asleep at ten was not romantic. Rachel rubbed my knee under the table, asked about my ride, blinked and leaned in as she did when trying, super hard, to listen. And I, dipping into dwindling reserves of raging sentimentality, told her how happy I was to be here with her, how amazing and exciting and wonderful it was that we'd been riding for a month, across four states, together. But the words didn't sound right. It felt like we were playacting. My head was up in the hills, Rachel's in Portland, and yet we were pretending this day, this trip, had brought us closer.

As we walked back to the hotel, Rachel took my hand and asked, "Is everything all right?"

I nodded a little too vigorously. "Of course. It was just a big ride today."

"You're sure that's all?"

"Yeah. What do you mean?"

She hesitated, then said, "I don't know. You just seem kind of distant."

I put my arm around her, and squeezed, and kept walking.

Back in the room, we poured glasses of wine and lay on the comforter. I'd been hoping that once we got back here, to this bed, this unambiguous place, a raw animal desire would ambush my apprehension, would rip it to shreds and spit it out the window. But now Rachel was putting her glass down and pushing her hand under my shirt, and I was shrinking away, was for maybe the first time ever thinking, I don't want this.

"Wait," I said. I grabbed her hand, through the fabric. I told her I was sorry. I'd overeaten. I was feeling farty and sleepy and not romantic.

She just sat there for a moment, blinking.

"I'm really sorry, Rach. I think I just need to pass out."

Now her lips said, "It's okay." But her eyes said no, it is not. We were asleep by ten.

After some crappy continental breakfast, we packed and headed outside. On the front steps, I paused. Sniffed. The air was heavy with wood smoke, the skies a gauzy gray. We rode up out of the valley, away from the pine, into another expanse of high desert, and now the gray was everything, everywhere. So much smoke. At the moment I had no idea where it was coming from, had somehow managed to miss every news headline and gas station conversation about the raging wildfires consuming most of western Montana. All I knew was that my eyes were stinging, and I was very thirsty, and a vast gray curtain hung over the horizon.

As we rode west, under a sky like a pile of dirty socks, my mood soured. We were finally at the foot of the Rockies, but if this smoke held, we'd never see them. There would be no sweeping views or sweet alpine air, just cold nights and tourist traffic and smoke-choked climbs. No distractions or destinations, just miles and miles of in-between.

I kept this up for quite a while, sucking on smoke and pouting, until something—I can't recall what exactly—brought the previous day's sojourn back into my head. I made myself remember how free I'd felt up in the trees, how content I'd been simply because I'd picked a destination and moved toward it and allowed myself to forget it when I found something real along the way. So now I sat back, took in the steel wool sky and weather-worn silos. I looked down, admired the taut knobs of muscle above each of my kneecaps, dropped a hand and gripped the Fuji's top tube, like a cowboy stroking his stallion's neck.

Fuck the stupid Rockies. I didn't need them. I liked spending all day in the saddle and sleeping in a tent and wearing the same two shirts and having a hideous farmer's tan and hearing people say "wow" when I told them what I was doing. I liked the stories I was accumulating, liked practicing how I'd tell my friends about escaping the Meth Muppet and braving killer headwinds and turning Cenex stations into breakfast nooks. I liked knowing how I was moving forward. And I liked knowing why: because I wanted to. It was a fleeting thing, having such a pure want, a want powerful enough to release me from my anxiety about where I wasn't going, and so even if it was stealing my horizon, I was going to enjoy this smoke, because it was mine, because it was real, because—

"I think we should stop soon." Rachel had crept up beside me. "This smoke is awful."

I didn't respond because, well, have you ever tried to speak while climaxing?

"Really," she said. "What do you think? Stop in Stanford?"

I kept my eyes on the road. "I guess. I don't know. That's not even fifty miles, and I kinda want to cover some ground—just get this over with and make it to the Rockies."

"We can't even see the fucking Rockies."

Uh-oh. F-bomb. In Rachel's conversational arithmetic, sincerity plus profanity equaled impending violence. Still, I kept at it. "I know. But I bet we'll be able to once we're in them."

"That doesn't make any sense."

"Well, can we just ride there and then see how—"

"Brian. I need to stop."

I looked at her. No trace of violence. She was just being honest. Her cheeks were flushed, her eyes saying, I am waving a white flag. I am being vulnerable. I am asking for mercy.

"Fine," I said.

And so we rode, through smoke and silence, to Stanford. We dropped our bikes in the park, and I pulled off my helmet and put on my fleece and told Rachel I wanted to take a walk.

"Look," she said. "I'm sorry. I just needed to stop."

"It's fine."

"No, it's obviously not. What's going on?"

I took a step back, toward town and away from the swing set where Rachel was now sitting. "I don't know. I just . . . I want to take a walk."

Before she could respond, I turned away and headed toward Central Avenue. I paced the downtown strip, all four blocks of it, and tried to focus. But my head was a mess. In the span of two hours, I'd pinballed from smoke-induced despair to oh-wait-the-smoke-is-mine mania to a deepened despair, a despair borne of Rachel's timely reminder that said smoke, and the decision about how to deal with it, was not mine but ours. And I was getting awfully tired of ours. I didn't even know what "ours" meant anymore. These miles had changed both of us, had changed everything, had demanded such attention that I'd basically stopped considering our long-imagined horizon, and now, quite literally, couldn't see it at all.

My pulse surging, I doubled back and power walked side streets to the town library. I slid in front of a computer, began googling jobs and creative writing programs in Portland and Chicago and Madison and Durango, Colorado, a town about which I knew almost nothing, except that an old friend had moved there years back. I even logged in to my e-mail and began writing a note to that friend, but halfway through I stopped and deleted the draft and stood and walked back to the park, where Rachel was still sitting on the swing.

I sat beside her, and she slid her hands up the chains and turned to me and said, "Please tell me what's going on."

"I'm not sure."

"Well, can you at least try?"

"Yeah. I'll try."

I paused. Collected my thoughts. And then I opened my mouth and began speaking fluent cliché. I-don't-feel-like-myself and sometimes-I-need-space and it's-not-about-you and—

"Brian. Please."

"Sorry." I looked down at the dirt and took a few pulls of wood smoke. And before I could think better of it, before I could think at all, I admitted that, okay, maybe this was about her, because more and more she seemed to hate what I loved, which was to say the challenge, the uncertainty, the spirit of this thing we'd set out to do together, and honestly that was making it hard for me to connect with her.

I looked up from my feet and found Rachel staring down at

hers. I had the sense I was going too far, had gone too far, but now I knew what I wanted to say, and she'd asked for honesty, and so I kept going, told her about joy and freedom, about lingering frustration and empty reserves of sentimentality, and once I'd finished, I looked at Rachel and she looked at me, and she asked if I was saying I wasn't sure I loved her anymore, and I just gave her the honest answer, the one I'd have given no matter what question she asked.

"I don't know."

CHAPTER 15

Into the Valley

Rachel was leaning forward, elbows on knees. I leaned with her, craned my neck and cocked my head and tried to catch her eyes. But she wouldn't look at me. She was just staring at the dirt, and her fingers were working at something small and brown, and I swear a single tear was trickling down her cheek.

"Rach," I said. "I'm sorry. I'm . . . I'm not sure I even meant that. Jesus. I'm just feeling confused, and I wanted to be honest."

She nodded.

"And . . . yeah, I guess I was just trying to say it's, well, it's hard. Sometimes. And I'm tired of pretending it's not."

Another nod.

I took this as an affirmation. "I feel better having said that. I'm glad I was honest."

"Well, I'm not." Her voice was barely above a whisper. "How the hell could you say something like that if you weren't sure you meant it?" She turned toward me. Her eyes were still glazed with tears, but the gaze underneath was smoldering. I'd never before seen this from Rachel, this mix of tenacity and vulnerability. To my total fucking horror, it was turning me on.

I shook my head, tried to focus. "I don't know."

"Oh, right," she said. "You don't know."

We sat like that, side by side on the swing set, for some time. I sputtered some more apologies and clumsy explanations, and she was pretty graceful about it, all things considered. Just kind of kept to herself. Eventually she got up and took a walk, and I stayed at the swing set, staring at my dirt-smudged hands, trying to figure out what the hell had just happened. I felt sick over what I'd said. That single tear had opened up this forgotten cache of tenderness, had yanked me out of my self-absorbed sob story, and now I was having one of those gut-sliming, mouth-desiccating, forehead-slapping epiphanies, was realizing that Rachel wasn't the problem. I was. It wasn't her fault she didn't enjoy being filthy and exhausted, wasn't her fault she simply couldn't ride as fast and far as I wanted, wasn't her fault that I, after a particularly acute attack of Galen envy, had examined my willful failure to compromise and dubbed it "freedom." And it definitely wasn't her fault that for well over a year I'd pinned my destiny to her back, or that I'd just had a "well, gosh, that's a really terrible idea" anxiety attack.

Even so, I'd taken that whole big shit pile and dumped it on her. And now, about eleven minutes too late, I was recognizing that I'd meant my "I don't know" in reference to everything—that I'd confused remembering myself with forgetting Rachel. And while I was glad I'd finally found these words, I really, really wished I hadn't said them out loud.

The next morning, the sky was a vast gray smudge. A weak wind blew from the west, its breath reeking of smoke. Rachel was silent, avoiding eye contact as she packed her things. She didn't appear angry exactly, just deflated. She'd already been struggling, and I'd made it worse, and now more than ever I wanted to take my words back. But I couldn't do that. So I cooked some cheap oatmeal, and we ate it, and then we rode out of town.

That day, our thirty-third on the road, we were headed for Great Falls, home to Sherri Bock, a friend of Kelly from Sidney, who had offered to put us up. It wasn't going to be a long ride— barely sixty miles—but a grocery clerk in Stanford had told us the traffic would be awful. And from the first, it was. West of Stanford, 200 merged with 3 and 87, and traffic multiplied exactly threefold. Long queues clogged both lanes, and riding along the crumbling shoulder felt like a tightrope act. I checked the rearview every minute, making sure I was holding a fair pace. And every time I looked up, Rachel was there, riding hard. I now thought her frown looked not glum but tough. She was so fucking tough. How had I forgotten that?

We stopped for a break in Geyser, a town about which I re- member exactly nothing, and got back on the road. This was maybe the nastiest stretch we'd seen yet. The smoke was as thick as the traffic, the elevation profile something like a healthy heart rate, and I relished every bit of it: the acid in my legs and smoke in my lungs, the truck-induced speed bursts and whatever else allowed me to forget about being an insensitive ass. I began to relax, so much that even when I wasn't able to forget my words, I was able to feel almost triumphant about them. Because I'd been honest, right? And honesty was good, even if it was clumsy, and even if it had hurt Rachel, and even if it wasn't exactly hon- esty but something more like second-degree attempted honesty.

Whatever it was, I'd tried, and I'd learned something: I might be able to have it both ways. My own sense of possibility and our big romantic story. Admittedly, it was not so romantic right now. But it would be again, somehow.

Sherri Bock's home was a monument to motherhood, to the people she'd cared for: photos of the kids next to photos of the

kids who were now adults, a Montana Teacher of the Year certificate on the fridge, books with titles like *How to Survive and
Thrive in an Empty Nest* stacked on the back of the toilet and
the table by the couch. "You guys can stay as long as you like,"
she said, within a minute of meeting us. I figured part of this
was loneliness and part was how defeated Rachel and I must
have looked upon arriving at her doorstep. But it seemed more
basic than any of that. You got the feeling this was just how she
operated.

That night, after Sherri did our laundry and showed us our
room and gave us big, fluffy towels for long, hot showers and
insisted on treating us to a meal, we all curled up to watch the
news. Sherri was worried. There were fires out there, raging
across western Montana, and we, her newly adopted babies,
were going to ride straight toward them. Okay, maybe not
straight toward them but nearby, and there was so much smoke,
and maybe we'd like a ride instead? We declined but gratefully
accepted her offer to host us for a second night.

Later, lying in our bunk beds, Rachel and I whispered about
how much Sherri reminded us of our moms. We kept talking—
about everything besides "I don't know." I got down from my
bunk, leaned down to kiss her, and she kissed back, pulled me
down beside her. After some time, she whispered good-night. I
climbed back to my bunk.

The next day we set out to explore Great Falls. We parked the
bikes downtown and walked the length of Central Avenue. The
street was fairly bustling with people, but it had this lonely quality
neither of us could name. Later Sherri would explain that the
bustlers were likely addicts, that Great Falls was ground zero in
the Montana meth war, that all the horrifically graphic roadside
billboards we'd seen were part of the Montana Meth Project, a

massive campaign funded by one crusading billionaire, which had in four years halved meth abuse among Montana teens. I didn't know any of that at the time. Just knew that after five minutes I was ready to retreat back to Sherri's.

But Rachel wanted coffee, and she spotted a little café, which ended up being as cozy as Central Avenue was creepy. This was a special skill of hers. You could blindfold Rachel and dump her in an Albuquerque exurb, and within a half hour she'd have located strong espresso and comfy couches. For hours, we tucked up on said couches, slugging coffee and reading while the barista curated a playlist of nonstop indie music. It was a lot of syrupy emo horseshit, but I drank it up, because I'd heard almost no music for a month, and because Rachel and I could maybe do with a bit of syrup, even if she had seemingly shrugged off what I'd said.

After less than a day in Great Falls, in fact, Rachel had again become her confident, competent self. She had asked Sherri all the right questions at dinner, while I'd lapsed into a midmeal food coma, and buzzed around the house all morning, calling friends and writing postcards and making a grocery list for the dinner she'd volunteered us to cook, while I'd spent a solid half hour sitting in a recliner, watching her and wondering what I wanted to do with the sprawling, empty day. Months earlier, this dynamic would have been grounds for an anxiety attack. But now I just felt relieved that Rachel could still make me feel cluttered and insecure.

From the café, we headed to a bike shop. Rachel was still suffering from buzzy hands and shooting back pain and was convinced she needed a taller stem, so she could sit more upright. One of the mechanics, the dudeliest of dudes, scrounged up what he could find, but didn't have what she was looking for. He shrugged and said, "Guess you're just gonna have to suck it up." Rachel made it out the front door, then burst into tears. I'd been expecting some good old-fashioned rage, but here, again, were the tears. And I understood, even more than I had on the swing set, or while I'd watched her fight the *Candid Camera* winds, that she was suffering, that it wasn't about her "wanting it enough." I felt I should tell her this, but I didn't know how to put it. So I just squeezed her hand and said, "Fuck that guy."

That night, we cooked up some gnocchi and marinara for Sherri, and after dinner, we joined her on the couch to watch the local meteorologist confirm that the wildfire smoke was, in fact, going to continue ruining Christmas. And then we all read our books, together in the living room, like real, normal, sedentary humans, before turning in.

I lay in my bunk, staring at the ceiling, and said, "I needed this."

"Me too," Rachel said. I heard her take a long breath and hold it. Choosing her words. "I'm really looking forward to Glacier."

"Uh-huh. Me too."

"I think we should stop there."

"Forever?"

"No. Just for a year."

"Cool."

"Or at least a week." When I didn't respond, she said, "Seriously."

Part of my brain was, as always, droning on about going forward. But why? It was mid-August, and we had nowhere to be. Better put, I had no idea where to be. And I owed it to Rachel to be way better about compromising. And, come on, it was fucking Glacier. How often would I get to decide, on a whim, to take a weeklong vacation in Glacier?

"Why not, right?" I said. "As long it's not all smoky."

"If it's smoky in Glacier, I'm chartering a plane to Portland."

"Fair enough. That's a good idea, though. Stopping."

"Yes," Rachel said. "Yes it is."

I lay awake for a while, thinking of Glacier. We would be

there in two days. And a week off would give us the chance to reconnect, to escape the on-the-road stressors. It was something real to look forward to. I prayed, to no one and nothing in particular, that the skies would clear.

Come morning, the smoke was thick, and traffic was nasty, and by the end of the first mile we were already fighting. We hadn't even made it to the farmers' market, where we were going to get snacks, and Rachel was already in tears, saying, "I can't do this," and, "You don't even want to be out here with me," and I was muttering okay-I-know-there-are-no-take-backs-but-what-do-you-want-me-to-do-now?

We did the only thing we could. Rode. That day our destination was the tiny town of Dupuyer, home to more friends of Kelly Markle, who had pretty much become our Montana booking agent. Dupuyer was ninety-two miles from Great Falls. And I was really hoping the next ninety-one would be a bit smoother than the first.

West of town, 200 merged with I-15 and two other major highways, so we were relegated to a frontage road. This was kind of nice, because the whining engines gave us a good excuse for not talking, but also kind of sad, because I knew that in a short while we'd finally be saying good-bye to the road we'd ridden for nearly a thousand miles. Once 200 split from I-15, the traffic calmed, and Rachel rode up beside me and asked if I remembered where we'd picked the highway up. Fargo? Sykeston? I knew she didn't particularly care, was just making conversation, and so I guessed with her, threw out more names, though I knew exactly, because I'd logged it in my journal, which I'd read cover-to-cover at Sherri's.

Soon we hit the junction with Route 89. We took the north fork, and I watched 200 fade toward the southern horizon, and though I'd been expecting teary eyes or nostalgia needles or at least the urge to sing "This Used to Be My Playground," I now found myself feeling not sentimental but relieved. I was ready to leave those miles behind. Ready to go somewhere new.

A few miles after the junction, we caught a light tailwind. Nothing to call home about, but it made for an easy enough ride to Fairfield, a quaint little town cowering beneath a half-dozen massive steel silos that held enough grain to give Fairfield the (self-proclaimed) title of Malting Barley Capital of the World. Said silos would have cast some pretty impressive shadows if not for the persistent smoke. It seemed a bit lighter now, but not light enough to betray the location of the sun, which we hadn't seen for four days. We picked up fixings for the trip's umpteenth sandwiches, and as we ate in Fairfield's well-treed park, I pored over our map. We were within thirty miles of the Rockies. And still no sign of them.

Past Fairfield, the traffic just kind of disappeared, and the wind kept rising, from pleasant to "hey now" to "holy shit I'm flying," until I was barely even pedaling, not a pilot but a passenger, just kicking back and appreciating the wind-tickled grasses and the distant, silvery splotch that appeared to be a lake and the gnarled cones of rock that were now rising around us like inverted tornadoes. It was one of those days when I felt I could actually see the land changing. When momentum felt like something I could photograph.

As we approached Choteau, a faint spot of gold stained the gray sky. "Do you see that?" I asked Rachel. She did. And together we watched as the stain deepened, the solitary patch of gold glowing brighter and brighter until, finally, it burst into flame. Scattershot sunshine poked through the smoke, touching down upon a knuckled heap of distant purple.

The Rockies.

We pulled to the shoulder, and I dug out the camera. I took a picture, shook my head, deleted it. Tried again, and again, until I got it right. And though the day was far from over—though we'd end up riding another forty miles, including a hellacious finale involving resurgent smoke and foothills that felt a lot more like mountains, such that we barely made Dupuyer by sunset—I felt then like we'd reached the end of something. The beginning of something else.

We sat with our hosts, Leanne and John, eating homemade granola and picked-from-the-property berries over a lacquered slab of hardwood, listening in rapt adoration as Leanne talked about yarn spinning and sheep farming while John quietly took his breakfast. I was picturing these two double-dating with Kelly and Forest, smiling at the thought, and wishing we had more time. We'd spoken little with them the previous evening, having arrived so late, but now, after just a half hour in their company, I wanted to stay a full day and learn how to spin wool and see all the cool shit they'd built on their property. Rachel, too, was enthralled by the pair. She was an on-and-off knitter—had never really diversified her work but could make a mean fucking scarf—and seemed to have a legitimate crush on Leanne.

But we couldn't stay. We'd seen the Rockies. Glacier beckoned.

Before we left, Leanne brought out a huge, multicolored mound of yarn, and Rachel bought a few skeins to stuff into her pannier. She wanted to knit a (wait for it) scarf by the end of the trip. While they talked knitting, I took a peek into Leanne's office, and hanging above her adorably huge computer was a sheet of paper with these words:

Life is not a journey to the grave with the intention of arriving safely in a pretty and well-preserved body. But rather, to skid in broadside, thoroughly used up, totally worn out, and loudly proclaiming, "Wow! What a ride."

At the time, I didn't have any idea where that quote had come from. I only knew that this woman—who I'd respected from the moment she shook my hand, who had tethered herself to property and committed to a singular pursuit, and who in all ways appeared to be a capital-A Adult—had this quote on the wall, in her office, in the place she'd be most likely to see it. This quote that pretty much encapsulated my whole philosophy. And, silly or not, it felt like an affirmation of what I was and wasn't doing. An affirmation that wherever I was headed was less important than how I was getting there.

Turned out my "this is the end of something" prognosis was off by one day. One smoke-drenched, agonizing, spirit-crushing motherfucker of a day.

It started well enough. The moment we left the driveway, we plunged into a valley, then dragged ourselves up and over the first of a great many foot-mountains. The terrain was now like a two-to-one enlargement of that roller-coaster hillscape we'd found in eastern Montana. The domes here were comically huge. Some seemed on the verge of popping. But we'd both had a good-night's sleep and a hearty breakfast, so we attacked the hills like Wheaties-box superstars. For about twenty miles. Then it was twenty more to Browning, the next town, and the hills kept coming, and the hearty breakfast worked its way through my bloodstream and bladder, and this funny thing happened. I started to feel like shit, and I just said so, verbatim, to Rachel.

"I feel like shit."

"Me too."

"Let's stop."

"Okay."

We stopped in a valley, had a snack, and while Rachel started casting on some yarn, I sprawled out and napped. Twenty minutes later, we were riding. And there was zero tension. It was that easy. Misery, when shared, became something less than misery. Of course. I knew the tired little aphorism. And it had only taken me 1,642 miles to remember it.

West of Browning, it was a ninja wind. I took two jabs to the right kidney, an uppercut square on the chin, a series of round-houses and leg sweeps, striking from all directions. I tried to stay vigilant and figure out where the attacks were coming from, but the air was hazy from so many smoke bombs, and I could see nothing but short grasses dancing every which way, feigning northwest but darting east, betraying nothing but the capriciousness of their tormenter.

By the time we stopped for a break, at a closed-down building that was the spitting image of the snack depot at a summer camp I'd once attended, the ninja wind had pulled off its mask and revealed itself as a freight train barreling down from the northern horizon. A mile back, Route 89 had turned ninety degrees, so we were now heading due north, which was unfortunate. And from our perch at the snack shack, I could see the pavement snaking up a ragged heap of earth, then disappearing into the thicker-than-ever smoke. Somehow I'd believed the mountains wouldn't start until Glacier. I'd been so very wrong.

You know how, in old-school side-scrollers, the ultimate megabosses always ended up being a constellation of every evil you'd faced over the course of the game? The final 18.9 miles were a lot like that. A boss fight. Rachel and I now faced a wind so violent that even the *Candid Camera* producers would have been like, nope, totally unrealistic, they'll never buy that. The grade was as steep as any we'd seen, the smoke a woolly mitten reaching down to smother us, the surrounding forest scorched to blackness, and in that blackness I pictured grizzlies and mountain lions and other somethings preparing to pick us off like à la carte items.

Rachel and I couldn't talk, couldn't even really scream, over the wind. But I could see—via the rearview and, in moments of exceptional bravery, via direct eye contact—that her eyes were bleary, reddened, defeated. I'm sure I looked just as haggard. After ten miles I was possessed by a seething hatred for the wind, struggling to keep my legs moving, terrified of the mountain lions and the setting sun and the knowledge that if this kept up much longer Rachel and I would never speak again. I tried so hard to go her speed and tell her I love you in eyelid Morse code, but it was worthless, and she was slowing more and more, until she just stopped, in the middle of the road, and got off her bike. I stopped too and stood beside her, and yelled encouraging words and asked questions and waited patiently, but she didn't respond. Just closed her eyes. Breathed. And after a few minutes, she got back on the bike.

When we finally crawled up to the summit and saw it, I braked so suddenly that Rachel almost rear-ended me. Before us were mountains upon mountains upon mountains, dusted in snow, bathed in glorious platinum light bursting through the overhead murk. After so many miles in the Plains, this landscape seemed logically impossible. I wouldn't have been surprised to see unicorns, Care Bears, Jesus on a golden chariot. The wind was still deafening, and neither of us could really think of much to say beyond "wow" and "fucking wow." So we just smiled giddy smiles, eyes glistening from the exertion or the wind or the relief or all of the above and more, and then we pushed off, tucked low, and dove into the valley.

PART IV

A PLACE VERY CLOSE TO WHEREVER WE WERE GOING

CHAPTER 16

An Arrival

In a hiker-biker campsite on the eastern edge of Glacier National Park, I sat on a picnic table, sipping Scotch ale and cataloging all the ways the hellride from Dupuyer had maimed me. My skin was windburned, my eyes puffy, my legs a molten mess. The muscles of my neck and back had fused into one throbbing megaknot, and my knuckles ached from hours of strangling the handlebars. Rachel was in even worse shape. Beyond the exhaustion, she was suffering from a needling burn in her right hand, a backache, and, as she put it, an acute case of crotch stink. But none of that mattered now. We'd made it.

Rachel began stripping her Fuji of its panniers. She placed them on the table, one by one, then wheeled her denuded bike away and parked it behind a big pine.

I nodded at the bike. "Behind the tree?"

"Yep," she said. "I don't even want to look at that thing."

"You're going to hurt its feelings."

"Well, it hurt my wrists. And my butt. And my sunny disposition." She came back to the table and dumped out her panniers. "Fair's fair."

I looked over at my Fuji, blew a kiss, and said, "Don't worry. I still love you."

Now Rachel began picking out the items she planned to use in the park: toiletries and towel, journal and pens, camp clothes and book, phone and yarn and needles. She repacked this pile in one of her panniers, then crammed the other three with Lycra, her gloves, her helmet, basically everything that might remind her she was on a cross-country bike trip. These bags she stuffed, rather unceremoniously, into the bear box.

"Much better." She opened a beer. "I am so ready to be off that bike."

"I get that about you."

I drained my can and pulled another from the six-pack. We'd stopped at a store in St. Mary, the but-for-the-grace-of-Glacier town just beyond the park's eastern border, and there we'd found a cooler brimming with microbrews. It had been nothing but Bud and Miller since we left Minnesota, and so I'd felt something close to arousal while considering that wall of stouts and IPAs, ambers and Scotch ales. We'd chosen a six-pack of the latter, and the first sip tasted something like my first orgasm had felt—surprising and personal and possibly life-changing.

"Wanna set up here?" Rachel asked. She pointed toward a spot behind the table.

I shrugged. So far, we had this hiker-biker site to ourselves. A fire pit, a couple of picnic tables, and a half-dozen sandy tent pads to choose from. For five bucks apiece. Back at the ranger station, we'd both made sure to note (loudly) that car campers were paying four times that much, just for a parking space and a bit of privacy. And, well, now we had this quite private site, and I'd parked my bike on a tent pad, which was kind of like a deluxe parking space. I smiled a smug smile. No one was around to notice, but I figured a little practice couldn't hurt.

The sun was sinking, the temperature with it, so I set up the tent while Rachel prepared a feast of boxed mac 'n' cheese, Fritos, and two beers. An hour later we were in the tent, well fed and half-drunk and groping for each other. And twelve minutes after that, I was asleep.

I woke to voices and crawled out of the tent to find people scrubbing dishes at the water pump and walking by with loaded packs. Up above, beyond the evergreen canopy, it was big sky. Blue and smokeless and beckoning.

I shook Rachel awake.

"What time is it?" she asked, yawning.

"Late," I said.

I had no idea what time it was. Didn't matter. Whether it was half past dawn or pushing noon, we needed to get outside. Because we were in Glacier. Because the smoke had cleared. And because Wisconsin's eight-month winters had conditioned me to regard sunshine with a sort of manic reverence. I'd have rather been caught masturbating than sitting inside on such a bluebird day.

Within the hour, we were on a bus, heading up Going-to-the-Sun Road, the fifty-mile miracle of engineering that snakes through the heart of the park. The views were stupefying. All around us were giant, ragged anvils streaked with the blackest of shadow and the whitest of ice, every one bowing toward the massive Saint Mary Lake, her heart a heretical blue, her shallows an upside-down still-life of shoreline evergreen and snow-dusted daggers. You could see why this place was called the Crown of the Continent.

The road itself was equally stunning. Also terrifying. More often than not, its narrow lanes were trapped between, to the north, a wall of dynamite-blasted rock, and to the south, just inches past the shoulder, a stomach-twisting drop-off. There were too few guardrails and too many blind corners, and the grade was steep enough that, when I faced forward, I felt gravity's pull less in the soles of my feet than in the small of my back.

I couldn't wait to ride it.

The bus had these floor-to-ceiling windows, and our fellow passengers were plastered to the glass, gawking at the views, which, okay, were definitely gawkworthy. Still, I couldn't help but pity these *tourists*. They couldn't see Glacier. Not like Rachel and I could. We had put in the work, had spent weeks searching for beauty in the beigest of beige-scale borescapes, and we could now see colors and textures that defied the imagination of your average American car camper.

I leaned into Rachel and whispered, "I can't imagine just driving here."

She put her hand on my shoulder. "You've got a pretty pathetic imagination."

We got off at the park's best-named trailhead, Gunsight Pass, and followed the path into the woods. Hiking felt weird. For the past month, we'd walked very little. We'd taken some strolls in the towns we visited, done some pacing around grocery stores, but mainly we'd been in the saddle. My legs now felt heavy in this peculiar way, as if I'd just returned to flat ground after an hour on a trampoline.

The trail descended into a river basin, then climbed to a broad plateau surrounded by mountains, all of them ice freckled and skirted in evergreen shag. Now I was the one gawking—slack-jawed and dizzy and mumbling in the general direction of Rachel. I'd gotten it wrong on the bus. My search for subtlety hadn't prepared me for anything. It had simply reduced my tolerance for grandeur. I felt like I'd spent three weeks nursing a snifter of scotch, only to wake in Glacier and slam an entire bottle.

I dropped my eyes from the mountains and saw that Rachel had stepped into a postcard. She was walking through high grass the color of a legal pad, about to enter a tunnel formed by the tangled fingers of a few scrubby pines, and in the distance snow-dusted mountains towered over an alpine lake. I pulled out my camera and framed a shot. Against the pine and powder blue and distant saw teeth, Rachel looked tiny. Engulfed.

Still holding up the camera, I began to think of a different photo, a photo I'd seen a million times, a photo very similar to the one I was framing. And . . . well . . . *click*.

Four years before his death, Sam Larsen went backpacking in Glacier with our mutual friend Josh. The two of them had the best time anyone has ever had doing anything anywhere. For weeks, they spoke of nothing else. They regaled our group of friends with stories of goat stampedes and sixty-foot cliff dives, force-fed us stacks of photos, used words like "epic" and "spiritual," finished each other's sentences and shared the kind of swoony gazes usually reserved for a couple newly pregnant with its first child.

I hated their stupid stories about their stupid trip, by which I mean I loved the stories and hated Sam and Josh for having lived them. Without me. Months earlier Sam had locked me out of his life. My offenses, as I understood them, included (a) serial one-upmanship, (b) flagrant sniffling about my first big breakup (because at least I'd *had* a girlfriend), (c) making out with a girl on whom Sam had a crush, and (d) being, on the whole, a self-absorbed jackass. I was eighteen years old. Years later, I would discover my own reasons for keeping him at a distance, would parse the ways in which he'd been right and wrong about my self-absorption. But that summer, I just felt like I'd been dumped. And I saw his trip with Josh as a targeted snub (see "self-absorbed").

The photo I hated most was a wide-angle shot of Sam crouched beside a goldenrod-yellow tent, his head raised toward a set of glacier-stamped saw teeth that rimmed the glassy lake on whose shores he and Josh had set up camp. The shot seemed to capture not only the visual majesty of Glacier but also the euphoria—profound and private—of my estranged friend. The first time I saw the photo, in Sam's company, I blinked away tears. The second and third and forty-first times, when it was framed and proudly displayed in Josh's apartment, I told myself I'd call Sam later that night. The forty-second time, Sam Larsen was gone.

Ever since, when I'd pictured Sam it was in Glacier, in that photo, his image reflected in glacial runoff, his mind full of big thoughts. Thoughts that transcended the grotesquely small bullshit that had pushed us apart. Thoughts that sprung from the firm and fertile ground where I'd hoped we might reconnect.

I was now standing on that ground.

I lowered the camera. Jogged to catch up with Rachel. "What day is it?" I asked.

"Tuesday," she said.

"No, what's the date?"

"Um. I don't know."

"Can you check the phone?"

"Let's see . . . It is the twentieth day of the eighth month of this, the year of the zebra." She held out an upturned hand. "That'll be three dollars, please."

I stared through her. "Wow."

"Okay. Two dollars."

I shook my head. "Sam died three years ago. Well, three years and a day, I guess."

"Oh."

"And he was here. I mean, right here."

"Didn't he . . . Didn't it happen in Lake Superior?"

"Well, yeah. But he was here a few years before, and Josh took this picture, and . . ." I looked off to the right, as I always do before saying something incoherent.

"And?"

What I wanted to say was this: And now I'm here, on this of all days, in this place Sam loved in a way I couldn't understand, and now I might kind of understand, and I wish I could talk to him, and maybe by being here I am talking to him, and—well shit, Rachel—I wouldn't even be here if not for you, you brought me here, and I know this is going to sound ridiculous, but I feel like I'm watching a movie of myself and this is something like an ending.

But those words weren't available. Not in that order. In any order. So I shrugged and said, "I don't know. I'm just happy we found this place."

I pocketed the camera and kept walking toward the lake.

We spent a full week in Glacier. For the first four days, we didn't even touch the bikes. Rachel may have even succeeded in not looking at them.

Mainly what we did was walk. And talk. See, Glacier was teeming with signs and pamphlets and ruddy-cheeked rangers warning us to BE ALERT and MAKE NOISE because DON'T SURPRISE BEARS, and though we felt bad about verbally polluting a landscape that all but demanded silent reverence, we felt even worse about the prospect of getting mauled by a surprised bear. So we made noise. We *conversed*, unlike most of our fellow hikers, who seemed to believe the only way to MAKE NOISE was, at ten-second intervals, to holler, "Hello, bears!" or "Yoo-hoo, bears! Here we are!" Which, I mean, yuck. Like everyone else, Rachel and I had a keen interest in avoiding violent death, but as seasoned veterans of the unstructured outdoors, we knew better than to be so fucking gaudy about it.

We decided, during that first hike to Gunsight Pass, that we'd MAKE NOISE by asking each other "big questions." This seemed easy enough, but then I tried to think of a single such question and blanked. I kind of felt like I knew all there was to know about Rachel.

And yet. BEARS.

I started simple, asked what she missed most about living in Xela. She answered (speaking Spanish, buying thirty-cent avocados, getting her ass kicked at soccer by Raúl, a seven-year-old boy who lived at the shelter where she volunteered) and then turned the question back on me (also the Spanish, piping-hot street-corner arroz con leche, and watching Soltura's sax player, Fernando, cheese it up while playing the melody to "My Way"). From there, the conversation started flowing. We talked about a two-week silent meditation retreat Rachel had been on years back. This had been mentioned but never described. Same for my clumsy college activism, and both of our vague daydreams about life in Portland, and even some of the whens and whys of our on-the-road frustrations.

These conversations followed us from the woods to the bus to the campsite, then back to the woods the next day, and the next, and I'd like to think we walked right past several grizzlies, all of whom were like, "Damn, that is one attractive and emotionally healthy couple, and even if they did startle me, they didn't insult my intelligence, and by golly I wish them well."

When we weren't hiking, we were drinking microbrew on the shore of Saint Mary Lake, or taking irresponsibly long showers, or having responsibly quiet afternoon sex, or eating breakfast pie at a little café just outside the park, all the while getting pampered by complete strangers. One morning a camp neighbor, with whom we'd spoken for like two minutes, handed us a twenty-dollar bill he'd found by his tent and told us to treat ourselves to a meal because "I think what you're doing is really cool." Another guy we met, who had the double virtue of being a fellow Wisconsinite and a fellow Brian, offered to drive us to the bus-inaccessible Ptarmigan Trail, and the hike ended up being our favorite of the week.

Everything felt easy. I wasn't thinking about where I was or wasn't headed, what I did or didn't deserve. I was just enjoying myself, my memories of Sam, the beauty of the park, the generosity of strangers, and, especially, I was enjoying Rachel. My frustrations seemed so distant. I'd just needed to step back and see her outside the rearview. I was seriously considering tossing that thing in the trash. It never showed me the Rachel I wanted to see: the woman who could land somewhere and instantly know how she wanted to spend her day, who had the most infectious laugh I'd ever heard, who knew who she was and wanted to be, who had such a voice that sometimes I got hard just listening to her speak.

In Glacier I'd been seeing a lot of that Rachel. I was now confident our on-the-road tensions hadn't been a harbinger of relationship doom. Quite the opposite. The miles had been a test, and we'd passed. We had figured out how to make tons of tiny decisions together and how to be painfully honest with each other, and now being in one place together was easy. It seemed like from here on out, everything would feel easy. Life in Portland, for example. Easy.

I must have on some level known the week in Glacier was not "being in one place together." It was a fucking vacation. But at the moment, I wasn't interested in that distinction. I was perfectly happy to take our vacation and call it an arrival.

———

I rested my elbows on the handlebars and considered the western horizon. I was ready for it. We'd taken a full day in camp to relax, so I had fresh legs and laundered clothes and was stir-crazy enough to do this—to climb up and over the Rockies.

"Ready to go?" I asked Rachel.

"Nope." She turned from Logan Pass and nodded toward town. "Why don't we go that way? There's pie that way."

"I do like pie."

"I'll buy you two pieces every day for the rest of your life if we just stay here."

All morning, as we'd pulled the bikes from their hiding places and repacked the bags and discussed our post-Glacier plans, Rachel had been saying stuff like this. I assumed she was kidding. How could she not be looking forward to riding through the park? It was gonna be *amazing*.

We set off. The initial miles were fairly flat, a warm-up for the climb, and I moved along easily, closing my eyes, drawing in mountain air, anticipating the scenery ahead and thinking, I am so lucky, so lucky, so lucky. I was about to tell Rachel that my legs felt surprisingly strong when—

"I already want this to be over."

I wasn't sure if she was talking about the climb or the entire trip. I didn't ask.

"I'm gonna go slow today," she continued. "And stop a lot."

"Sounds good," I said. "It'd be a shame to rush this. Kind of nice that we have to go slow, actually. We'll enjoy the views more."

"You sound like Calvin's dad."

"This will build character, Calvin."

"Keep it up, and me and Hobbes will let the air out of your tires."

This was about as jovial as it would get all day.

At about the ten-mile mark, the road started climbing, and we pulled above the trees and got our first big views, and though we'd seen the sights from many a bus seat, and many a back-country trail, on the bikes everything felt more immediate, more accessible, more . . . Well, just more. It pains me to admit this, but I had that old Skittles slogan in my head. I was looking up at the mountains, feasting upon greens and blues and purples and feeling like I'd finally learned what it meant to "Taste the Rainbow."

"This," I said, "is amazing."

Rachel didn't reply. I thought I saw her roll her eyes. I wasn't sure if she was disagreeing with the overall sentiment or simply my choice of words. Again, I didn't ask.

The actual climb was only six miles. But we were averaging 3.7 mph, and so it took us the better part of two hours. By the time we hit the 6,646-foot summit and pulled into the Logan Pass Visitor Center, I was giddy. We'd climbed the Rockies, and it had felt almost easy, and I was all oh-wow-look-at-those-mountains, and whoa-it's-a-bighorn-sheep, and hoo-boy-I-am-going-to-get-closer-and-then-I-am-going-to-frolic-in-that-meadow-do-you-want-to-frolic-with-me? Rachel did not want to frolic. Rachel wanted to knit. Here we were, seconds removed from riding one of the prettiest roads anywhere, perched atop a pass in the Crown of the Continent, and it was a cloud-less day, and there was a sheep within shouting distance, and she was knitting.

"You're really going to knit right now?" I asked.

"Yep."

I nodded thoughtfully, as if I were thinking, well, sure, that's a reasonable thing to do, when I was in fact thinking, there is something deeply wrong with you. And then I went to the meadow, which, honestly? Not that exciting. A lot of sandal-wearing, photo-snapping tourists who had driven or taken the bus. They couldn't understand what it meant to be here.

I found a somewhat solitary spot, sat down, and tried hard to make this a moment. I'd hopped on my bicycle, come all the way from Wisconsin, and now I was here, atop the Rockies, my head spinning from these stunning panoramic . . .

It wasn't working. This wasn't a moment for me alone.

I walked back over to Rachel. She'd probably just needed a bit of space. By now she had to be ready to momentify with me. But her head was still tucked to her chest, her fingers working at the yarn. She was muttering something.

"Hey," I said. "Want to take a walk?"

Rachel didn't look up. "This fucking yarn is all tangled."

"Oh. So, do you want to take a break? The views over there are pretty incredible."

She glanced up, then looked back at the yarn. "I'm getting this untangled."

"Right," I said. "Well, hey, when you finish, I'll be over there. In Glacier National Park."

A half hour later, I'd come back, and we'd talk. Rachel would say she'd been dismayed by how hard it had been to get back on the bike, that she hadn't wanted to ruin my good time—though she resented me for it—and that she'd buried herself in the yarn in a failed attempt to center herself. And I'd say that, yes, I'd noticed all that but was too wrapped up in myself to be sensitive and empathetic. We'd both offer apologies, and they would be good, honest apologies, and soon we'd be back on the bikes, smiling and laughing together, and though I'd like to chalk this up to the apologies, it probably had more to do with the fact we were now going downhill.

CHAPTER 17

Where I Was and Where I Hoped to Be

The descent from Logan Pass was a blur of tight corners and dive-bombed straightaways, arthritic brake pumping and metaphor-defying scenery, and it left me so giddy and breathless that it wasn't until evening, after Rachel and I had settled into our campsite on the shores of Lake McDonald, that I felt the tickle in my throat. The soupy weight in my chest. By dark, my tongue was coated in a tacky film that tasted of ammonia.

This was not part of the plan. The plan had been that Rachel and I would spend two days on Glacier's west side, hiking and swimming and being in love, before waking on a bright blue morning and riding from the park side by side whilst saying, "That was perfect" and "Now I'm ready for anything." Instead, I lay in the tent, pouting. Life was so unfair.

By our second morning at Lake McDonald, my throat was ragged, my lungs were heavy, and I was cranky in that I'm-an-American-male-with-a-head-cold-and-therefore-the-sickest-person-in-the-history-of-the-world kind of way. But we had to get moving. We'd made plans to spend that night with an old Wisconsin friend who now lived in Whitefish. Charlie and his wife, Micaela, had offered to host us, even though they had a newborn child, and even though I'd given them like two days' notice. I didn't want to flake out and abuse their grace.

So we rode. Slowly. We stopped three times in the first eight miles. First to gaze across the lake from a slightly different vantage point, then to steal toilet paper from a park bathroom, and finally at the same "Welcome to Glacier National Park" sign we'd seen at the east entrance a week earlier. I wished I felt like I had before Logan Pass: renewed and triumphant. Wished I could say, "Thank you, Glacier National Park, for changing everything." But this didn't feel like a new beginning. It felt like starting over.

Whitefish was a railroad-turned-logging-turned-tourist town, and while it retained some old-time flavor—a wide central boulevard, a few saloons, some sagging sidewalk overhangs and handsome brick buildings—it also had a ton of kitschy shops and faux-frontier eateries and was sprawling ever outward, the rustic inns and not-so-rustic box stores and timber-framed mansions encroaching upon the forest and, especially, Whitefish Lake, the five-mile, mountain-crowned beauty whose shoreline was the city's "desirable neighborhood." Ground zero in a rapid rural gentrification.

I wasn't surprised to hear that Charlie—who back in high school was the life of the party, the guy who knew every bartender and back road—had all the dirt on the lakeside goings-on. After years of pounding nails for his uncle, a contractor who built megahomes for the über-rich, Charlie had swindled his way into some cush caretaking gigs. Our second day in town, he drove us by the most ostentatious mansions, told us the juicy backstories about this celebrity or that billionaire, showed us around one of the homes he looked after. The place had an elevator. And like ten bedrooms. And zero inhabitants for much of the year. We pulled drinks from the stainless steel fridge and repaired to the basement, where we sat in a plush theater and watched the opening scenes of *Die Hard*.

As he locked up, Charlie laughed and asked, "Isn't this absurd?"

The question didn't quite sound rhetorical.

Later, as we lay in bed, Rachel said she couldn't tell if he'd been proud or ashamed of the homes. I said, "I don't know," which was a lie. Having grown up revering lake country while benefitting from its gentrification, I knew perfectly well that the answer was "both."

Besides that insider's tour of the lake, I didn't get to see a whole lot of Whitefish. Mainly what I saw was the ceiling of Charlie and Micaela's guest bedroom. My cold had taken a turn for the worse and, as I put it in my journal, reduced me to a "low-energy, sneezy, snotty, feverish, diarrhea-afflicted, bed-ridden" blob. I felt like an awful guest, but Charlie told me over and over again that I should rest, that he and Micaela were happy to host, that we could stay as long as we liked.

And so while I festered in bed, Rachel hung out with Charlie and Micaela and Baby, whose name and appearance and (let's just be honest here) gender I cannot recall. Rachel instantly clicked with them, and I woke from many a fever dream to hear her belly laugh in the living room. She had always been great with kids, and loved Baby, and whenever Baby was awake, she was right there, cooing and holding and giggling.

Our second day in town, I came into the kitchen to find her helping Micaela change a diaper, and my life flashed forward in a mental montage. I saw a home and a wedding, Rachel in a hospital gown, and me behind a stroller. I shuddered. Too much future too fast. But then I hit rewind and brought the tape back to the part where it was me and Rachel, in our own place, sipping coffee and reading the paper. I played that scene over and over, and thought about the dream we'd deferred. The dream of staying.

By our fourth night, I was at last feeling better, and so Charlie and I—Rachel and Micaela and Baby declined to join us—headed to a bar with the stated goal of shooting pool and getting drunk. After a few games, we racked the cues and holed up at a table, where we stayed for hours, talking about Wisconsin and the West and Sammy and how much we missed him. I told Charlie about encountering Sam at Meyers Beach and Gunsight Lake, and he seemed to get it when I said it had felt like finding key clues in some kind of existential scavenger hunt.

"Man," he said. "I bet your trip has been full of stuff like that."

"Yeah." I stared dreamily into my pint glass. "It really has."

"What's been your favorite part?" he asked.

I took a gulp of beer. Time for my big speech.

"Well," I said, "I guess I just love how it feels out there, you know? Even on the ugliest of days, there are these moments where I sort of pull back and see us from above. We're riding an empty road, and there's a brutal headwind, and the sky is smoky, and there's a totally fucking mangled raccoon on the shoulder, and I remind myself that even if this looks—and actually, okay, is—pretty miserable, Rachel and I are the only people in the world who know where we are and what we're doing. And knowing that, for whatever reason, just makes me really happy."

I paused, then said, "I'm probably not making any sense at all."

This was where Charlie was supposed to politely say, "No, I

think I might get it." For extra credit, he could even follow up with, "It sounds like the experience of a lifetime."

But instead he was nodding furiously and saying, "No, I totally understand. Micaela and I feel the same way. We've got our house and our family. We change shitty diapers and go to bed really early, and when I try to talk about it to my friends, it's weird, because pretty much none of them are in the same place. I bet they all think I've gotten old and boring. But I'm happy. I love where I am. I'm just leading a very different life from everyone I know."

"Huh." I massaged my increasingly massageable beard.

"What?" Charlie asked.

"Oh. Uh. I guess that's a good point. I can't think of any friends who have kids."

This, of course, wasn't what I was really thinking. What I was thinking was: Hey, that's my line. I am the one who's different.

We had a beer and headed home, and after brushing my teeth, I lingered in the bathroom. I stared at my reflection, at the windburned face and unruly beard and shaggy mop of hair, then executed a slo-mo pirouette, took in the big fluffy towels and the artfully decorated walls and the half-dozen magazines stacked on the back of the toilet. And just as I was on the cusp of thinking a deep thought, I hiccuped and decided it was maybe time to go to bed.

Like any self-respecting son of rural Wisconsin, Charlie had traveled every back road within a forty-mile radius of his home. So when Rachel and I, after four days in Whitefish, loaded up and said we were just planning to take Highway 93 south to Kalispell, he shook his head and said, "Nope, no way, not on my watch." He gave us handwritten directions that involved a half-dozen turns and roads with names like Lodgepole and Farm to Market, and though his route ended up being five miles longer, I'm sure it was at least fifty times better.

Aside from the purple-mountain backdrop, the ride reminded me of home: towering evergreen giving way to sprawling pastureland, air smelling of Pine Sol and manure, decorative mailboxes and gravel driveways, sparse traffic and hands waving from car windows. The wind was weak, the terrain flat, and even the resurgent smoke felt forgiving. It was a hushed and gentle world, and I was happy to be riding through it once again. Then we hit Kalispell. We'd decided to take a route that bypassed downtown, and so the Kalispell we encountered was just a mess of stoplights and car lots, gas stations and golden arches. It looked like everywhere and nowhere. Halfway through town, we turned west on Highway 2, and just like that a brutal wind was lashing my chest. I pushed into the current, now on the shoulder of a four-lane highway clogged with RVs and 18-wheelers, and Rachel hugged my tire, her head bobbing with every pedal stroke, her eyes saying exactly what I was thinking: I did not miss this one bit.

For five, ten, fifteen miles, everything that was bad got worse. The smoke smokier, the wind windier, the trucks truckier. Soon Highway 2 was crawling with logging rigs, its shoulder littered with bark strips. Also, I was exhausted. After the long break, my legs had gone all saucy. My taint had lost its toughness. I was feeling miserable, and in the rearview I could see that Rachel was equally miserable, not to mention falling a bit behind. I slowed my pace. Before long I was fuming about how unfair it was that she was making me endure extra minutes of otherwise avoidable misery, but then we stopped at a gas station and I ate chocolate and realized I was, for the thousandth time, being a hangry martyr.

We got back on the road, refreshed. But within the hour, I

was again tanking and pouting, and so when Rachel suggested we stop and camp on the shores of McGregor Lake, even though we'd only ridden fifty miles, and even though the camp-site cost a whopping ten bucks, I agreed. We swam in the lake and sat on the dock and cooked macaroni and cheese and had a beer, and by the time we lay down in the tent, I was back to happy and I think Rachel was too.

On day forty-nine, we woke at dawn to clear skies and sun-kissed water. For the first few miles, we traced the shoreline of McGregor Lake. Traffic was sparse, and the lush Salish Moun-tains humped up around us like giant Chia Pets, and at the lake's west end was a store where we stocked up on fruit and pretzels and sugar water and trail mix with yogurt-covered raisins.

As we packed the panniers, Rachel said, "If every day started like this . . ."

She didn't finish. Didn't need to. Whatever she'd been think-ing, I agreed.

Ten miles in, we crossed from Flathead County to Lincoln. The latter must have had a healthy tax base, because right at the border the pavement turned from bumpy and potholed to perfect. In a car you might not notice the difference, but on a bike there are few things more satisfying than leaving cheese-grater chip seal for baby's bottom blacktop. We stopped at the border, and I tried to take a picture of the change in the asphalt's surface. But it didn't show up right; just looked like asphalt and then some more asphalt. I put the camera away. This was yet another thing that couldn't be explained with a picture, if it could be explained at all.

And that day the smooth pavement didn't end up making much of a difference. For forty miles, all the way to Libby,

Highway 2 was relentlessly hilly. I loved every minute. This was the landscape I'd long dreamed of, the one I envisioned every time I stared at our Montana map. On paper and in person, it was green space: Furry mountains overhead, freshwater all around. Breath-stealing climbs and plunges. Big sky and big horizon, little me and little Rachel. As I took in the cedar and spruce, the rivulets of water drip-dropping from roadside clumps of loamy mocha soil, I thought, *this* is the West. And my heart quickened. Because we were close. Close to being done and needing to know what "done" looked like. I squeezed my eyes shut and pushed the thought away. For now, I just wanted to be where I was.

West of Libby, the highway cozied up to the Kootenai River. It was a mesmerizing thing to behold—silty water tumbling over rock, surging through canyons, pushing twenty-foot logs over waterfalls—so we stopped at a trailhead and walked to the river's edge. While Rachel wrote in her journal, I looked back and forth between the Kootenai and the train tracks alongside it. When I'd visited Portland, almost a year earlier, I'd ridden the Empire Builder along this very route. The train had passed through this stretch in the night, and I'd sat in my seat, resting my head on the glass, unable to sleep, peering into the black and wondering what was out there. Now I knew.

A few miles up the road, we hit the intersection of Highway 2 and Route 56. For weeks, I'd been hoping we might take the northern fork here, ride 2 all the way to Bonners Ferry and cross into Canada. But we no longer had time. We were on a schedule. Back in Whitefish, we'd called Galen and finally made plans to meet. In four days, we were to be in Moscow, Idaho, some 252 miles to the southwest. Even without a northerly dog-leg, we'd need to push it to arrive on time.

Near the intersection was a rest area with bathrooms and a pavilion split into four partitions, each with its own picnic table. Rachel wanted to camp there, because the light was dusky, and it had been such a nice day, and why take chances? I wanted to press on, because the light was dusky, and it had been such a nice day, so let's take chances. Somehow my logic won.

We made it about a mile, just far enough to see that the ride down 56 was going to be breathtaking, when I got a flat tire. After almost nineteen hundred miles, this was the trip's first flat. Pretty remarkable, really. As I removed my bags and fished for the patch kit, Rachel and I talked about how lucky we'd been. No flats, no crashes, and except for a few stray drops, no rain. Sure, I'd blown a bunch of spokes in Wisconsin, and North Dakota had been windy, and in Montana we'd maybe almost gotten murdered, but really, overall, the world had been kind to us.

I fixed the flat quickly, but by the time I'd reloaded my bags the light had all but faded from the sky. Rachel suggested we maybe do the sensible thing and just head back to the freaking rest area already, and I agreed. We chose a table, cooked some pasta, lit up a candle, and pulled out our journals. Perhaps because I was thinking more about the end of the road, or because I'd just fixed that flat and was feeling a little flush, I wrote:

> *I've been thinking lately (i.e. today) that I might want to get a job at a bike shop in Portland. Yeah, it would probably be low-paying and a poor use of my university degree, but it's something I really enjoy doing.*

Which, to this day, is one of the funniest things I've ever written in a journal.

When the candle burned out, we threw our pads and bags

on the concrete and lay down. This wasn't legal, nor was it comfortable, and throughout the night I was startled from sleep by alarmingly close sprinklers and the patter of foot traffic. But we didn't get arrested or accosted or soaked, and when the sun came up, we rose with it and headed into the valley.

Route 56 was a stunner. Its perfect pavement wound slow and easy, nuzzling up alongside a smattering of still-as-glass lakes and the Bull River Valley's eponymous river, a burbling beauty that meandered through grasses of every imaginable green. In the river were men wearing oily brown waders and waving fly rods, and over the river were weather-worn bridges bound for weather-worn barns, and to either side were mountains—the Cabinets and Coeur d'Alenes—whose faces, when I took them in slowly, bottom to top, blurred from a peppering of pine to a sweet green fuzz to a purple-tinted smear that made me feel warm and hopeful in a way I still can't explain.

Fifteen miles in, we stopped for a snack on the shores of Bull Lake, and I decided to call my friend Vijay. Big mistake. Because after I shared some choice anecdotes, and tried with little success to describe where Rachel and I were, and tried with even less success to convey what it really felt like on the road, I asked how he was doing. And then I listened as Vij, with maddening precision, told me about his challenging, rewarding job and his weekly guitar lessons at a neighborhood school and his recent shit-show night of drinking with our mutual friend Carl and all the new hip-hop he was listening to and how he was overall feeling really happy in Chicago.

I hung up, stared at distant purple, and daydreamed. About a planner. An iPod. A café where the baristas knew my name, and some new pants, and a rewarding job, or really any old . . .

I snorted. Here I was, sitting in the Garden of Eden, and

somehow I was feeling not content but jealous—torn between where I was and where I hoped to be.

I stood and forced myself to focus on the lake and the mountains, the bike and the Rachel. She was standing on a rock and munching on a carrot and staring at me with this cocked, curious expression that seemed to say, Whatever you're thinking about, it isn't worth ignoring *this*. Or maybe she was just looking at me and I was doing the rest, because when she did open her mouth, she just said, "Ready?"

South of Bull Lake, the mountains crept closer and rose higher, and the greens got greener, and there was no wind, no traffic, no reason to do anything but ride side by side and spew rapturous goo like "This is so beautiful," and "It's like we're in a painting," and, well, I guess I don't really remember. What I do remember is breathing deep and looking left to right to left, trying to consume it all at once. I remember feeling the particular sadness that anticipates joy's disappearance, remember seeing Rachel in sharp focus against the blurred blues and greens, and thinking: This is it. This is what I wanted. This is where I hoped to be.

By the time 56 dead-ended at Highway 200—yes, that Highway 200—we'd ridden thirty-six miles on two bowls of oatmeal and a dozen baby carrots. A gnawing hunger was beginning to threaten my precarious euphoria. I'd figured we wouldn't find food until Clark Fork, Idaho, some twenty miles to the west, but now we were pulling up to 200, and right at the intersection was an Amish bakery. I turned to Rachel and said, with some conviction, "This is the best day of my life."

We bought soup and sandwiches and cookies and lemonade and took our meals to the shaded porch. For purely sentimental reasons, I pulled out the Montana map and looked over our route. I'd been tracing it, day by day, and the inked line now looked not unlike a Rocky Mountain skyline. Rachel pressed her thumb to the westernmost stretch of 200, which we'd be riding to the Idaho border.

"Just one more finger," she said. "Good-bye, Montana."

Behind us, someone asked, "Did you do all that on bikes?" I turned to find a guy eyeing our map. He had striking features— barrel chest, strong jaw, icy blue eyes—that all but ensured he was a news anchor, lawyer, or doctor.

"Sure did," Rachel said.

"Where'd you start?"

"Northern Wisconsin."

"Wow."

He turned to the woman beside him, and she gave us this intensely warm smile that seemed to exercise her entire body. A real-life Care Bear stare. The two of them just sat there, grinning and nodding. Then they asked more questions, and Rachel offered up our boilerplate monologue. The pair listened attentively, looking somehow proud, as if we were their children.

"Sounds like some trip," the man said. He extended a hand. "Robert Yost. This is my wife, Cindy. We're camping down on the Clark Fork with the family, but we live across the border, in Coeur d'Alene. Have you been?"

We had not.

"Well," Cindy said. "You'll pass through Coeur d'Alene on your way to Moscow." She glanced at Robert for a microsecond, then said, "We'd love it if you stayed in our home."

"We might not be back by the time you get there," Robert said, not missing a beat. "But there's a spare key around back. Do you have any paper? I can write down the info for you."

He scribbled an address and a phone number and a map to the spare key, and he and Cindy stood and said it sure was nice to meet us and to make ourselves at home even if they weren't home. The whole interaction lasted maybe four minutes. And then they said good-bye and left Rachel and me on the porch.

"I feel like we should be creeped out," Rachel said.

"But we're not," I said. "Right?"

She looked over at the Yosts, who were now herding some children into a mint green minivan. "No, I guess not. I think they're just that nice."

Robert waved at us, and I waved back, watched him drive away. "I keep wondering," I said, "what exactly we're doing to deserve this."

"I don't know. But whatever it is, I say we keep doing it." She piled up our soiled napkins and plates. "Well. Shall we?"

I was still watching the van as it headed east, toward the Cabinet skyline. "Can we stay a bit longer?" I asked. "I need to space out for a few minutes."

By which I meant: I need to remember Montana. We'd been in the state so long, and I felt I owed it a final wistful gaze. Unsure of what else to do, I opened my journal and compiled stats. Over twenty-three days—ten at rest, thirteen on the road—we'd ridden 763 miles; spent sixty-two hours in the saddle, moving at an average speed of 12.3 mph; slept at five campsites, four homes, one hotel; survived one near breakup, one googly sketchball, and an unknown number of speeding semis and unseen grizzlies. And all of this meant . . . maybe nothing. I shut the journal.

As we rode west, I replayed memories, still casting about for a Montanan moral, a neatly packaged story I could tell for years to come. But I only saw a messy collage of moments. And all I could think was that this was something like saying good-bye to an old friend. The kind you've known through sunshine and shit. The kind you know you'll see again.

CHAPTER 18

The View

Border crossings hadn't exactly been a trip highlight. We'd entered Minnesota on a traffic-clogged bridge that ferried us from the industrial squalor of Superior to the industrial squalor of West Duluth. North Dakota had welcomed us from one dreary city (Moorhead) to its twin (Fargo) via a rotted wooden sign peeking from behind underpruned oak. And at least those two borders had the decency to grant us the symbolic act of crossing a river. Where North Dakota met Montana, there had been nothing more than an invisible line in the quite literal sand and, to either side, sagebrush and oppressive heat and rolling hills and the sense that whichever direction you went, you'd end up in the same place.

But Montana to Idaho? I swoon just thinking about it.

As soon as we left the bakery, we began climbing, up from the Clark Fork River and into a tangle of evergreen. Then we climbed more. And more. The highway kept switching skyward, feigning summits but surrendering nothing of the sort, and just as my sugar buzz was mutating into cookie coma, just as I was questioning whether we'd ever reach the top—whether we'd ever escape Montana—I rounded a bend to find the highway disappearing into shadowed bramble. In a falsetto whoop, that singular language of descent, I called out to Rachel, and then I pedaled hard, tucked low, and plunged downward, whipping around blind corners and past signs with graphics of runaway box trucks, going thirty, now thirty-five, now forty miles per hour. The air was reddening my cheeks, drawing tears from my eyes, tickling my tongue's sweet spot, and as I hit what felt like peak euphoria, I came around a long sweeping turn and saw, beneath a stand of pine, the sign. White serifs on a blue rectangle: "Welcome to Idaho."

We coasted back down to the river and stopped at a boat landing, where a guy with tree-trunk legs and Burt Reynolds chest hair was leading a gaggle of raft-and-paddle-toting college kids down to the shore. We parked the bikes near their piled gear, and as we dug for our towels, two guys came back for a stack of life jackets. Though they were clad only in board shorts, and were walking in silence, something about their gait just screamed frat boy.

The shorter, scruffier one looked at Rachel and asked, "Where are you going?"

"Portland," she said.

I glared at her. We hadn't specifically talked about Portland that day, which, according to my logic, meant it no longer existed. I took a breath, blinked, reminded myself that we'd chosen Portland like a month ago, and that a couple of days earlier, in Whitefish, I'd had vivid daydreams about life there. I produced a smile and nodded.

"Whoa!" said the taller, Waspier guy. "Did you just start?"

"No," Rachel replied, still digging in her pannier. "We're coming from Wisconsin."

"No way." They exchanged this adorably doofy look and turned back to Rachel. "That's like a thousand miles, right?"

"I think," Rachel said, "it's more like two thousand." She

smiled at the pair, and as I watched them watching her, I saw Rachel through their eyes: ultraconfident, beautiful, self-possessed, and strong enough to have biked two thousand miles with a guy who was taller and more muscular and quite possibly mute.

I snapped out of it and said, "It'll be about twenty-five hundred by the time we're done."

"Whoa!" they said in unison. And then Burt Reynolds called them down to the shore, and they wished us good luck and trotted back to their group.

We dropped our camp towels on some riverside rocks and waded in. The current was surprisingly fierce, the water painfully cold, so we both forced baptismal dunks and returned to the rocks to warm ourselves in the afternoon sun. Now Rachel started flexing her legs, directing my attention to the knots above her knees, the swell of her calves. She rolled on her side and said, "And take a gander at these taut buttocks." I grabbed said buttocks, and though I intended it to be playful, her wet skin felt good. One of those intent-versus-effect things. I traced a finger over her hip, across her stomach, but she grabbed my hand and set it beside her, pulled away my newly tent-poled shorts, and gave me this look that said, "I'm in charge here, pal."

And so then that happened.

I opened my eyes just as a two-passenger rowboat came floating around an upstream bend. Rachel noticed it at the same time and started laughing. I kind of crossed my arms over my stomach, and she pretended to search for something she'd dropped. The boat floated by, and its passengers kept their eyes on their reels and their beers, looking up only briefly to give us the tight-lipped nods that men employ to say nothing and everything. I nodded back and turned to Rachel, who had picked up her journal. I followed suit, and we sat there, side by side on the riverbank, writing about glorious Idaho, and this all felt absurdly normal.

Viewed via prop plane or Google Maps, Lake Pend Oreille—from *pendant d'oreille*, French for "ear pendant," a supposed reference to shell earrings worn by the Kalispel Indians, who, despite having fished Pend Oreille for millennia, get only passing, white-guilty treatment in this and every other mention of the lake—does, to the extent a lake can, resemble an ear. It was formed after the last ice age, when glacial Lake Missoula blew out an ice dam and charged clear to the coast, the violent churn forming and filling a mountain-rimmed, snaking, fjordlike abyss that is now the country's fifth-deepest lake. Pend Oreille has been a naval sub test site, has inspired lore of a lurking monster, known not so monstrously as the Pend Oreille Paddler. It is intensely, bewilderingly deep, the kind of place that—much like Lake Superior and the Oregon coast—inspires you not so much to swim as to sit and stare and wonder at what it might contain.

Pend Oreille sits at the mouth of the Clark Fork River, and the minute Rachel and I saw its sun-dazzled surface, we knew we needed to camp on its shore. But the shoreline was cluttered with fenced yards, and so we rode the water's edge for several miles before finding a spot that, in the forgiving sepia of dusk, looked discreet: a cradle of grass hidden from home and highway by the sprawl of a skyscraping ash. We parked our bikes behind the tree, sat in the sand, cooking quinoa and watching the sun push shadows across the lake, and only when the sky went black did we put up the tent. Even the sex was stealthy.

Dawn came and passed. And when we woke, hours after a sunrise muted by overhead foliage, we found ourselves camped on a recently mowed lawn, quite visible from the road and more so from the water and more so again from the lawn itself, where, a few hundred feet away, a man was pouring gas into what looked like a Weedwacker. We started packing.

Back on 200, the lanes were narrow, the shoulder rotten, the traffic sparse but belligerent, a staccato parade of growling trucks rarely leaving us more than a foot of breathing room. I could hardly have cared less. Was far too bloated, on bandit-camp bluster and deep depths and a hunger for all things Idaho, to be punctured by something as banal as mortality. Between passing pickups, I watched sunlight strobe on wind-rippled water, smelled dead weeds and gasoline and teenage Wisconsin. It was a beautiful day.

We passed through the tiny town of Kootenai, followed by the less tiny but adorably phonetic Ponderay, and by nine o'clock we were in Sandpoint, which, according to Robert and Cindy Yost, we were "just going to love." And I did. I loved it. Immediately. Just like so many Wisconsin towns, Sandpoint sits on the shores of an über-lake and is nestled into dense forest. But unlike my hometown and, I thought, quite like Portland, it had bike lanes and a theater that showed foreign and indie films, and young people on the sidewalks and a cozy, curving central boulevard and a farmers' market and what looked like a community pharma—

"Hey." Rachel pointed at the pharmacy. "Can we stop here? I want to see if they've got arnica. My back is killing me."

I'd been zooming thirty thousand feet above our future, and it took me a moment to touch down and orient myself and tell Rachel I'd just wait outside. We were short on time, and there was much to see, and I think my logic was that if I stayed put, outside and above the particulars, I could see everything at once, could live a Sandpoint lifetime in a passing afternoon.

When Rachel emerged from the pharmacy, I followed her up the street and into the café she blindly sniffed out. I dispatched my bagel sandwich in five bites, and while Rachel read Allende and savored her oatmeal, I pinballed around the room. There were young people at every table, and handwritten invites to jazz jams, and twin towers of a weekly rag called the *Sandpoint*

Reader, and posters advertising a microbrew festival—happening *that day*—in some place called Schweitzer Village, which I assumed to be Sandpoint's Swiss neighborhood, even though Sandpoint only had eight thousand residents, and thus no ethnic enclaves, and even though Schweitzer is actually a German name.

I slid into a chair across from Rachel and started babbling. I told her I wanted to stay for a couple of nights, and that Galen could wait, because we needed to go to the brew fest and catch a Nepali film, and also I wanted to look into volunteering on this organic farm I'd read about on a thumbtacked index card, because, really, farming would be a great complement to writing for that weekly rag, and as for Rachel, well, I was sure she'd find a million things to do, because she was Rachel, and she always found what she wanted, and, seriously, what did she think? Should we stay?

She sipped her coffee. "I thought we were going to Portland."

Portland. Suddenly it sounded like a dirty word.

"Well, yeah," I said, "but there's no reason we have to, right? Wouldn't it be amazing to, I don't know, not go? What if we stayed here? It's new to both of us, and it seems awesome."

Another sip. "I'm kind of excited about Portland. And I thought you loved it."

"I do love Portland," I said. "It's just . . . "

Rachel was staring into her cup, tracing her fingers along the ceramic handle.

I leaned back in my chair and shrugged and said, "You're right. This is probably the coffee talking." And then I got up and grabbed a *Reader* and focused on figuring out where Schweitzer was anyway.

Schweitzer was the mountain—or rather was the ski resort nestled in the Selkirk Mountains—that towered over town, and its chalet, where the brew fest was being held, sat at forty-seven hundred feet, a half mile above Sandpoint. This I knew because a guy in the café, a Wisconsinite by the name of Quinn, had overheard our conversation and asked if we were really trying to bike to Schweitzer. When I'd nodded, he'd smiled up from under beard and baseball cap, then pointed skyward. This seemed odd, until he explained about the ski hill. Then it just seemed sad.

Quinn began asking the standard questions, and I told him where we were coming from, what states we'd crossed through. He nodded slowly. He was speaking slowly, breathing slowly. Being slowly. I got the feeling Quinn meditated a lot.

"So," he said, "northern Wisconsin. I went to school in Ashland. And I spent a lot of time on the Bayfield Peninsula."

"Really?" I asked. "I love it up there!"

"Yeah," he replied. "Long shot, but do you know Andrew and Jennifer Sauter Sargent?"

Turned out that Quinn had lived in Corny for a few years and spent a good bit of time with Jennifer and Andrew. He even knew Ann Christensen, who taught at Northland College, his alma mater. Quinn and his wife, Moh (I initially heard Moe, and since he said "partner" pictured not a petite, curlicued brunette but a raspy, balding bartender), had moved to Sandpoint a few years back, planning to ski a few seasons and move on. But they'd fallen in love with the place and were now looking to put down roots, raise their newborn girl, and do something involving herbs that I didn't even remotely understand. Quinn had barely sized us up before sharing that he and Moh and the baby lived in a rented condo in Schweitzer Village, that they were presently mansionsitting south of Sandpoint, and that if Rachel and I thought we could make the climb, we'd be welcome to stay in their condo for a night. In fact, he was about to head up there and would be happy to carry our bags.

Ten minutes and twenty thank-yous later, we'd stripped the

bikes and set off. We gained twenty-five hundred feet in nine miles. This was the biggest climb of the trip, including our Glacier summit, and while I'm sure it was grueling, I only remember smiling and laughing and standing from the saddle, pumping the pedals, seeing how long I could hold ten miles an hour on a 4 percent grade. Without the panniers, I felt weightless, superheroic, and Rachel was right with me. Every time we stopped, she'd say, "I feel so strong" or "I figured this would be harder," and I'd nod and wonder why it couldn't have been like this all along, before reminding myself that "all along" was the reason it could be like this now.

It was six miles of dense evergreen before we burst free to head spinning views of Sandpoint and Pend Oreille, the Cabinets and Coeur d'Alenes—all the miles we'd covered during the past few days. We stopped and gaped for a minute, then kept pushing, higher and higher, up ever-steeper grades, until we were there, at the door of the condo. We thanked and hugged, showered and changed, and made for the beer.

The festival was packed. Hundreds of people were lined up at the beer tent, dancing to reggae, sprawling on the grass. Rachel and I were in the latter camp. We were feeling the climb. Also, the beer. After one pint, we were giggly, cuddling in public, and when we went for a second round, we got to talking with a volunteer, who, when she learned of our trip, filled our cups for free. Same deal for our third round. Our fourth and fifth and I-don't-remember-how-many cups we filled ourselves, in the tent, into which we'd been invited by the event manager, and we kept on drinking even as the tents and tables disappeared into box trucks. Eventually it was just me and Rachel and a half barrel and five volunteers, one of whom Rachel was grilling about local jobs for Spanish-speaking social workers. She even got his business card. Around midnight we stumbled home, had sex about which I would remember little besides bashing my head into the frame of the bed's upper bunk, and passed out in a heap of arms and legs and blankets.

The next morning started very, very slowly. We managed to get out of bed by eight, only to collapse back onto the window seat, where we ate granola and waited for the ibuprofen to kick in. When I could keep my eyes open, I stared out the window. It was a typically stunning view—jagged mountains under deep-pile pine, popcorn clouds over pale blue water—but, mostly, I was looking at myself, at all the miles that had brought me here. Being up so high up made it easier to understand how far I'd come. And while I'd more or less accepted that we couldn't stay here—not on this mountain, not in the town below—I hoped I could at least hold on to the view.

South of Sandpoint, the only real option was Highway 95, a potholed, car-choked yawn inducer connecting scrubby pine to dusty lot to four-pump gas station. This was one of those drop-your-head-and-deal-with-it stretches, and so we dropped and dealt, and at one point I checked the rearview and noticed I'd been dealing quite a bit faster than Rachel, so I pulled over and waited, and when she caught up, we sat on the shoulder sharing elk jerky and comparing hangovers, and then we got back on the bikes and resumed riding at our own speeds, and I wondered why the fuck we'd ever fought about any of this.

It was late afternoon when we hit the outskirts of Coeur d'Alene. Thanks to the Yosts' enthusiasm, and also this beautiful Josh Ritter song that mentions the city as a place one might ride to on a stolen mule, I had pictured Coeur d'Alene as a quaint lakeside village. I bet it once was. But now it just appeared to be another sprawling city. Four-lane roads and gaudy billboards. Cul-de-sacs and strip malls.

"I think they live out here," I said to Rachel. "We aren't even going to see the city."

"We *are* going to see a bed."

"Yeah. But I almost want to keep riding. We could check out downtown and head to the lake after sunset. I bet we'd find another camp spot down there."

I meant these words. But fifteen minutes later—after Cindy had met us at the door of the Yosts' tremendous home (she had "just walked in!") and given us each an orange and showed us to our private air-conditioned basement and explained that we should plan on staying at least until dawn, when Robert would return, and at most forever—I found myself in the bathroom, oblivious to the city outside, thinking only, I'm so glad we're here.

That night, over Cindy's life-changing lasagna, we learned that she, a nurse, and Robert, a doctor, had dreamed for years of taking a trip like ours, that they still hoped to once they'd raised their kids. She asked question after question about how we'd met and why we were doing what we were doing and where we thought we were headed, and by the time we'd wrapped up our now extensively rehearsed story, she was twinkly eyed and smiling, was saying maybe we ought to just ditch Portland and stay in Coeur d'Alene, where we could live with her and Robert in their plush, private basement, rent-free, forever.

Later, as we lay in bed, it was Rachel who started talking about what life might look like if we said yes. I egged her on, and soon we were plotting, in pulse-quickening detail, about finding work and playing music and exploring Idaho and seeing where all that took us.

We just had to say yes. And if not for the plans with Galen, we really might have.

Robert had been home for all of fifteen minutes, and already he was on the phone, planning our route.

"Jon says there's a big climb right away." He had the phone

to his ear, his hand over the mouthpiece. "Then it's just a nice, hilly ride through the Palouse."

"The Palouse?" I asked.

"Gentle rolling wheat fields," Cindy whispered. "You've never seen the Palouse?"

Two heads shook.

"You're going to love it." She nodded at the box of pastries on the table. It was barely eight o'clock, but she'd already driven to the bakery to buy them for us. "Don't be shy about those. You'll want all the calories you can get."

Robert hung up the phone. He'd called Jon, an avid cyclist, to get his opinion about the best route to Moscow. Jon had said to definitely avoid Highway 95, which, though it was by far the most direct road, was a nightmare of traffic and topography. We still didn't have an Idaho map, and refused to take one from the Yosts, so Robert scribbled some numbers on a piece of paper and placed it on the table between us.

"Jon recommends taking 97 to 3 to 6 to 95," Robert said. "I've driven this route many times. Well, part of it, at least. My folks live in St. Maries, which is about halfway to Moscow. Beautiful spot. I will say that even in a car it feels pretty hilly, but Jon rides all the time, and if he says it's the best route, I'm sure it is."

We accepted these words without question. So far as I remember, we didn't even look at a map, just thanked Robert and memorized the directions: "97 to 3 to 6 to 95." Easy.

Because this scenic route would add over thirty miles, making it a 125-mile ride to Moscow, Robert insisted on driving us through the city, thereby shaving off a dozen miles. He and Cindy further insisted on loading our bags with granola bars and Gatorade and string cheese, and as we drove away in Robert's car, Cindy stood on the porch, waving and smiling. Just before nine, Robert dropped us at the north end of 97 and said good-bye in a whirl of bear hugs and repeated offers to "come back whenever you'd like." Rachel and I sat there for a minute, looking over the lake and wondering aloud at the Yosts' generosity. We were no longer questioning whether we deserved it, just agreeing that it was about time to start paying it back.

The "big climb" wasn't so bad. It lasted a mere mile, and I was so distracted—by the lake beneath us, by the palatial homes tucked into its shoreline pine—that I was almost surprised when it ended, and then even more surprised when the road began to climb again. And again. By the fifteenth mile, and the third gnarly uphill, I was starting to wonder if this guy Jon had actually ridden a bicycle on these roads and, assuming he had, if he was an Olympian.

For thirty miles we rode the shore, then followed 97 up into highland meadow. Yellow grass and graying barns, small homes with greenhouses and shake siding. This, I figured, was the Palouse, but it sure was hillier than I'd expected. Mountainous, even. My legs were on fire, and I guessed Rachel's were too, and we had another sixty miles to go. Still, we were in good spirits, enjoying the scenery and the luxury of having a third party to blame for our suffering.

"I bet Jon has one of those nine-pound carbon bikes," I said, when we stopped for a snack at what seemed like the peak.

"And a steroid problem," Rachel added. "By which I mean a tiny wiener."

"Which maybe explains the sadism of sending us out here."

Rachel bit into an apple and nodded. "Glad we got that all figured out."

"Anyway," I said, "it should be downhill from here."

"Brian."

"What? You can see the valley."

"I bet we'll have a tailwind too."

"I hate you."

As it turned out, we did drop into a long downhill, just a half mile up the road. But during the descent, my bike started feeling skittish, and by the time we bottomed out at the Saint Joe River, I could hear rim scraping pavement. It was midafternoon, and we still had a long way to go, so I rushed the flat fix, carelessly stuffing the tube back in the tire. After a few pumps, I heard the telltale hiss. A pinch flat. Swearing under my breath, I searched for the new puncture, did the whole thing over again, and after forty-five minutes, I'd at last fixed the flat. Suffice it to say that I was no longer dreaming of being a bike mechanic.

I put my bike-tank back together, and we returned to the road, and soon we were tracing the Saint Joe through an achingly pretty valley, which I can't in good faith describe here, given how actively I ignored it in the moment. My flat had cost us precious time, and we needed to rush to make Moscow. We were no longer in a position to stop and enjoy small surprises. To search for beauty would have been to set ourselves up for heartbreak.

What I do remember of those miles is Rachel—cracking jokes through the climbs, passing me a granola bar as I patched my flat, expressing keen interest in the speedometer, and texting Galen to update him on our progress and say, "We'll be there. Might be after midnight, but we'll be there." By the time we reached St. Maries—where we sat in the town park, inhaling junk food and trading massages and calculating how fast we had to ride (13.5 mph) and how much break time we could afford (one hour) if we were going to arrive in Moscow by sunset—I was beat from all the climbing and wary of what lay ahead, but mostly I was happy. Giddy, even. Because Rachel and I were aiming for the same place, for the same reasons, using the same language to talk about the miles that would take us there. This was all I'd wanted from our trip. What I'd feared we'd lost in the Plains. What we'd found our way back to.

Straight out of St. Maries, we came upon a big yellow sign that read, "Chain-Up Area Ahead." At which point I knew, just as Rachel must have, that we were totally fucked.

The next six hours were maybe the most punishing of the entire trip. Jon, for reasons I shall never learn, had sent us not through the Palouse—that gorgeous, glacially massaged hillscape I'd soon fall in love with and, of course, describe as "lunar"—but instead into the Saint Joe National Forest, which, like all western national forests, was characterized by surging rivers, old-growth evergreen, and topographical violence.

The climb out of St. Maries was four miles at a 6 percent grade. It took us an hour. Still fixated on Moscow, we decided not to rest at the summit, but just bombed downward, tucking low and laughing, until we spilled out into a river valley and saw the next ridge. That climb was five miles. It took another hour. The grade in some places was so steep that we had to zigzag from shoulder to shoulder just to keep moving, and by the halfway point I felt like someone was crosscutting my quads with a butter knife. When we finally reached the summit, the sun was sinking, and we were both tanking, and as we inhaled our last bit of food—stupid *almonds*—we cursed ourselves for not buying more snacks in St. Maries. We'd figured we'd re-up in Potlatch, some thirty miles up the road, but we hadn't banked on all this climbing. Now we were both ravenous, and a dozen almonds didn't satiate the hunger, just spotlighted it.

We plunged into another downhill, bottomed out in another valley. There, at last, the earth stayed flat, and we rode side by side under darkening skies, each of us searching for encouraging words, still believing we could make Moscow. We'd now been on the road twelve hours, had ridden ninety miles, including twenty of climbing, and maybe we could have dragged ourselves through thirty more if we hadn't come upon that trailer park with its brightly lit vending machine.

We stopped. "Just for a minute." But as soon as I sat and felt sweet relief in my every atom, as soon as I looked at Rachel and saw her looking back at me, I knew we were done for.

I called my friend Anna, who lived in Moscow and was the whole reason we'd decided to meet Galen there. More than a little embarrassed, I asked if she could pick us up in Potlatch.

"Oh my God, yes," she said. "I can't believe you're still riding!"

Which, just after quitting, is pretty much exactly what you want to hear.

We rode the six miles to Potlatch. Six miles, compared to ninety-two, may sound like small peas. But after ninety-two, and after your muscles have been led to believe it's beer thirty, six miles is pure agony. By the time we pulled up to the gas station where we'd planned to meet, Rachel and I were barely functional. We hobbled inside and bought day-old burgers and candy and cocoa. Back outside, we leaned against an ice chest and laid into our feast, and there we sat, in an empty parking lot, under fluorescent light, in the company of a mangy dog, rehashing details like it was the end of just another day. Only when a familiar car pulled up before us, when I saw Anna and Galen's smiling faces through the windshield, when I foresaw a week of laughing and relaxing and, yes, of course, riding with dear friends, only then did I realize our trip had basically ended.

CHAPTER 19

Horizon Country

I woke well before the others, and as soft morning light spilled through Anna's kitchen window and washed over sleeping bags and bodies, I lay on my back, staring at the ceiling, trying—and failing—to keep my eyes off that stupid fucking duffel.

The duffel belonged to Galen, who was now snoring into a pillow near my left foot. Ever since he'd shared his plan to one-bag it across the country, I'd indulged wicked fantasies about the bag in question: had envisioned a seam-splitting mess, full of unnecessary gear, rising up behind him like a mushroom cloud. But now here it was, lying beside Anna's couch. Just a simple green duffel, the size of one of my panniers. No side pockets, no water-resistant coating. I'd carried bigger, nicer bags to high school soccer games. To college classes. To the Laundromat.

And his bike, presently locked up on Anna's stoop, was just as maddening: a silver-blue aluminum-frame Giant. I'd heard over and again that loaded touring on an aluminum frame was a bad idea. But Galen wasn't loaded, just duffeled. And as such, he was free to ride an aluminum hot rod that, beside our bloated earth-tone pack mules, looked impossibly light and fast. I was starting to wonder whether people might mistake Rachel and me for his Sherpas. Or, come to think of it, whether they'd notice us at all. Galen—who, as we'd now heard many times, had ridden "*alone*?" and "from *Boston*?"—had a way of making us disappear.

I rolled over and buried my face in the pillow and swamped the case with a particularly fragrant blast of morning breath. For some time I lay there, facedown in my own rot, telling myself what I'd been telling myself for months: that Galen—who had spent next to nothing on food and gear, had slept in abandoned homes and falling-down barns, had topped a hundred miles like a dozen times and stopped wherever he pleased and never even considered buying a rearview mirror—had traveled not just farther but better.

I pulled my face from the fabric and turned to look at Rachel. She was lying on her side, her hair fanning out from the pillow and spilling over an upturned palm. I shimmied closer, freed a hand from my bag, and grasped hers. She gave a light, reflexive squeeze, but her breath stayed slow, her eyes shut. I held on, traced my thumb over her fingers. This had been the one uncomplicated sweetness in Moscow. Being with Rachel, off the bikes, in the consistent company of others, had felt so easy. For months, we'd had all the time in the world, but now we had to seek out space just to talk, to furtively make out like a couple of seventh graders. Even if everything else felt fuzzy, I was surer than ever I was going wherever she was.

I let go of Rachel's hand, stood, and surveyed Anna's wrecked studio. The floor was covered in unfolded maps and gutted panniers, scattered clothes and twist-tied bags of bulk granola. Anna, I thought, had been awfully gracious about hosting us. Sure, she was one of my oldest, dearest friends, but she was also in the first semester of an MFA, buried under the books she was reading and the memoir she was revising and the adorably awful Freshman Comp essays she was grading, and though she'd said a dozen times over that "You can stay forever," the bags under her eyes said something quite different.

I walked to her bookshelf and pulled out a Steve Almond paperback she'd put in my hands the night before. She insisted I'd love him, and I'd only had to skim a few pages to know she was right. I flipped to a random story. Halfway through the first paragraph, I shut the book and shelved it, feeling not grateful but insecure. Why hadn't I heard of Steve Almond? Of half the authors on Anna's bookshelf? Oh yeah. Because while she'd been reading and writing, I'd been fucking around, avoiding commitment.

I tiptoed back to my bag and resumed staring at the ceiling. I'd been prepared for the Galen envy, but had been blindsided by this longing for Anna's life. For the past few months, I'd pictured her wading through the exhausting tedium of grad school, and while she certainly was doing that, she was also taking herself seriously as a writer. Her shelves teemed with great books, and books about how to write great books, and I'd read her stuff, knew how talented she was and how hard she worked, daily, to get better.

I looked back at the duffel. Then the bookshelf. Closed my eyes. These four days in Moscow had been enough to remind me that I was incapable of ignoring the existential background noise. Maybe what I wanted, really, was to keep moving, forever, so as to avoid comparisons with Anna and Galen and everyone else who seemed to be doing better, more worthy things. I honestly didn't know.

Rachel stirred beside me, and I rolled over. Her eyelids were still stuttering, her hand lying where I'd left it. Again I took hold and waited for her to wake.

We were aiming to ride a hundred miles that day—Rachel had made plans to meet some friends at a park near Walla Walla—so we were on the move by eight, pedaling west on a separated bike path that cut straight through the Palouse. I could see why Cindy Yost had been so wide-eyed and whispery about this place. Everywhere you looked, it was a sea of perfectly rounded, elegantly tilled silt dunes, something like a giant child's sandbox. The winding roads seemed traced out by pudgy fingers, hills shaped by cupped palms and textured with the teeth of a twenty-foot comb.

The bike trail was fairly wide, and we initially tried to line up three abreast. But as with most threesomes, this got awkward, and so I dropped back and let Galen and Rachel talk. Soon I was staring off at the wheat fields, watching the stalks tumble and twist, thinking that it wasn't so bad, being the odd man out, that in fact it was kind of . . .

Rachel was laughing. I mean, really laughing.

I pulled closer, tried to eavesdrop, but I couldn't hear much over the wind and traffic. I craned my neck, tilted my head, got my ear a tiny bit closer, and now I picked up more rolling giggles, and Rachel, in passable cockney, talking about her "bits." Instantly I thought of those early days in Xela, when I'd watched bashfully as she and Galen conversed in octogenarian Cuban Spanish and babbly Brooklyn Jew. I'd never been any good at accents, and had always been eager for those conversations to end. Now I found myself trying to recall the last time I'd heard Rachel bust out one of her voices. Nothing came to mind. Maybe it was the difficulty of the trip, or maybe I just couldn't bring out that side of her. Whatever the case, for the first time in a while I was feeling shut out, left behind.

After a few miles, we crossed into Washington, and right at the border Galen's front tire went flat. He'd bought super cheapos, opting against the bombproof wallet-emptiers Rachel and I had chosen, and as a result he had been getting flats almost daily. While this allowed me to feel a certain sense of superiority—I'd had only two flats, and Rachel none—it was also kind of annoying. We had a long day ahead, and changing flats took a while, and what if we had to ride until two in the morning just because Galen had been too stingy to buy the right equipment?

Ten minutes later, I got a flat of my own. I patched it, and we made it a mile before I got a second flat, this due to my shoddy repair of the first. As I waited for the glue to set, I watched Galen and Rachel leaning over his teeny travel Boggle set, laughing and scribbling on grocery receipts. I decided that maybe flats weren't so annoying, after all. Just part of the experience. Still watching them, I began tracing my fingers around the tire. I felt something odd and looked down to find that the treads were sporting some red streaks and fibrous whiskers. This was new. The word "threadbare" popped into my head. Also, the word "replace." But I just had to make it a few more days, right?

We rode forty miles of farmland flats and corduroy rollers, then turned onto Route 127, heading south toward the Snake River Valley. Galen pulled on headphones and rode ahead, and Rachel and I pedaled side by side in carless quiet. Auburn earth mounded up around us like a bunch of desiccated Creamsicles, and ahead I could see deep into the valley. Could maybe even see Oregon. "I can't believe how close we are," I said, or Rachel did, a dozen times.

The bomb into the valley was a lifetime top ten. I caught up to Galen, and we tucked tight and leaned into the curves and sent echoing shrieks down the canyon. It was a six-mile downhill, and it took at least ten minutes, just enough time to move through all four stages of descent: relief, mania, self-awareness, and regret. And when we reached the river and laid the bikes down and looked at what we'd just done versus what lay before us, I found myself unable to say anything but "Oh shit," on repeat, my inflection somewhere between celebratory and anxious.

The five-mile climb up from the Snake was unfairly steep, into headwinds, under a suddenly blistering sun. One of those hills where you can see, way off in the distance, a wavering black ribbon that, you tell yourself, is not—cannot possibly be—the road.

It was the road.

We fell into what was quickly becoming our go-to formation: Galen charging ahead, Rachel on the flank, and me in the middle or, more precisely, in the first third, hanging closer to Rachel because (a) it seemed like the sensitive thing to do, and (b) I couldn't go any faster. The climb took over an hour, and by the time we hit the peak, it was pushing five and we'd ridden sixty-three miles and we were woozy and suffering from varying degrees of pudding leg.

It was thirty-five more miles to the park. This would have been a slog even without the vicious headwind that slammed us once we turned west on Route 12, and had it been just Rachel and me—any twosome, really—these miles could have been disastrous. But now we had a gang of three, and if two of us were crashing, the third was hitting a second wind, cracking jokes, telling stories. We rode hard under fading light, and by the time we pulled up to a picnic table covered in kebabs and beer and s'mores fixings, I could barely remember why I'd been nervous about sharing these final miles.

The next morning it was mile after mile of perfect Palouse. Blue sky over golden brown rollers, distant combines kicking up clouds of wheat dust. After so many weeks in the mountains, I was happy to be back in such open, sprawling country. Horizon country.

By noon we'd reached Walla Walla, where, in the span of a couple of hours, we checked out downtown, visited the library, sent some final postcards, and ate in the park. I loved how ingrained these routines had become and, just as much, loved seeing how they matched up against Galen's. He didn't seem to buy postcards or coffee, or treat gas stations like home, but did loiter in libraries and nap in parks. He preferred canned beans, gas station hot dogs, and generic strawberry Newtons to our deli meat, trail mix, and Nutty Bars. He was clearly spending way less than we were, but now that I was back on the road, I didn't care. Relativity felt irrelevant. I knew what I wanted, knew that canned beans were boring and Nutty Bars were awesome.

Just past Walla Walla, I got another flat. This time it was a goathead thorn, a sort of 3-D ninja star that's ubiquitous in the area and the bane of local bikers' existence. I fixed the flat quickly enough, and we rode for a half hour, and then I got another. There was no obvious cause this time, except for the tire's ever-larger patches of red, its mess of exposed threads. I was kicking myself for not replacing it in Walla Walla, where I'd seen at least two bike shops.

At dusk, a few miles east of Wallula, Galen got a call from the CouchSurfer host he'd lined up that morning. She said she'd been cool hosting one person, but now that she thought about it, three was an awful lot. So we pressed on, toward the setting sun, and soon we were kissing up to the east bank of the Columbia River, and I was time-traveling back to the previous year's train ride. It was upon first seeing this storied river that I'd felt truly close to Portland. Now I felt the same way, especially because we were turning left, tracing the river south toward the Oregon border. Just six miles away.

We rode south on the empty highway, chatting and laughing, high on that particular energy borne of impulsive choice. Galen and Rachel started talking about whether three people were enough to establish a bicycle gang, and what exactly a bicycle gang might do, and after offering a few suggestions, I drifted back and closed my eyes and tasted the night and thought about exactly what I wanted to think about, which was nothing.

By the time our lights fell upon the sign, the sky had gone starry. The air was thick with sweet vapors, the southern horizon surrendering faint, hulking suggestions of a coming dawn.

The sign said, "Welcome to Oregon."

Day sixty was what you call a real scorcher. We were back in high desert, and there was nothing approaching shade. Not so bad when we were moving, but soon enough we weren't, because after eight miles I got yet another flat. My tire now looked like it might not survive a particularly strong gust of wind. There was no way it would make it to Portland.

"Can you do the Google text-magic thing?" I asked Galen.

The day before, he'd told Rachel and me about this new-fangled service where you could text Google a question—something like "Where is the closest bike shop to Umatilla, Oregon?"—and expect an answer within minutes. This was a year before smartphones would make their debut. It seemed like the cutting edge of technology.

Galen found a shop in Hermiston, seven miles from Umatilla. I pulled off the panniers, left him and Rachel at a café, and sprinted south. It felt good, riding solo without the bag weight, and I pushed hard. When I arrived at the shop, I was sweaty and dizzy. And embarrassed. The mechanic was just plain tickled by my tire. He called over coworkers and invited them to "get a load of this." It seemed my tire was, in technical terms, totally hosed, and Mr. Mechanic told me I should have replaced it hundreds of miles back. He couldn't believe it hadn't blown out on me. I replied, in a shoe-gazing mutter, that, okay, I got it, but I was kind of in a hurry, so . . .

As I watched him work, I recalled the journal entry I'd written a week earlier and grunted a laugh. Forget working in a bike shop, I thought. I don't even want to enter one.

West of Umatilla, I-84 was the only Oregonian option. Riding the interstate sounded nightmarish, so we opted to cross back into Washington and take Route 14. On this stretch, shade trees were few and far between, and there were no towns aside from Paterson, a three-shack cluster where we stopped to refill water bottles and inhale diner pie, and it was outside said diner that we met Emily, the first fellow cyclist we'd seen in a month. She was heading east, from Portland, and when Rachel mentioned we were headed that way, Emily dug around in her handlebar bag and produced a glossy pamphlet.

"Have you guys heard of Adventure Cycling?" she asked. "A friend gifted me the maps for the Lewis and Clark route, and I don't need the gorge section anymore. Want it?"

I was about to launch into a poignant monologue about finding my own way when Galen said, "Totally! We've just got this crappy Washington map."

Galen and Rachel huddled up as Emily pointed out the spots

where she'd camped, the roads she'd ridden. I folded my arms and looked away. After twenty-four hundred miles of principled resistance to prepackaged experience, I wasn't about to give in now, wasn't going to pollute these final—

"There's a nice free campground in Roosevelt," I heard Emily say. "It's pretty much the only good spot in the next fifty miles, so you should definitely stop there. Also, there's a sweet little fruit stand right by this bridge. Great peaches."

I inched a bit closer and peeked at the map. I liked peaches. And free campgrounds. I kept listening, and as I watched Emily point out more of her favorite spots, I had this epiphany. The map in her hands, it was not a threat, not a constraint. It was a fucking map.

We thanked Emily, wished her well, and got back on 14. West of Paterson, it was more heat and headwind. I'd somehow expected the final miles to be easy, but I was as exhausted and bored as I'd been on any Dakotan day. My eyes were sweat stung, my legs aching. By the time we reached the aspiring ghost town of Roosevelt, I was thrilled that we'd met Emily, that we knew we had a safe place to sleep.

We made our way to the park and found the camping area. It was ugly and rocky, and the park was empty, and none of us could see why we shouldn't set up in the lush grass that hugged the river, so we did, and we slept good, heavy sleep, until about two o'clock, when I woke to what sounded like a metallic heartbeat. I unzipped the tent door just in time to catch a faceful of water. A whole lot of shrieking and stake pulling and tent dragging followed. Rachel and I ended up on the beach, safe from the attacking sprinklers, and Galen tucked up in the corner of a little gazebo, his hammock just out of the blast zone. I dried off, spooned Rachel, and smiled up at the stars, thinking of how and to whom I'd tell this little anecdote. And then I fell asleep.

The next morning, it was more dry heat and grinding climbs, gorge-force winds and infinite dirt. We fell into formation and pushed, stopping only for snack breaks, riding past the wineries, the scenic viewpoints, the cliff-top Stonehenge replica. We were so close, just a hundred-some miles from Portland, and could no longer be bothered with frivolous detours.

By midafternoon we'd crossed back into Oregon for good. It wasn't exactly a hero's welcome. The bridge from Maryhill to Biggs Junction had no shoulder and a glut of traffic, and by the time we'd reached Oregon, a half-dozen growling cars were queued up behind us. Since Biggs was just a concrete island amid a sea of dirt, we ate our gas station sandwiches, loaded up on Newtons and Nutty Bars, and left as quickly as possible.

Emily had prepped us for the next stretch: ten miles on a frontage road, which she described as "meh," then thirteen more on I-84. The interstate. She'd insisted there was no other option, unless we wanted to climb a thousand feet on gravel roads, and that the highway wasn't so bad. "The shoulder is super wide," she'd said, "and I had this great tailwind . . . Oh. Dang. Yeah, tomorrow's gonna suck for you guys."

The frontage road did indeed suck. It was one of those ferociously gusty stretches where I wondered why the hell we'd chosen to ride cross-country against prevailing winds. For well over an hour, we pushed into the wind, leapfrogging at mile markers, taking turns facing the current.

But I-84? A revelation.

The shoulder was six feet wide, and we rode right along the Columbia, and the thick traffic ended up generating this localized tailwind that pretty much canceled out the westerly we'd been battling. Locked as I was between cars and water, between

Rachel and Galen, I felt this unnatural momentum, like I was being sucked westward, like everything was definite and life was acceleration and all that lay before me was perfectly inevitable. For the hundredth time, I dropped my eyes to the Fuji, my hand to the top tube, and I said, if only to myself, thank you.

A few miles up the road, just east of The Dalles, Galen got another flat. While he patched his tube, and Rachel called her folks, I climbed atop some roadside rocks and looked across the river at the train tracks that had first carried me to Portland. I remembered this stretch. I'd been staring out the window, peering into mist and fog, squirming in my seat and wondering what lay ahead. A year later, here I was again. Approaching. Wondering. I didn't know what, if anything, it meant to have traveled so far only to arrive at such a familiar place, and with such familiar questions. I just knew I'd traveled.

The plan had been to make Hood River by sunset, or midnight, or sunrise. Just as long as we got there before tomorrow, so as to begin day sixty-two, our final day, within sixty miles of Portland. But Galen's fix took a long time, and as soon as we got back on the road, Rachel got her first flat and, shortly thereafter, her second. By the time we'd ridden through The Dalles, the sky had gone black, and only when we escaped the glow of the town's last streetlamp did I realize how dark it was. Also, windy. And cold. I shared my observations with Rachel, and we had a quick conference, then told Galen that this was nuts, that we were going to stay in The Dalles. And though I'm sure he would have continued on had he been alone, he just nodded and said okay.

There was nowhere obvious to camp, so Galen set off in

search of abandoned buildings while Rachel and I sat in a grocery deli, eating mealy fried chicken and lukewarm mac 'n'
cheese and justifying why it was acceptable, even appropriate,
for us to drop the cash and get a room on this, our final night.
Galen could do his vagabond-hobo thing, and we could buy a
bottle of wine and do what you do with a wine drunk and a
cheap hotel room, and then the three of us could meet up in
the morning and head for home. I was about to call Galen and
break the news when a short, bespectacled guy asked if those
bikes outside were ours. Five minutes later, we had an offer for
a backyard campsite and a home-cooked breakfast.

Our benefactor, Dale, was a former Marines sharpshooter
who now spent his days throwing pottery and smoking salmon
and making thinly veiled references to having killed people. He
insisted that he never slept, and indeed, when I got up at two
thirty and stumbled inside to pee, I found him sitting in the
dimly lit kitchen. He looked up from a *National Geographic*
and asked if I'd ever seen a puma in the wild. Four hours later,
he woke us with salmon-and-goat-cheese omelets and sludgy
coffee and wild-eyed, pure-hearted reminders to "Pay it forward, okay, guys?" And an hour after that, he stood on the
front porch and waved until we disappeared from sight.

It was September 14. Exactly two months, and 2,428 miles,
from the day Rachel and I left Conover. The skies were clear,
the air cool. We'd all had a good sleep and a big breakfast, and
we were ready. Ready to ride ninety miles to Portland. Ready to
arrive. Maybe.

Galen, at least, was dead set on making it by nightfall. He'd
even made plans to cook dinner with his cousin, a Portlander.
Rachel, too, had let her folks know to expect us, and the previous night, during our romantic deli dinner, she'd talked about

how excited she was to get off the bike and into her bed, her favorite sweatshirt, her routines. I'd nodded and mumbled my agreement, though I wasn't sure I meant it. Even if part of me was ready to find out if these miles had mattered, if they'd vested me with whatever powers one needed to stay somewhere, a far more familiar part of me wanted to be here, on the brink, in anticipation, forever.

We were on the road by seven thirty. Per Emily's suggestion, we took Route 30, and about a mile past The Dalles, pretty much exactly where we'd turned around the night before, the road disappeared into a nest of evergreen. The change was instant. Arid to lush. Autumnal to vernal. More than the border crossing, more even than the sight of tracks tracing the Columbia, this felt like the end. Or the beginning. Either way. I was glad we'd waited for daybreak. I wanted to see where I was going.

For five miles, Route 30 wound through rock and pine, deep into the gorge—eroded bluffs to the north, the sprawling Columbia to the south, and between, picket fences and thirsty pastures, chirping birds and whining engines. I-84 was just a few hundred feet away, and though it was noisy, it was also a magnet for all but the most local of traffic, and so the three of us rode side by side by side, talking about Dale and Portland and the etymology of the word "gorgeous," until the road started to climb and we all went quiet. I felt lactic acid saturating my legs, a throbbing knot between my shoulders. I took a long, slow drag of pine and time-traveled back to the Mesabi Trail, the hills above Lewistown, the crossing into Idaho. This felt right. As much as I'd enjoyed the propulsive tumult of the interstate, I wanted to spend the final miles here, in the quiet carless nowhere, in the in-between.

It was one o'clock when we pulled into Hood River—plenty of time to make it to Portland, provided we skipped the scenic highway and banged out the final miles on I-84. Galen was all about this plan. I was not. Sixty miles of interstate headwind seemed like the wrong kind of ending. I wanted more grinding climbs, more carless quiet, more time to reflect, to ponder, to figure out what all these miles had meant and where they should take me and what I really wanted and who I could and should and would be. So when we stopped for bagels and coffee, I proposed staying the night in Hood River, then taking the final day slow.

"What do you guys think?" I asked.

Rachel nodded. "I'd be into that."

Galen took a slow sip of coffee, looked back and forth between us. "Nope," he said. "I'm getting there tonight."

He stood and excused himself to call his cousin, and Rachel and I leaned over the table and whispered, even though he'd gone outside, about what to do. She said maybe we should let him go it alone, and I said yes, we should, we should stay here and rent that room and buy that wine, should end how we'd begun, alone and apart, but then Galen came back to the table, and we hadn't settled on an answer, and it seemed weird to keep discussing it in front of him, so we made a sort of nondecision to just keep going.

As I followed Galen and Rachel down the on-ramp, as I merged with the motorists, I told myself I'd keep my head up, mind clear, eyes on distant purple. But soon enough I'd surrendered my precious attention to broken glass and rumble strips, to swirling winds and foot-to-forehead aches, to signs whose names and numbers were changing too fast for my mind to process but too slow for my body to bear. The farther we rode, the more I felt like I'd made a bad choice, like Rachel and I should head back to Hood River and get that room and end this thing right. But somewhere in there I looked down at my legs, watched them pumping like pistons, and then off toward the water, where I could barely make out what looked like a crumbling old dock. And I started thinking that maybe this river-gorge-highway hellride, this mile-by-mile slog through something I couldn't quite see, was in fact the perfect ending, if it was an ending at all.

Epilogue

I rise from the saddle, lock my knees, and coast. My quads scream, but I stay standing, because my ass has never, ever hurt this much. The pulsing, tip-to-tail throb I can deal with, but as of the past few days, I've also been suffering these eye-popping, localized jolts. Whenever I so much as shift a centimeter, it's as if I just sat on a pack of lit cigarettes.

The term, I believe, is "saddle sore."

I can't say I'm surprised. It's been two weeks since I last took a break. A couple of days ago, I rode 102 miles. Yesterday, it was 128. And today, if my legs don't melt, I'll be hitting 140.

I pull off at a gas station, inhale five bucks' worth of corn syrup, return to the road. It's going to be dark soon. The sun dipped behind the pines a half hour ago, and the light is grainy. Passing cars are switching on headlights, and drivers are slowing and staring, furrowing brows, waiting for me to raise a hand or a white flag. I'll do nothing of the sort. I'm finishing this ride.

It's September 14, five years to the day from that final push to Portland. I'm back on the road, heading east, on a breakneck solo ride that's taken me through Oregon and Idaho, Montana and Dakota, Minnesota and Wisconsin. I've been riding fast, faster than I thought I could, faster than I ever will again, not because I like midnight calf cramps or heatstroke dry heaves, not because I'm trying to prove something, but rather because I'm equal parts impulsive and ragingly sentimental, and so, even though I didn't decide to do this until mid-August, even though it's meant riding twenty-two hundred miles in a month, even though I know it matters to no one but me, I've been racing time to make it home on this day, in this way.

I no longer own a speedometer, but if I had to guess, I'd say I'm now going somewhere between nine miles per hour and backwards. My joints are full of concrete, back spasming, quads liquefying and pooling in my socks. I know I'm close— twenty-some miles close—but I can't fathom actually riding this final stretch. And yet, I'm going to.

I drop my head and bite my cheeks and make myself think about something. About anything. About Rachel. About how I probably wouldn't be out here if she hadn't—on a crisp November night, just as I was emerging from that first Portlandian year, a year full of anxiety attacks and depressive funks and incessant moaning about how we should get back on *our* bikes and leave *her* city and ride somewhere, anywhere, forever— stopped and turned and met my eyes and said the worst words in the English language: "I need to talk to you about something."

And I get it now. Though I wasn't ready to see it then— not that night, that week, that year—I get it now. I get that, just as I'd never have found Portland without Rachel, I'd never have left it with her. I owe her my second trip as much as our first.

The air is getting downright autumnal, too cool for short sleeves, so I pull over and dig around in a pannier for my flannel. I've still got the same panniers. They're a lot dirtier now, and I've had to repair hooks and clasps, but I've still got them, just as I've still got my sleeping bag and pad, my dented tin cookware, my trusty beer-can stove. I pull the flannel from the top of the rear right bag, and underneath it is a mess of unwashed clothes, including the soccer shorts I haven't worn for days. For much of the past week—for much of the trip, really—I've been hiding the Lycra under a pair of frayed jean shorts. I've similarly ditched the sweat-wicking shirt and dorky fleece, the cleated shoes and expensive sunglasses, have ridden most of these miles in a baby blue Donald Duck T-shirt, a red and white flannel, a pair of Sambas, and some chipped yellow shades I found on the ground at a music festival.

On second thought, maybe I *am* trying to prove something.

I tug on the flannel, get back in the saddle, and force my legs to push the pedals. My legs are not happy. My legs are saying things like "never forgive you" and "permanent damage." But I'm so close, and I don't think my legs, or any other part of me, really want to ditch-camp beside a county highway on a sub-forty night, and so I pedal on, and as the pain dulls from "I might cry" to "I still might cry but who cares?" I try to recall if riding a bike has ever hurt this much. And, yes, as a matter of fact it has; as a matter of fact that's why I'm not riding the Fuji.

Exactly one year after Rachel left me, I was riding downtown on a Portland-population-control kind of night—rain pissing sideways, wind torpedoing down from the West Hills and shoving me toward a queue of honking, lurching cars—when out of nowhere a big black box flashed in front of me. I strangled the brakes but still I hit hard, my shoulder into metal, my head through glass, and then I was on my back, feeling rain and something thicker on my forehead. Much later that night, after the police report and ambulance ride, after the drugs and stitches, I lay in bed, unable to sleep, because my shoulder was melting, forehead throbbing, mind racing, trying to make sense of why I wasn't more busted up about the grisly death of the bike that had carried me all the way from Wisconsin. But I didn't care. At the time, I couldn't quite say why. I just didn't.

And now, I especially don't, because I'm riding *this* bike. Riding Rudolph. I chose the name in honor of my gramps, who, upon joining the army to fight in World War II, noticed that all the other infantrymen had middle names, and, in a bout of self-conscious genius, chose Rudolph on the spot. My Rudolph is lighter than the Fuji—and with his matte blue powder coat and copper-bedazzled leather saddle, much prettier—and his wheels, which I myself built, have blown exactly zero spokes.

I lean forward, and though this shift in balance shoots off fireworks in my groin, and causes me to swerve left, then right, then left again, I persist, until I manage to plant a kiss on Rudolph's headset. I don't miss the Fuji at all. I adore Rudolph. I chose him. I built him. Well, okay, I mostly built him. Admittedly, I had a lot of help from some seriously patient coworkers at the nonprofit bike shop where, for the better part of four years, I'd worked as a volunteer manager–cum–event organizer–cum–everything else. The day after arriving with Rachel, I'd googled "portland+community+bicycle" and found the shop, a scrappy nonprofit that got bikes to people who couldn't afford them. I fell in love with the place, and its volunteer program in particular. They had these drop-in nights when dozens of people came together to fix old bikes, and they tolerated, even welcomed, doofy unskilled hacks like me. The guy in charge of the program was effusive and charming and clearly loved what he was doing, and I soon decided that his was the best job ever. So I haunted the place, and applied for every position they posted, and when, a year after I'd arrived in Portland, the best job ever opened up, I actually got it, and I was euphoric, until two months later, when Rachel said the worst words.

I lean back from the bars, look up past the pines, catch a few timid stars peeking through deep purple. Suddenly I'm getting nostalgia needles; I'm remembering those Dakotan nights when Rachel and I had pedaled side by side, alone, our solitude like a secret. It's the same sweet secret now, has been for an entire month, really. Because the whole time, it's just been me out here, moving forward, not needing or wanting anyone else to know how or where or why.

That's not to say I haven't been lonely. I've missed my sister. I've missed my friends. And I've missed my job, which I've loved almost as blindly and fully as I loved Rachel. For a long, long time, I thought it was perfect—absurdly fitting. A bike brought me to Portland, gave me joy and purpose, and somehow I found a way to get paid to basically cheerlead the world's kindest people as they—joyfully, purposefully—built bikes for the bikeless. I loved knowing I was making their work possible, loved knowing I was doing right by Dale from The Dalles, was "paying it forward," was giving what I had to people I hardly knew.

Um, wow. I'm really sucking air now. Seeing stars both natural and man made. My pinkies are numb, and the pain in my legs is whatever pain-scale number means "unable to think clearly." I recalled County K as a carless, quiet, pine-lined beauty, and though it is indeed all of those things, it is also mercilessly hilly. Well, bring it on, I say. I've got thousands of miles behind me, and no more than ten to go, and I want this final push to hurt. I want to feel every inch. I want to end this trip by remembering why I chose it. That I chose it.

It was a sunny Saturday morning, and I was sitting at my favorite café, trying to squeeze in a few fleeting hours of writing. After three-plus years, my job was no longer energizing, just exhausting, and I'd been having bimonthly panic attacks about where it was taking me, about where I was going, and why, and why I could no longer answer such a simple fucking question. I was too scattered to really write, on that and every morning, and so I was just clicking through the street view of Washburn, Wisconsin, calling it research, when, without quite knowing why, I slid the cursor over the minus sign and tapped the party end of the zoom bar. In the span of about twenty seconds, I floated from Washburn to Bayfield County, from Chequamegon Bay to Lake Superior, from trees and towns to green space and white space, from a two-year gut twist to the sudden realization that I knew exactly where and why and how I needed to go.

And so here I am, turning right onto West Buckatabon Road, under familiar pine boughs, over familiar pavement. Until today, I made a point of making my own route, steered well south of the roads I rode with Rachel. But now I want the beacons, the reminders of where I started and where I've ended up. I've already passed the site of the spoke explosion, a sign for the loon capital of the world, a shimmery lake that, though it's still cattail peppered and evergreen rimmed, has surrendered one small, sun-bleached dock. And now, as I ride past roadside pine I once thought I was seeing for the last time, I'm thinking what I've thought every day for the past month: that maybe this is how I move—in search, in circles, incessant.

It's pitch-black now. My light is low on batteries, flickering and fading, and so I turn it off. I can't see more than ten feet in front of me. I don't need to. I just listen to my tires on the pavement, my chain on the cogs. I take a deep breath, and the air smells like pine tar, like dried sweat, like aged summer. My calves are seizing, my eyelids sandbagged. My neck is packed with glass shards, and I don't even have words for my crotch. But I keep riding, at a jogger's pace, past the tiny lake whose breath I can feel through the trees, past the marsh where Rachel and I watched the eagle, past the boat landing and over rolling hills and up to the foot of the driveway. It's dotted with tiny pillars of dancing light. I pull up beside one, see that it's a candle. My dear, ragingly sentimental parents have lined their driveway with candles. For a moment, I hesitate, because I kind of wanted to end this night alone, wanted to have myself a moment. But I've already done that. I'm doing it. And, anyway, my folks are up there, waiting, as are the things I left behind, the things I hope to carry back to the city I hope is home. And so I get back in the saddle, and I follow the lights, one by one, toward something like an ending.

AUTHOR'S NOTE

This is a work of narrative nonfiction. It is true. It is also a story. In telling it, I make use of certain tools (section breaks, snappy transitions, narrative distance) that were unavailable while I was living it. I have done my very best to use said tools artfully—to tell a good story—without in any way misrepresenting my experiences or mind-set at the time of the trip.

In an effort to best recall those experiences and that mindset, I pretty much memorized my bike trip journal, and spent untold hours re-creating our route on Google street view, and re-rode or drove many of the miles we covered, and called everyone we met along the way to say hello and compare recollections and make sure I wasn't totally full of shit.

Still, most of this story comes from memory. I'm sure I got something wrong. If you live in Richey, Montana, and can't believe I'd call those buttes "blue-brown," or if you are dismayed that I've labeled *you* a serial killer when you were just trying to help, or if you, the something that was lurking outside our tent in Minnesota, would never *ever* describe yourself as a snorter, well, I'm sorry. I did my best.

Some of the dialogue is exact quotation, but much of it has

been re-created based on my memories and my consultations with the characters involved—especially Rachel, who sat down for many a rambling conversation and shared journal entries and even responded to an absurd, written-by-her-ex-boyfriend survey that included the question, "I guess what I'm asking is: why'd you fall for me?"

I compressed time a bit in the first two chapters, so as to get us on the road sooner, but I wrote no composite scenes. Neither did I form composite characters. Matter of fact, every name in the book is the character's name in real life: these people are all that generous and good. Hearing their voices made me want to drop everything and do it all again. And again.

ACKNOWLEDGMENTS

The prospect of honoring everyone who helped me write this book is utterly overwhelming, and I'm not sure where to start or end, or how to best balance humor with sincerity, or whether I'm better served by short, simple declarations or effusive looping run-ons, or . . . Actually, I guess writing acknowledgments is not so different from writing a book, and on that note maybe it's best I begin with Karen Karbo and Cheryl Strayed, both of whom are even now perched on my shoulder, whispering advice like a pair of literary Obi-Wans.

Karen, from the first you asked infuriatingly good questions and helped me learn the language with which to answer them. You went to bat for this book and its author well before the book felt like a book and its author like an author. "Gratitude" is such a puny word.

Cheryl, thank you for a mantra called "dig," for invisible last words, for being nice to my mom, for having the grace and presence of mind to, in the middle of your whirlwind rock-star book tour, pick me out of a standing-room-only crowd and say five words I very much needed to hear. You deserve statues and parades.

A big thank-you to David Biespiel for helming the Attic Institute, where this book was born, and to Liz Prato, who pulled me aside at the end of her fantastic workshop to tell me about a train I ought to hop on. A salute to David Forrer, my agent, for his unwavering belief in this book, his patient fielding of my naive questions, and his refreshingly liberal use of exclamation points. And a deep bow to Denise Roy, my editor, for expertly, gracefully, downright Socratically leading me back to the story I set out to write.

I am forever indebted to Laura Koch, Brian Rae, Jessica Harrison, Neil Schimmel, Nate Schlingmann, Emily Gowen, Noah Beck, Michelle Helman, Joe Greulich, and Janelle Bickford, all of whom welcomed me into their guest bedrooms and family cabins and furnished basements when I was too focused on writing to be bothered with securing my own housing.

I'm buying the next round for Emilee Booher, Kristin Bott, Breesa Culver, Celeste Hamilton Dennis, Carl Gustafson, Julia Himmelstein, Ted Lee, Ashley Mitchell, Vijay Pendakur, Sarah Royal, Gram Shipley, Melia Tichenor, Nick Williams, and everyone else (you know who you are) who, during the writing of this book, offered a well-worded critique or well-timed note of encouragement, or who maybe just leaned across a table full of empty pint glasses and grabbed my hand and told me to shut up already.

To everyone who offered a bed or a meal or a ride or a power wave from a passing car, thank you for reminding me how good people can be. I talk of you all often and think of you even more.

Rachel, you have been unbelievably graceful and supportive throughout this process. In more ways than you'll ever know, you made it possible for me to write this story.

Beau and Joe and Joe and Josh and Anna and Bethye and Danny, you are and always will be home, and you know it, just like you know the name that's absent from this sentence but present everywhere else.

Galen, your conviction is a contagion. You've made so many of us better.

Leah. You're my favorite.

Mom and Dad. Everything, always, unequivocally.